John Esten Cooke

Stories of the Old Dominion

From the Settlement to the End of the Revolution

John Esten Cooke

Stories of the Old Dominion
From the Settlement to the End of the Revolution

ISBN/EAN: 9783744751148

Printed in Europe, USA, Canada, Australia, Japan

Cover: Foto ©ninafisch / pixelio.de

More available books at **www.hansebooks.com**

STORIES OF THE OLD DOMINION

*FROM THE SETTLEMENT
TO THE END OF THE REVOLUTION*

BY

JOHN ESTEN COOKE

AUTHOR OF "LEATHER STOCKING AND SILK" "PROFESSOR PRESSENSEE"
"HENRY ST. JOHN, GENTLEMAN" ETC.

NEW YORK
HARPER & BROTHERS, PUBLISHERS
FRANKLIN SQUARE
1879

TO MY BOYS

EDMUND PENDLETON COOKE
AND
ROBERT POWEL PAGE COOKE

*These Stories from the History of Virginia
are*
𝔇𝔢𝔡𝔦𝔠𝔞𝔱𝔢𝔡

THE BRIARS, VIRGINIA, 1879.

A FEW WORDS TO MY OWN AND OTHER BOYS.

In these stories I mean to tell you some interesting incidents in the history of Virginia, which, in former times, was called the "Old Dominion."

Many of these I look upon as more striking than fiction—that is, than stories which are not true, and only written to amuse people. You cannot find them easily in the long histories of Virginia; and when you do find them, little is said about many of them, and that little is buried in words. I do not mean to speak ill of the histories, but I must say they are not very interesting to me. As much time is taken to tell us what is dull and commonplace, as to relate the striking events which everybody should know about.

This is wrong, I think. There is wheat and there is chaff, and if you mix them both together the wheat is of no value. It is better to clean up the wheat and skim the cream from the milk of history—that is, dwell on the interesting scenes, and say little of the unimportant ones.

This I mean to try and do in my book. I shall aim to tell you the most striking events in the annals of the "Old Dominion," and leave the rest to take care of themselves. There are plenty such incidents. Virginia history is full of remarkable scenes, and she has produced some of the greatest men who have lived in America. By telling you of these I hope to interest you, and, what is better still, to inform and improve you.

I call my stories a book, but I wish you to feel as if I were talking to you like an old gentleman in his arm-chair, with his young ones gathered around him. Easy talk of this sort is often better than long words; but you must not think that I talk carelessly, without minding what I say. I wish all to listen to me—even the "grown-up children," as men and women are sometimes called; and with these I must be careful. They will know if I am telling the precise truth, and I can only say I have made every effort to do so. I have written a number of books in my life, and this has been one of the hardest of them—for nothing is more difficult than to be simple.

This is all I have to say before beginning my stories, which are meant for my own boys, and for any others who will read them. I even hope, as I have said, that grown-up persons will like them, and here and there meet with something which will be new to them.

CONTENTS.

About my Stories..Page 7

I.
THE ADVENTURES OF CAPTAIN JOHN SMITH.

I.	How he made himself a Soldier................................	17
II.	His Fight with Three Turks..................................	20
III.	Is taken Prisoner, and Escapes.............................	26
IV.	Sails for Virginia...	29
V.	The Settlers at Jamestown...................................	32
VI.	He Visits Powhatan..	36
VII.	Pocahontas..	40
VIII.	He Explores the Chesapeake.................................	47
IX.	His Last Meeting with Pocahontas...........................	50
X.	His Death...	54

II.
WHY VIRGINIA WAS CALLED THE "OLD DOMINION."

I.	Richard Lee's Visit to Breda................................	56
II.	The Surrender to Parliament.................................	60

III.
THE GREAT REBELLION IN VIRGINIA.

I.	Sir William Berkeley and Bacon..............................	65
II.	The Scene in front of the State-house.......................	71
III.	The Fight at Bloody Run....................................	73
IV.	The Battle at Jamestown.....................................	75
V.	The Death and Burial of Bacon...............................	77
VI.	The Governor's Cruelty......................................	79

IV.
THE KNIGHTS OF THE GOLDEN HORSESHOE.

I.	Alexander Spotswood...	82
II.	The March of the Knights....................................	85
III.	Over the Mountains...	89
IV.	The Horseshoe...	92

V.

GEORGE WASHINGTON, THE YOUNG SURVEYOR.

I. George and Lord Fairfax...Page 94
II. The Ride beyond the Blue Ridge... 101
III. Back to Greenway Court.. 107

VI.

WASHINGTON IN THE WILDERNESS.

I. He Visits the Chevalier de St. Pierre.................................... 110
II. The Indian Guide.. 114
III. On the Raft in the Ice... 117
IV. The Surrender at Great Meadow....................................... 119

VII.

BRADDOCK AND HIS SASH.

I. At Cumberland.. 123
II. The March... 126
III. The Battle.. 130
IV. The Retreat... 135

VIII.

POINT PLEASANT, AND THE DEATH OF CORNSTALK.

I. Andrew Lewis and his Men.. 140
II. The Battle with the Indians.. 145
III. Cornstalk... 149
IV. Cornstalk and his Son... 153

IX.

PATRICK HENRY, THE "MAN OF THE PEOPLE."

I. His Early Years... 158
II. His First Speech.. 162
III. In the Burgesses.. 167
IV. In the Convention... 173

X.

THOMAS JEFFERSON, THE "PEN OF THE REVOLUTION."

I. His Youth and Marriage... 180
II. The Declaration.. 184
III. His Old Age, and Death... 187

XI.

A BALL AT THE CAPITOL.

I. In the Capitol... 193
II. Henry, Pendleton, and Jefferson... 197

III. Mason, Lee, and others ....Page 199
IV. The Council-chamber........................... 202
V. The Ball.. 203

XII.
LORD DUNMORE AND THE GUNPOWDER.

I. Robbing the Magazine 205
II. The Battle of Great Bridge................. 211
III. Lord Dunmore's Flight....................... 214

XIII.
ELIZABETH ZANE: THE STORY OF A BRAVE GIRL.

I. The Border People........................... 219
II. The Fort at Wheeling....................... 223
III. The Attack of Girty........................ 227
IV. The Keg of Gunpowder....................... 230
V. M'Culloch's Leap............................ 231

XIV.
THE FATE OF COLONEL ROGERS.

I. How I found out this Story.................. 236
II. Down La Belle Rivière...................... 238
III. The Surprise 242

XV.
THE CAPTURE OF VINCENNES.

I. George Rogers Clarke........................ 245
II. Kaskaskia................................... 247
III. The Drowned Lands of the Wabash........... 251
IV. Vincennes................................... 253

XVI.
JOHN MARSHALL, THE CHIEF-JUSTICE.

I. Lieutenant of "Minute-men"................. 257
II. The Old Gentleman and the Turkey........... 260
III. Marshall and the Sceptics.................. 263

XVII.
JOHN RANDOLPH OF ROANOKE.

I. The Boy and his Mother..................... 267
II. Randolph and Patrick Henry................. 271
III. How he looked in Old Age.................. 273
IV. His Character.............................. 275

XVIII.

ROSEWELL, AND SELIM THE ALGERINE.

 I. Governor Page and his House..Page 278
 II. The Wild Man's Story 280
 III. His Portrait.. 283

XIX.

MORGAN, THE "THUNDER-BOLT OF THE REVOLUTION."

 I. His House and his Battle... 289
 II. The Old Soldier.. 294

XX.

CORNWALLIS, AND "THE BOY" LAFAYETTE.

 I. Arnold the Traitor in Virginia... 298
 II. Phillips, and his Death.. 307
 III. Tarleton 310
 IV. Cornwallis and Wayne... 315

XXI.

THE SURRENDER AT YORKTOWN.

 I. In the Trap... 319
 II. The Sea-fight.. 323
 III. The Attack.. 327
 IV. The Attempt to Escape.. 329
 V. The Surrender, and Washington's Farewell to his Generals ... 331

A LAST WORD TO THE BOYS... 335

ILLUSTRATIONS.

	PAGE
CAPTAIN JOHN SMITH MAKING TOYS FOR POCAHONTAS	*Frontispiece*
CAPTAIN JOHN SMITH	18
HOLLAND IN THE OLDEN TIME	20
SHIP IN A STORM	21
FLIGHT OF THE SARACENS	23
FORM OF RALEIGH'S SHIPS	31
CHESAPEAKE BAY	32
JAMESTOWN	34
INDIANS	37
POISONED ARROWS	38
POCAHONTAS INTERCEDING FOR JOHN SMITH	44
POCAHONTAS	46
MARRIAGE OF POCAHONTAS	52
LOG-CABIN	57
THE KING AT BOSCOBEL	62
JAMESTOWN ISLAND	67
BACON ADDRESSING THE COUNCIL	69
INDIANS FIGHTING	74
BLOODY RUN	75
BLACKBEARD, THE PIRATE	84
A RIVER VIEW	88
YOUNG WASHINGTON'S MILITARY ASPIRATIONS	96
RESIDENCE OF THE WASHINGTON FAMILY	98
GREENWAY COURT	102
INDIAN WITH SCALP	106
OHIO RIVER	112
WASHINGTON ON HIS HOMEWARD JOURNEY	118
BENJAMIN FRANKLIN	124
ON THE MARCH	127

ILLUSTRATIONS.

	PAGE
MILITARY ENCAMPMENT	129
BRADDOCK'S DEFEAT, 1755	138
INDIAN COUNCIL	141
IN THE MOUNTAINS	143
AN INDIAN ATTACK	149
PORTRAIT OF PATRICK HENRY	159
PATRICK HENRY'S STATUE	161
HANOVER COURT-HOUSE	167
STAMP ACT RIOTS	170
ST. JOHN'S CHURCH	174
"GIVE ME LIBERTY, OR GIVE ME DEATH"	177
THOMAS JEFFERSON	180
RALEIGH TAVERN	182
MONTICELLO	183
THE APOLLO ROOM	186
UNIVERSITY OF VIRGINIA	190
THOMAS JEFFERSON'S STATUE	191
THE OLD CAPITOL	193
REMAINS OF GUARD-HOUSE	194
RICHARD HENRY LEE	200
PEYTON RANDOLPH	201
INDEPENDENCE HALL, PHILADELPHIA	206
MINUTE-MAN	208
THE OLD MAGAZINE	209
CULPEPER FLAG	210
VIEW OF GREAT BRIDGE	213
GWYN'S ISLAND	215
SPANISH FORT	239
AMERICAN FLAG	240
GEORGE ROGERS CLARKE	246
JOHN MARSHALL	257
OLD TAVERN	264
JOHN RANDOLPH	267
DANIEL MORGAN	289
FLAG OF MORGAN'S RIFLE CORPS	291
MONTGOMERY'S MONUMENT	292
GATES'S HEAD-QUARTERS AT SARATOGA	295
BENEDICT ARNOLD	299
JOHN ANDRÉ	301

ILLUSTRATIONS.

	PAGE
CAPTURE OF ANDRÉ	304
ANDRÉ'S MONUMENT	306
LAFAYETTE	308
BOLLINGBROOK	309
CORNWALLIS	311
GENERAL ANTHONY WAYNE	314
LE COMTE DE GRASSE	319
WASHINGTON AS COMMANDER-IN-CHIEF	322
VIEW AT YORKTOWN	325
CORNWALLIS'S CAVE	327
NELSON HOUSE	328
SURRENDER OF CORNWALLIS AT YORKTOWN	331
MOORE HOUSE	332
MOUNT VERNON	333

STORIES OF THE OLD DOMINION.

THE ADVENTURES OF CAPTAIN JOHN SMITH.

I.

Virginia was founded by Captain John Smith, and I ought to begin my stories with an account of his wonderful adventures.

At that time nearly all the Western world was called Virginia. This name was given to it in honor of Queen Elizabeth, who was never married, and therefore was called the "Virgin Queen." The country was known to be rich, and adventurous Englishmen attempted to settle it; but for a long time these attempts all failed. The Indians drove away the settlers, but the plan was not abandoned; and at last, in December, 1606, three small vessels sailed from England to establish a colony in Virginia.

Among the men in the ships was a young soldier of remarkable character. He was not quite twenty-eight, but he had seen many countries, and fought in nearly every part of Europe. His life from boyhood had been a series of romantic adventures, and he was destined soon, as I will show you, to meet with more adventures still in Virginia. You must have heard of this celebrated man—Captain John Smith. He was the founder of the United States, we may say, as Jamestown was the first English settlement in the New World, and everything about him is interesting. In addition to this, he was so brave and devoted to his duty that his life is an example for boys to follow. I will therefore tell you his story; and his adventures were so singular that they are certain to interest you.

He was born at a town called Willoughby, in England, in the month of January, 1579. Nothing is known about

CAPTAIN JOHN SMITH.

his parents, except that they died when he was a child, and he was left alone in the world without any one to take care of him. But young John Smith was not cast down by his lonely situation. He was a brave and independent boy, and resolved to make his own way in the world. He was fond of adventure, as most boys are; so, while he was still a youth, he wandered away to Holland, a country of Europe, and spent some years of military service in an English army there. This made him long to become a soldier. He therefore came back to Willoughby and set about training himself; and you will be interested in hearing how he did so.

Instead of passing his time in idleness with other young men in the town of Willoughby, he went out to the woods near, and built a sort of house for himself of the boughs of trees. In this he intended to live, and as to supporting himself, he meant to shoot deer and live on the venison. He then got together as many books as he could on warlike matters, and retiring to his "Bower," as he called it, set about studying them. By this means he taught himself the art of war; but as he knew that a soldier must fight with his own hands, he resolved also to learn how to use every sort of weapon. At that time men fought on horseback often, and one of the most important of their weapons was the lance. This was a long wooden affair with a sharp iron point, and soldiers held the head straight in front of them, to strike their enemies as they rode against them at full gallop. Young John Smith had a horse and lance, and he now practised to make himself skilful. This he did by suspending a ring to the bough of a tree, after which he went off to some distance and rode at it at full gallop, pointing his lance at the ring, in order to carry it off from the bough. By repeating this over and over, he at last became expert in it, and then he knew he could strike an enemy on horseback. He also practised with his sword to make his eye keen and his wrist tough, and fired at the trees with his pistol to become an expert marksman. By this means he grew to be a skilful soldier; and then he set out in search of adventures.

These adventures, he knew, would not be wanting, if he only had a brave heart to seek them. War was going on

HOLLAND IN THE OLDEN TIME.

with the Turks in Eastern Europe, and all good soldiers were welcome there, to help the Christians. So Smith set forth gayly with the design to fight hard, and, if he could, make a name for himself.

II.

Wherever young John Smith went, something singular happened to him. His life was crowded with strange adventures; and though I cannot tell you the whole of them, I will relate the chief ones, which will give you a good idea of them all.

THE ADVENTURES OF CAPTAIN JOHN SMITH.

He crossed the Channel between England and France; but as soon as he had landed on the other side, three Frenchmen who had come over with him in the ship took advantage of him. They saw that he was a mere boy, and stole a small trunk containing his money and clothes. This left him in great distress, as he was in a strange country, without friends; but he kept up his courage, and soon showed that he could take care of himself. The Frenchmen had escaped; but he afterward met one of them, and as he knew him at once, he drew his sword and ran it through his breast, killing him. He then wandered on, meeting many kind persons on the way who helped him,

SHIP IN A STORM.

and at last came to the city of Marseilles, on the Mediterranean Sea.

You know that his plan was to go and help the Christians to fight the Turks, so he went on board a ship bound for Rome, which was on his way. A strange adventure now happened to him. The ship set sail, but soon a violent storm arose, and the vessel was tossed about and in danger of being wrecked. On board were some Roman Catholics going to Rome, and they soon discovered that Smith was a Protestant, or *heretic*, as their term was for anybody who was not a Roman Catholic. This brought them bad luck, they said, and there was nothing to do but to get rid of him; so they seized him and threw him into the sea. The waves were running very high at the time, and there was great danger of his being drowned. But he was an excellent swimmer, and struck out for the nearest land. This was a small island, called the Isle of St. Mary's, off the coast of Nice, and here the waves threw him on shore. As the weather was cold, he nearly froze, and he had nothing whatever to eat. But another ship at last came in sight, and Smith made signals of distress by waving to them. They saw him, and a boat was sent, which took him on board the ship, where he was overjoyed to find that the captain was an old friend of his. The ship was bound for Egypt; but as Smith was in search of adventures, he did not care for that. He agreed to go to Egypt, and, as usual, something happened to him on the way. They met with an enemy's ship, and Smith's friend the captain attacked it. A sharp fight took place, but the enemy's ship was captured; and as young Smith had fought bravely, he received about two thousand dollars in gold as his share of the "prize-money."

This made him quite rich, and he determined to go on and fight the Turks. His friend the captain put him ashore in Italy, and he set out joyfully for Transylvania, east of Austria, where the fighting was then going on. He had to pass through a rough wild country, but he did so safely, and at last reached the Christian army, and was enrolled as a soldier in it.

He was now among strangers who knew nothing about him, but they soon saw that the young Englishman was a man of brains as well as courage. There was a fortress called Olimpach, in which some Christians were besieged by the Turks, and the rest of the Christian army came to assist their friends. The trouble was to get a message to the people in the fort, but Smith thought of a means of making signals to answer the purpose. This was done by

FLIGHT OF THE SARACENS.

raising and lowering large flaming torches from the top of a hill at night; and by this means he spelled out a whole sentence, which was understood by the Christians in the fortress. The result of this was that the Turks were attacked on both sides and defeated; and Smith was made a captain, and given a company of horsemen called the "Fiery Dragoons."

This probably filled the young man with delight, and he longed to show that he was ready to fight hard. He soon had an opportunity. The Turks had shut themselves up in a fortress called Regal, and the Christians surrounded the fortress and besieged them. As no fighting was going on, the times grew tedious, and a Turkish lord named Turbashaw sent out word that he was ready to fight any Christian soldier who would meet him. This offer was accepted, and the Christian soldiers drew lots who should fight him. The lot fell on John Smith; and when the day came he rode forward to meet his enemy. Turbashaw was ready, and presented a splendid appearance. His rich armor was covered with jewels, and two large wings made of eagles' feathers sprung from his shoulders. Martial music went before him as he came out of the gates of Regal, and a great crowd of Turkish soldiers and ladies was seen on the walls. The two enemies then rushed upon each other; but the fight was a very brief one. Smith's lance pierced the Turk's forehead, and he was hurled back dead from his horse. Smith then leaped to the ground and cut off his head, and the whole Christian army burst forth into shouts of triumph.

A second Turk then appeared to revenge his friend. His name was Grualgo, and he and Smith rode at each other. Both their lances were shivered, but Smith fired his pistol and broke his enemy's arm. He fell from his horse, and Smith once more leaped down, and struck off his head as he had struck off Turbashaw's.

The young soldier was now in high spirits, and sent a challenge to the Turks. If any of them would meet him, he said, they might have the heads of their friends, and his own, too, if they overcame him. The challenge was accepted by a famous Turk, called Bonnymulgro. It was agreed that they were to fight hand to hand with their swords, pistols, and battle-axes; and on the day appointed greater crowds than before assembled to see the two champions meet. They rushed at full gallop on each other, firing their pistols, and then began to fight hand to hand with their battle-axes. Bonnymulgro was a powerful man and a dangerous enemy. He struck Smith so heavy a blow on the head that he reeled in his saddle and dropped his axe. At this a loud shout rose from the Turks on the walls, and they shouted louder still as they saw Smith wheel his horse and fly, with the big Turk after him. But this was only pretence with the young soldier. As soon as Bonnymulgro caught up with him and raised his axe to beat out his brains, Smith suddenly wheeled his horse, and ran his sword through the Turk's breast. He fell from the saddle, but tried to fight still. But Smith cut him down, and struck off his head, which he held up by the hair to show that the combat was ended.

This was the last of the fighting. There were no more challenges, and the whole Christian army escorted Smith in triumph to the general's tent. The three fine horses of the dead Turks were led in front, and the ghastly heads of the warriors carried aloft on the points of pikes. In this manner they came to the tent of the general, and he made his appearance, and embraced Smith in his arms. He then gave him a fine horse and sword, and made him a major; and the Grand Duke Sigismund, who was carrying on the war, sent him his portrait in a golden frame. He also promised Smith a reward of three hundred ducats, or about two thousand dollars, a year, and told him he might wear on his "coat of arms," as it was called, three Turks' heads, in memory of his exploits.

Whether he ever received the money I do not know, as princes often forget such things; but for this he probably did not care. He had fought for fame, and not in order to be paid for it; and he no doubt looked upon the honor and glory he had won as far better than the golden ducats.

I will now go on, and soon finish with his adventures in Europe.

III.

John Smith was now a distinguished young soldier, but he was soon to find that war is not entirely made up of triumphal processions and rich rewards and success.

A day came when ill-fortune befell him. In a book which he afterward wrote he speaks of "the dismal battle of Rottenton, in the valley of Veristhorne, where the soldiers of Christ and his Gospel did what men could do; and when they could do no more, left there their bodies in testimony of their minds"—by which he means that the Christians fought as long as they could, and fell instead of retreating, in order to show that they were in earnest in making war on the Turks. They were defeated in this "dismal battle," and young John Smith was wounded and left on the field. He lay there until night, when some prowling thieves, who had come to rob the dead bodies of anything they found upon them, heard him groaning from the pain of his wound, and stopped. He had on a very rich suit of armor, and from this they supposed that he was some great lord. They therefore did not kill him, but resolved to carry him away, and keep him prisoner until he paid a large ransom for his freedom again.

John Smith did not tell them that they were mistaken in this, as his life depended on his saying nothing. They then carried him to a city called Axiopolis, and here they found that he was only a poor soldier. He was therefore sold in the slave-market as a common slave, and was bought by a Turk named Bogall, who sent him as a present to a lady in Constantinople named Charatza Tragabigzanda. On the way he was driven along, chained by the neck to other Christian prisoners, and at last they reached Constantinople. Charatza received him kindly, and soon became very much attached to him. Smith found that his master, Bogall, had written a letter pretending that he had made the young man prisoner himself, by which he hoped to persuade Charatza that he was a great soldier; but Smith told her the truth. At last she grew so fond of him that she determined to make a Turk of him and marry him. He was in danger, however, in Constantinople, so she sent him to a brother of hers, called the Tymor of Nalbritz, living on the shores of the Sea of Azov, requesting him to treat Smith kindly for her sake.

This by no means pleased the Tymor. He thought it highly absurd in his sister to take so much interest in a slave. So he stripped off Smith's clothes, and ordered him to put on coarse sheepskins. He next shaved his head, and put an iron ring around his neck, after which he ordered him to go to work among the rest of his slaves.

His situation was now very miserable. He was the "slave of slaves" to all the rest, he says. He therefore determined to take the first opportunity to escape. At last this opportunity came. His work sometimes took him to a lonely barn on the Tymor's large estate, where his business was to thresh out grain with his flail. One day he was thus engaged, with no other person with him, when the Tymor rode up to the barn. He was in a very bad humor; and at such times, you know, people like to have some one to quarrel with. As he looked upon Smith as only a miserable slave, he began to curse him and offer him every insult. This excited the young soldier's anger, and he looked around. Not a soul was in sight, and he had in his hand his heavy flail, which consisted of two pieces of wood joined by a leather thong, and was quite a dangerous weapon. At last the Tymor, after cursing him for some time, struck him with his riding-whip; at which John Smith sprung upon him and dashed his brains out with his flail.

The great thing now was to get away, and the young fellow did not hesitate. He stripped the clothes from the Tymor's dead body, and then took off his own coarse sheepskins. He next put on the Tymor's suit, and hid the body under the straw; after which he leaped on the dead man's horse and rode off at full gallop. He meant to make his way to Russia, where he knew he would be safe, but he did not know the route. Day after day he wandered about, not daring to ask his way of anybody, and nearly starved. But at last he saw, along the road which he was travelling, a number of wooden crosses, and by this he knew that he had at last found his way. The crosses showed that he was coming to a Christian country. He followed the road joyfully, and at last reached a Russian fortress; and here he saw that he had nothing more to fear. He was received with the greatest kindness, as the Turks and Russians were enemies; the iron ring was struck from his neck; and at last he went on his way toward Austria, "drowned in joy," he says, at his deliverance.

His sufferings were now over. His old friends met him in the warmest manner, and the Grand Duke Sigismund made him a present of three or four thousand dollars in gold as some recognition of his services. He then set out for Paris, and then for Spain, where he embarked on a ship to go and fight the Moors in Barbary. What he heard of the war there, however, disgusted him, and he resolved that he would take no part in such heathen proceedings. He therefore left the Mediterranean and made his way back to England, which he reached without further adventures.

IV.

Young John Smith was now only a little more than twenty, but he was already a famous man. He had left his home at Willoughby a poor unknown boy, and had come back a distinguished young soldier.

All London was talking of the brave young fellow who had passed through so many wonderful adventures. They even made his life the subject of plays in the theatres, for he says that "his fatal tragedies were acted on the stage." It is therefore highly probable that he made the acquaintance, among other people, of the great dramatist Shakspeare, who was always looking out for men of remarkable characters. At that time the "Mermaid," and other London taverns, were full of swaggering soldiers returned from the wars. They walked about rattling their swords, curling their mustaches, and boasting of their exploits, while in some quiet corner Mr. William Shakspeare, as he was called, looked at them with a quiet smile on his lips, and listened to all they said. We know that this was his habit, as he has drawn the portraits of a number of such persons in his plays. He made fun of them; but if he knew Smith, he must have seen that *he* was a very different sort of person. No doubt he did know him, as I have already said, and, if so, he must have had a great respect for him. The rest were swaggerers and boasters, passing their time in drinking and idleness, while Smith did nothing of the sort, and was a brave, modest young soldier.

Young John Smith soon found that London was no place for a man like himself. He could not remain idle, and his restless disposition made him long for new adventures. He had seen life in Europe and Asia, and now turned his thoughts to America. This was discovered, you know, by Columbus, in the year 1492, but little was known of it, except that it was a wonderful country. The strangest and most exciting stories were told about it. Now and then sailors had visited it; and when they came back they reported that the earth was full of gold and precious stones, and that the rivers ran over golden sands. More singular things still were believed about the New World, as it was called. There was said to be a fountain there which made old people young again, if they only bathed in it. It was called the "Fountain of Youth," and many people really believed in it. The gold attracted others; and the educated people, who knew that the Fountain of Youth was mere folly, were just as anxious to see the country settled as the rest.

In fact, the whole world of Europe at that time was excited in the highest degree. There had been a great movement called the Reformation, and everybody's mind was in a sort of ferment. People longed for something new: they were tired of old times and things. The world was like a man who has had a long sound sleep, and gets up strong and refreshed, and ready to begin some great business. The rulers of England saw this, and they determined to take advantage of it. For this they had two main reasons. One was to increase the power of England and get ahead of the French and Spaniards, who were looking toward this new world; and another was to convert the Indians to Christianity. They were earnest about this latter thing, little as was afterward done; but they had at heart first the enlargement of English territory. Among these great men was the famous Sir Walter Raleigh, who was so eager for such voyages that people called him the "Shepherd of the Ocean." And all these persons Smith no doubt knew.

He was quite ready to sail for the western land as soon as an expedition was ready; and this event soon took place. James I., who was king of England now, granted the right to Sir Thomas Gates and others to form a settlement in the New World; and in December, 1606, the three small ships which I have mentioned set sail for the shores of America.

John Smith was on board one of the vessels, and I will soon tell you what happened to him. First I will speak, however, of the voyage, which was over what was called the "old track." The ships, with one hundred and five men in them, crossed the ocean in safety, and reached the West India Islands.

FORM OF RALEIGH'S SHIPS.

They then sailed northward along the coast of Florida and the Carolinas, looking for a good harbor. When they reached the mouth of Chesapeake Bay they were tossed by a violent storm, but managed to get in without being wrecked. This was in April, 1607, and some time was spent in looking for a place of settlement. Before them was a broad river, which was called the Powhatan by the Indians, and this they sailed up, delighted with the beautiful prospect before them. Spring had come, and all was fresh and attractive. The shores were covered with green trees, and white-winged water-fowl skimmed the waves. The skies were blue, and the birds were singing, and the weary storm-tossed sailors must have thought that they were near a peaceful harbor at last, perhaps not far from the wonderful Fountain of Youth.

Some Indians came down to the shore and stared at the ships as they sailed by; but they went on up the broad current until they reached a sort of island close to the shore, where they resolved to stop. Here the ships cast anchor on the 13th of May, 1607, and the new settlement was called Jamestown, in honor of the king.

To-day an old ruined church is still standing on this spot, to show where Virginia began.

V.

In a short story like this I cannot tell you everything, you know—that would make my book too long. I shall

CHESAPEAKE BAY.

only relate a few incidents of those old times; but these will prove interesting, I think, and will show you how bravely Smith struggled for the good of the colony.

The English sailors were now in that famous "virgin land" they had heard so much of, and had nothing to look to but the help of God and their own arms to guard them. Some persons have supposed that they were a rough, irreligious set, only greedy for gold. But this is not true. As soon as they landed at Jamestown and pitched their tents, they stretched an old sail between four trees to shade them from the sun, and under this they held religious services night and morning. They had a minister with them, and his pulpit was a bar of wood nailed to two trees. Here he held regular prayers, and preached two sermons every Sunday, and every three months administered the Holy Communion. A regular church was afterward built, and a bell was placed in it; and when this bell rang, at ten o'clock in the morning and four in the afternoon, every man stopped work, and knelt down and said his prayers.

I tell you this to show you that the colonists were not bad men. They had many faults, but they respected religious things, and did not forget that "the end of this voyage was the destruction of the devil's kingdom"—that is, to live good lives themselves and convert the Indians to Christianity. They did not work hard enough, and were too anxious to pick up the gold they expected to find; but they began in the right manner, by attending to their religious duties, you see.

One great reason why they were lazy was the character of the men who led them. Most of these were perfectly worthless, and John Smith was almost the only man among them worthy of any respect. But he could do nothing for the settlers. He had been arrested by the leaders, while the ships were crossing the ocean, on some foolish charge that he intended to make himself king of Virginia, and iron fetters were placed upon his wrists. These they now had to remove. King James I. had not told any one the names of the "councillors" who were to rule over the colony. The paper containing their names was sealed up in a box, which was not to be opened until the ships reach-

2*

ed Virginia. But the time had now come: the box was opened, and the name of John Smith was found among those who were to be councillors, or leaders. They therefore released him, but refused to let him sit in the council;

JAMESTOWN.

so he found that he had no more authority than the poorest of the settlers.

But in this world brains and courage will show themselves, in spite of everything. The colonists soon saw that Smith had more sense and energy than all the worthless council put together. From the first he was the real leader in the colony. His martial figure was seen moving about everywhere. The settlers felt that he was a true soldier, and the man to look to. And this is a good opportunity to tell you what his appearance and character were at that time.

Any one could see at a glance that John Smith was a thorough soldier. He was just twenty-eight, and a handsome, brave-looking man. His forehead was broad and high, and his bright eyes looked everybody straight in the face. He wore long mustaches and a full beard, and his dress was martial. It consisted of a steel hauberk, which was a sort of armor covering the body down to the hips, and his boots came to his knees, and the tops turned over. Around his waist was buckled a belt, from which hung his heavy broadsword; and he generally carried a carbine, that is, a short gun with a large barrel. He had to use this carbine more than once, as you will see, against the Indians; and one look at him showed that he was ready to fight with it or any other weapon. He was polite and friendly, but he was not a man to be trifled with. He had come to do hard work, and he meant to do it. His bold off-hand manner showed that he was a soldier, and people were forced to respect him, whether they liked him or not. The best and bravest of the colonists, however, liked him very much, for they saw that he was worthy of it. He was not only a resolute and unselfish man, but had no vices whatever. He never uttered an oath, or played cards, or drank, and did not even use tobacco, which was then the fashion as now. He was content to live roughly and do his duty, and never seemed to be thinking of his own pleasure in the least. He hated idleness, and set an example by working himself. In fact, hard work and hard fighting seemed to be his idea of the right way of living in this world. If he said he would do a thing, he always kept his word; and a man who establishes that character is looked up to and trusted. His "old soldiers," as the men called themselves, loved him, and had the highest respect for him; and you will see that these old soldiers who fought under him and shared his hardships were right when they said that he was one of the bravest and truest of men.

Rough houses of felled trees were soon built at Jamestown; and then Smith began to think what it would be better to do next. The councillors were a poor set, and nobody had any respect for them. They passed their time in idling and eating and drinking, and seemed to have no idea of the dangers all around them. They had seen little of the Indians, and very foolishly paid no attention to them. Besides this, nothing was done to raise corn for food; and Smith looked on in astonishment at such childish folly. He knew that the woods were full of Indians, who would soon attack them. He also knew that the food in the ships would not last forever. He therefore resolved to go and explore the country, and find what they had to expect by making the Indians a visit.

With a small party of men Smith, therefore, rowed up James River, as they had called it, to visit the emperor of the Indian tribes, who lived in that direction.

VI.

The name of the Indian emperor was Powhatan. He was an old and famous monarch, who ruled over all the Indians of tidewater Virginia, amounting at that time to about eight thousand in number.

The Indians were a strange people, and not at all like other savages—those of Africa, for instance. They were tall and powerful, and as brave and cool as they were bloody. They were very fond of hunting and war, and when they were going into battle, painted their naked bodies in a frightful manner. As to their arms, these were bows and arrows, and a sort of hatchet made of flint, which they called a "tomahawkee;" and they lived in wigwams or rough log-cabins. Wigwams were made by bending together the heads of saplings, and tying them with bark. Skins were then stretched around them, and a hole was left at the top to allow the smoke to rise. The food of the Indians was game, chiefly deer and wild turkeys or ducks, and their bread was made of corn-meal, as they had no wheat. They smoked tobacco in long stone pipes, and when any one visited them in their wigwams or cabins, they would take a whiff and then pass the pipe to their guest, which was looked upon as a proof of friendship. They had a sort of money made of shells, which they strung on a string; and their clothes were deer or raccoon skins, rarely worn except in winter.*

This will give you some idea of these singular people; but I ought not to forget to say that they also had a sort of religion. They believed in a god of their own, whose name was Okee,

INDIANS.

or Kiwasa, and thought the thunder was his voice, and the lightning the flash of his eyes. They also believed in a future world of happiness or misery. If they were good, they expected to go to the "happy hunting-grounds" of heaven; and if they were bad, to a great fire in which they would burn forever. They were savage, and when they took their enemies prisoners, either killed or burned them by tying them naked to a stake in the ground, and piling wood around them; but they were not entirely bad. The men were dignified, and bore pain without a word, and the women were often pure and affectionate. All were brave, and they would not allow any one to rule over them who was not as brave as themselves: and the old emperor, Powhatan, was obeyed and respected because he was a man of dauntless courage.

You will meet with this remarkable old emperor, Powhatan, hereafter. I will only say now that he had many places of residence throughout the country, where he lived at different seasons, and that his summer resort was near the Falls of James River, just below where the city of Richmond now stands. It was a little village of about twelve cabins, on a hill opposite three islands in the river, and the spot is still called "Powhatan" after him. Here Smith and his companions, who had come up from Jamestown, found the old emperor; and he pretended that he was very glad to see them. He was a tall, strong old man, clad in a royal robe of skins, with moccasins (a sort of shoe decorated with beads) on his feet, and on his head he wore a plume of feathers. Thus clad, he received the white people, surrounded by his many wives, and a hundred bowmen, who always guarded his person night and day.

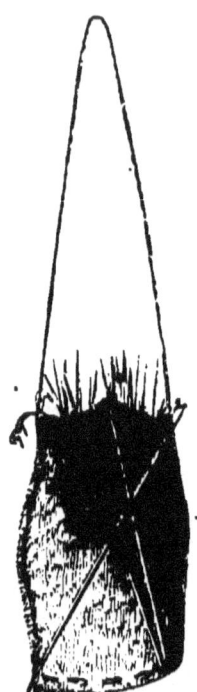
POISONED ARROWS.

Their meeting was friendly, as I have said, and they talked by means of signs. What took place during the interview we are not informed, but Smith soon found that he had a cool and cunning old enemy to deal with. Having finished his visit, he and his men rowed back down the river; but they had no sooner reached Jamestown than they found how treacherous the Indians were. In their absence the savages had made an attack on the place. No doubt Powhatan had sent them as soon as he heard from his spies that Smith was coming up the river. One of the settlers had been killed by an Indian arrow and several wounded; but a cannon-shot was fired into the band from one of the ships, and this made such a noise, as it crashed through the woods, that the Indians fled and did not return.

John Smith now became every day more and more the head of everything. The worthless "Council" were the face of the clock for people to look at, but he was the mainspring which moved the works. He was the master-mind, and everybody could see it. The hot summer had made them all sick, and the Council were doing nothing; so Smith resolved to take things into his own hands. This he did at once. He demanded a trial on the charges against him, and forced them to acquit him. He then took his place in the Council, and made every one go to work. Not long afterward he went on an expedition down the river, but on his return found that some of the councillors meant to run off with one of the ships to England.

Smith made short work of them. He aimed the cannon in the fort at Jamestown against the ship, and sent word that if they tried to escape he would fire upon them and sink them. This brought them to their senses. A short fight took place, in which one of their party was killed, and then they came ashore and surrendered. A change was made in the Council, another president being elected; and as cool weather now came, the colonists grew well. The river was full of wild-ducks, which come to feed at this season, and these supplied fresh food for the colonists. Smith had also obtained corn from the Indians for bread; so the prospect before them was far brighter than before.

VII.

We come now to the famous rescue of John Smith by Pocahontas, the daughter of Powhatan; and of this I will give you an account.

One of the orders of King James was that the New World should be carefully explored, and all the information possible obtained of it. Smith always remembered this; and as he had gone some distance up James River, he now determined to explore another river not far above Jamestown.

This was the Chickahominy, and he set out to visit it about the beginning of winter. With a few men he rowed up and entered the wide mouth of the stream, and then went on until it grew so narrow and shallow that his boat could go no farther. He did not know, probably, that the "Chickahominies" were the most daring and warlike of all the tribes; but he soon found that they were dangerous enemies. Some came down to the bank of the river, and professed to be very friendly. They made signs that if he wanted a smaller boat to go higher up, they would supply one, and also guides to show him the way.

Smith accepted the offer, and the skiff or canoe was brought. He got into it, with two of his men and two of the Indians; and then ordering the rest of his men not to leave the big boat and go ashore, set off in his canoe to explore the stream higher up. He was soon out of sight behind the tangled vines and undergrowth, the place where he left them being near the great White Oak Swamp; and then the men disobeyed him and went on shore. The Indians attacked them at once, driving them back to the boat, and taking one of them prisoner. He was at once put to death, and then the Indians hastened up the river in pursuit of Smith.

They soon found him. He had gone on up the Chickahominy, forcing his way through the vines and low-hanging boughs, until he was near an Indian place called Orapax. Here he stopped and landed, and, taking one of the Indian guides, set out on foot to look at the country. He had ordered the two men in the canoe to keep a sharp lookout, but they foolishly disobeyed him. They were cold, and kindled a fire, beside which they lay down and went to sleep. The Indians in pursuit found them and killed them at once, and then they went on to put an end to Smith.

He was going through the woods with his guide, an Indian boy, when a flight of arrows came from the undergrowth, and the Indians rushed upon him. His situation seemed desperate. He was alone in the heart of the woods, far from help, and surrounded by the savages; but he was a cool man, and not disposed to lose his courage. He saw that his only hope was to get back to the boat; so he tied the Indian boy to his left arm, as a protection from the arrows, and hastened back in the direction of the river. He fired his carbine at the Indians, and this startled them so much that he would probably have escaped. But he did not know the danger of the swamp he was hurrying through. The ground was soft and treacherous, and before he knew it he sank to his waist. The Indians then rushed upon him, and in a moment disarmed him and took him prisoner.

Things now looked hopeless. Smith was in the power of his enemies, and had very little doubt that they would at once put him to death. Their chief was named Opechancanough, and at first he seemed to have made some impression on this warrior. He had a small pocket-compass with him, and this he explained to him, and made him a present of it. But they soon bound him to a tree, and the bows were bent to shoot him, when Opechancanough waved the compass around his head, and ordered them to stop.

Smith was then unbound and taken to Orapax, where the Indian women and children danced around him with wild shrieks. The band then set out, and travelled day after day toward the Potomac. They walked in single file, with Smith in their midst, and an Indian guard beside him kept their bows bent ready to shoot him if he attempted to escape. As they passed through village after village, the women and children shrieked and danced around him as they had done at Orapax; and this march seems to have been a sort of triumphal procession, to show that they had made prisoner the great leader of the "Pale Faces."

At last they reached the banks of the Potomac River, and then they marched back toward the royal residence of the emperor Powhatan. This was on the banks of York River, in what is now Gloucester County. The Indian name for it was Werowocomoco, and Powhatan spent his winters there to enjoy the fish and oysters, as his summers were passed near the Falls of James River, for the benefit of the cool breezes.

Smith was now once more in presence of this famous old warrior, and saw him surrounded by his woodland court. The hundred bowmen of his guard were grouped around, and he was lying down in his large wigwam, in the midst of his wives. On his head he wore a rich plume of feathers; a string of beads was around his neck, and he was wrapped in a large robe of raccoon skins. At his head sat one Indian girl and another at his feet. These were his favorite wives, and quite young, as the Indian women often married when they were only twelve or thirteen. They wore dresses of fur, which were highly orna-

POCAHONTAS INTERCEDING FOR JOHN SMITH.

mented, and their arms and shoulders were painted a deep red. In their straight black hair they wore plumes of sea-fowls, and white bead necklaces around their necks, probably pearls from oysters. Other women were ranged around the wigwam, in which was a fire, and behind were a crowd of warriors, who uttered a wild yell as Smith was brought in.

Powhatan looked at him keenly, and gave an order to a young Indian princess near him. She was the "Queen of Appomattox," and brought him a wooden basin to wash his hands in. This he did, and she then presented him with a bunch of feathers in place of a towel; and then meat and corn-bread were set before him, while Powhatan consulted with his warriors what to do with him.

His fate was soon decided. The Indians hated the whites; and as they had the leader of them in their power, they determined at once to put him to death. At an order from Powhatan, Smith was therefore seized, and his arms were bound together behind him. A large stone was then brought in and his head was laid upon it; and at another order from the emperor a tall savage raised a club to beat out his brains. In another moment the club would have fallen, and Smith would have died cruelly; but a kind Providence watched over him. An Indian girl of twelve or thirteen sprang toward him. From her dress, it was plain that she ranked as a princess. The plume in her black hair was similar to that worn by Powhatan, and her moccasins were embroidered like the old emperor's. On her arms were bracelets of shells, and from her shoulders fell a robe of doeskin, covered with the plumage of birds, and lined with down from the breasts of wild pigeons.

This girl was Pocahontas, or "Bright-Stream-between-two-Hills," as her name meant in the English language, and she was the favorite daughter of the old emperor. She was filled with pity for the poor prisoner, and ran and clasped her arms around him, looking up to her father with beseeching eyes as she did so. The heavy club did not fall. The blow would have killed Pocahontas, as Smith's head was clasped to her breast; and Powhatan ordered that the prisoner's life should be spared. He was therefore unbound, and found himself free; and Powhatan soon showed him that he had nothing to fear. He entertained him in a very friendly manner, and not long afterward allowed him to return to Jamestown. And that was the fortunate ending of this famous adventure.

POCAHONTAS.

I have related it without exaggerating anything—that is, making it out finer or greater than it really was. Pocahontas was only a child, but acted nobly, and like a true woman. There was no especial reason why she should rescue the young Englishman. He was a perfect stranger, and she must have heard that he was a dangerous enemy. Nevertheless, she risked her life for him, and she deserves our love and respect. Looking back to those far-off times now, we can see the brave girl, and the fearless young soldier whom she saved; and Virginia is fortunate in having two such figures on the threshold of her history.

Pocahontas often came to Jamestown afterward, we are told, with her "wild train" of Indian boys and girls, and gambolled about in the market-place and on the grass. She was a mere child, full of high spirits, and there was no reason why she should not do so. But she was a woman in her feelings too, and showed it in times of trial. Once Powhatan determined to attack the English; but Pocahontas overheard him consulting with his warriors about it, and stole off through the woods at night, in the midst of a violent storm, to tell them of the danger to which they were exposed. She then stole back in the same way; and when Powhatan came he found them ready for him, so he gave up the idea of attacking them.

This is nearly all we know of Pocahontas, or "Matoa," as her other name was, when she was a little girl and proved herself so good a friend to the English. As I have said, she deserves our love and respect for her devotion and courage; and among all the legends, as they are called, of history there is none more beautiful than her rescue of Smith.

VIII.

I cannot follow John Smith through all his adventures in Virginia. You will one of these days read the long books in which they are related. With a few more words, I will pass on to other stories I have to tell you.

He and Powhatan had many dealings with each other. Sometimes they bargained about swapping a grindstone for some corn. At other times they visited each other, though Powhatan would not come to Jamestown; and they had numerous battles. At last Powhatan grew tired, and said he wished to live in peace. What he said to Smith showed how much sense he had, or how cunning he was.

"I have seen two generations of my people die," the old

copper-faced emperor said, "and not a man of these two generations is alive now but myself. I know the difference between peace and war better than any man in my country. I am now grown old, and must die soon. Why will you take by force what you may have quietly by love? Why will you destroy us who supply you with food? What can you get by war? I am not so simple as not to know that it is much better to eat good meat, sleep comfortably, live quietly with my wives and children, and laugh and be merry with the English, and trade for their copper and hatchets, than to run away from them, and to lie cold in the woods, feed on acorns, roots, and such trash, and be so hunted that I can neither eat nor sleep. In these wars my men must sit up watching, and if a twig breaks they cry, '*Here comes Captain Smith!*' So I must end my miserable life. Take away your guns and swords, the cause of all our jealousy, or you may all die in the same manner!"

John Smith, no doubt, listened to this speech quietly, without putting any great faith in the old fellow's words. He knew him too well to trust him; but perhaps the old emperor was sincere. He probably saw that Smith was too brave a soldier to be defeated, and that the best thing would be to make peace with him. This is not opposed to what we know of Powhatan. He was a long-headed old ruler, and not a mere stupid savage. An Englishman named Ralph Hamor paid him a visit once, on the Pamunky, and gives us a very good idea of him. He was hospitable and liberal after his wildwood fashion. He grew angry at something, but went away and got over it; and when something amused him he laughed heartily. He was a real king, and governed all around him: the only person who gave him any trouble was Smith.

I cannot tell you, as I have said, all Smith's adventures

with Powhatan and the rest. Once he had a single-handed fight with his old enemy Opechancanough, and caught him by his hair and dragged him off prisoner. At another time he fought and captured an Indian giant named Paspahey; and I might go on and tell you of other exploits of his, if I had the time.

His most important act, however, was his exploration of the great Chesapeake Bay. He made two voyages in an open boat, going at least three thousand miles, and drew a map of the whole country, which was so true that it has never needed any correction. He went up all the great rivers, fighting the Indians wherever he met with them, and landed and cooked his dinner where the city of Baltimore now stands. He then came back and went up the Potomac, past the city of Washington, and up the Rappahannock and all the rivers along the coast.

One day he came very near losing his life. The boat ran on a sand-bank, and he saw some strange-looking fish in the water. They were odd-looking creatures, with long tails like a saw, and Smith stuck the point of his sword into one of them, and attempted to take it in his hand. As he did so, the fish writhed its sharp tail around and stung him in his wrist. Soon the place turned blue, and his arm began to swell. The swelling went on growing worse and extending toward his shoulder; and at last he was convinced that he was going to die. He was so certain of this that he picked out a spot on the shore where he told his men they must bury him. But the swelling at last went down. It was rubbed with a certain oil, and finally disappeared; and in memory of the incident Smith called the place "Stingray Point," a name it bears still.

Soon afterward the brave boatmen got back safely to Jamestown. They had made a remarkable voyage, and when people heard of it in England they wondered at it.

But this was only one of Smith's remarkable exploits and adventures in the New World. He had many others, which you will read of when you are older. In spite of all his exertions for the good of the colony, there were some base persons who hated him, and even tried to destroy him. An attempt was made to poison him by these wretched creatures, and at another time a plot was formed to murder him.

All this he would not have cared for, as he was a fearless man, and knew that he was doing his duty. But at last a painful accident brought his career in Virginia to an end. As he was rowing down James River one day, a bag of gunpowder in his boat exploded, and he was terribly burned. He was all in flames, as his clothes had caught fire, and the pain was so fearful that he leaped into the water to extinguish the fire. In this he succeeded, but he came near being drowned, and his men could scarcely get him into the boat again and take him home. He at last reached Jamestown; but his burns were terrible. There was no surgeon to dress them, and he determined to go back to England and find one. As a ship was about to sail, he embarked upon the vessel; and that was the last of John Smith in Virginia.

He had come over in the spring of 1607, and went back in the autumn of 1609. It seemed a very short time—not three years in all; but in this time he had laid, broad and deep, the foundations of the Commonwealth of Virginia.

IX.

I must not end my story of the adventures of John Smith without telling you the fate of Pocahontas, and of Smith's last meeting with her. Everything concerning this devoted girl is interesting, and I will proceed to tell you what became of her.

Some years passed, and the little girl of thirteen was now a maiden of seventeen or eighteen, and quite good-looking, as her portrait, which was taken soon afterward, shows. She had straight black hair (for the hair of the Indians never curled), bright black eyes, regular features, and was not too brown to be very pretty. She often came to Jamestown, as I have told you, and remained friendly to the English. But they requited her for this in a very poor way. While she was on a visit to some of her friends toward the Potomac, she was betrayed by them for a copper-kettle to the English, and taken back prisoner to Jamestown. Their object seems to have been to hold her as a hostage, as it is called, and thus make her father remain quiet. She was kept for some time, and a young gentleman named John Rolfe became very much in love with her, and she with him.

Rolfe scarcely knew what to do. The Indians were looked upon as an inferior race of people, and mere heathens; and at that time it was considered a sin to intermarry with such persons. Rolfe was therefore much troubled, and wrote a long letter to Sir Thomas Dale, who was then governor. He knew, he said, that in the Bible men were forbidden to marry "strange wives" who were heathens, but that Pocahontas was ready to become a Christian. He loved her, he said, and he was acting for the good of the colony and the glory of God. He was sincere in this, he declared, and he gave a high character to Pocahontas. His words were: "Likewise adding hereunto her great appearance of love to me, her desire to be taught and instructed in the knowledge of God, her capableness of understanding, her aptness and willingness to receive any good impression, and also the spiritual besides her own incitements stirring me up hereunto."

There is no reason to believe that John Rolfe was not

honest in what he wrote. Every word came from his heart, as any one who read his letter could see; and those who knew him spoke of him as a "discreet gentleman" and a man of high character. The governor gave his consent, and soon afterward Pocahontas became a Christian, and was baptized at Jamestown under the name of Rebecca. She and Rolfe were then married, and he went with her to England, where she was called the "Lady Re-

MARRIAGE OF POCAHONTAS.

becca," and treated like a princess. It is even said that King James looked upon her as the daughter of a real emperor, and grew angry at one of his plain subjects having married into a royal family.

In England, about three years afterward, Pocahontas again met with John Smith. He paid her a visit, and they talked together for two or three hours. She was then twenty-one and he was thirty-seven; and though they were thus both tolerably young people still, it seemed an age since they had last met. They must have remembered old times in Virginia, where they knew each other so well; and Pocahontas was ready to meet him with the same joy and affection as before. But Smith would not allow this, or permit her to call him "father," as she had been in the habit of doing. It is probable that he had heard of the king's foolish ideas, and thought that there might be trouble. He therefore addressed her as "Lady Rebecca," and treated her with great respect.

At this Pocahontas covered her face with her hands and began to cry. It was unkind in him, she said, in a faltering voice, to speak so coldly to her. In Virginia she had called him father, and he had called her his child, and she meant to call him father still. What had become of him all this time? she asked: they had told her he was dead. She murmured these low words from behind her hands, which she never took away from her face. And that is all we know of her last meeting with John Smith.

Some persons have supposed that when he left Virginia, she loved him and expected to marry him, as the Indian girls became wives often when they were very young. It is also said that the friends of Rolfe knew this, and therefore told her that Smith was dead, in order to induce her to give up the idea. Of this nothing is known at this far-off time. Smith was young and handsome, and Pocahontas saved his life; so it is not improbable that she had formed a deep affection for him.

The meeting I have spoken of was their last. About a year afterward she and her husband were about to sail for Virginia, when Pocahontas was taken ill, and soon afterward died. She left one son, whose name was Thomas Rolfe. He returned to Virginia, where he afterward married; and among his descendants were the great orator

John Randolph of Roanoke, and some of the most respectable people in Virginia.

Such was the end of this "tender virgin," as John Smith calls her in a letter to the king. She was only a child of twelve or thirteen, he says, when she saved his life, and he adds: "Her compassionate, pitiful heart of my desperate estate gave me much cause to respect her; she hazarded the beating out of her brains to save mine; ... and during the time of two or three years she, next under God, was the instrument to preserve this colony from death, famine, and confusion."

Could praise be much higher than this? If we think of Pocahontas and of what she did—of her "aptness and willingness to receive any good impression," and her "desire to be taught and instructed in the knowledge of God"—we have before us a very beautiful character to love and admire.

X.

I have thus related the chief events in the life of the brave soldier John Smith, and with a few more words will go on with other stories.

He continued to make voyages, and received from King James I. the title of "Admiral of New England;" but at length he went into retirement, and spent his last days in quiet. He died in 1631, at the age of fifty-two, and was buried in St. Sepulchre's Church, in the city of London. His grave was just in front of the chancel, and two flat stones were placed in the floor above it. On one of these was carved his coat-of-arms, with the three Turks' heads upon it; and on the other these words were cut,

"HERE LIES ONE CONQUERED THAT HATH CONQUERED KINGS."

Under this was a prayer that when God came to judge him he might "with angels have his recompense." And there the dust of the brave soldier remains to the present day.

My story must have shown you the true character of John Smith. He lived in a remarkable age, and was one of the foremost men of his time. The Middle or Dark Ages, as they are called, were giving way to the modern world, and John Smith seemed to have in his character what was best in both. He was a romantic soldier, but a man of business also. He loved fame, but was ready for the hardest work. We find him talking at one moment with dukes and princes, and then, axe in hand, cutting down trees to build palisades. He was ready to fight the Turks, or to bargain with Powhatan for a grindstone. In all this he showed his good-sense and readiness to do his duty. He looked to Heaven to help him always, but he meant to do his best also to help himself; and this makes him a noble example.

WHY VIRGINIA WAS CALLED THE "OLD DOMINION."

I.

Virginia received the name of the "Old Dominion" about fifty years after the settlement at Jamestown. What led to it was somewhat curious; and as you ought to know about the events, I will tell you what they were in a very few words.

The colony went on increasing in these first years, in spite of every difficulty, as to which I will say more when I come to my next story. I need only tell you now that at the middle of the century—that is to say, about the year 1650—there were twenty thousand people in Virginia, and the land was prosperous. Many persons of high character had come over after the death of Charles I., for fear of being persecuted by their enemies in England; and I will show you how much courage they exhibited in times of trial, which were now near.

The trouble grew out of affairs in England. About 1640 a great struggle took place there between King Charles I. and the Parliament. They complained that the king was a tyrant, and he charged them with rebellion and treason; and the result was that a bloody war began, which for some time was doubtful. At last the king was defeated and made prisoner by the Parliament, when they went through the form of trying him, and beheaded him in front of his palace in London.

A new government was now established, and Oliver

WHY VIRGINIA WAS CALLED THE "OLD DOMINION." 57

Cromwell, the leader of the Parliament party, was made "Lord Protector of England." He was a man of great genius, and made a powerful ruler; but the Virginians were by no means pleased at the manner in which he had gained his power. Many of them were "Cavaliers," as they were called, and had fought for King Charles, and the Virginians generally were in favor of royal authority. They were proud enough, and ready at all times to fight for their rights, against the king or anybody else, as you

LOG-CABIN.

will see when you have read a few pages farther; but they looked upon the execution of Charles I. as murder, and, like brave men, openly said so, in spite of Cromwell and the Parliament, who ruled affairs with an iron hand everywhere.

I will now give you the proof of this. Charles was executed in the month of January, 1649; and in the following October the Virginia Burgesses passed a law which

I will tell you of. In this law they said that if any one went about in Virginia declaring that the execution of "the late most excellent and now undoubtedly sainted king," Charles I., was justifiable, such persons should be arrested and punished as traitors, just as if they had taken part in the king's death. And in the law there is another very remarkable passage. It speaks of "his sacred majesty that *now is*," and threatens with bloody punishment anybody who denied "the inherent right of *his majesty that now is* to the colony of Virginia."

You may not understand what these words, "his majesty *that now is*," meant, and I will explain them. The friends of royal rule believed that kings were entitled to authority by birth, and that if one died or was put to death, the next heir began to reign from that hour. He might not be able to assert his claim and make himself king, but he was the true king for all that, wherever he was; and this was the meaning of the law passed by the Burgesses. Charles I. had a son, who had been driven out of England. He was a careless young fellow, very good-hearted, but rather worthless, who was lurking at this time in Holland. He was only about eighteen, and scarcely had clothes to wear, such was his poverty; but homeless as he was, and almost an object of charity, the followers of his father looked upon him as the real King of England.

In this feeling the Virginians shared, you see; and in spite of the great Parliament, they said what they thought. I have shown this by quoting the words of the law passed by the House of Burgesses. They spoke of the boy who was lurking and dodging about in Europe as "his majesty that *now is*," and denounced the penalty of treason against any one who denied that he was the true King of England and Virginia. This, of course, was a dangerous proceeding. Oliver Cromwell was one of the most powerful rulers of Europe—for he ruled from the very beginning—and was a bitter enemy. Scarcely a man in all England dared to whisper that the execution of Charles I. was unjustifiable; and as to asserting that his son was entitled to the throne, they knew that short work would be made of any one who did so. Parliament hated the very name of Charles, and hunted down his friends everywhere; and it was in the midst of all this that the Virginia Burgesses stood up for the young man in exile. An offer was even made to him that if he would come over, the Virginians would fight for him; and I will tell you how and by whom this offer was made.

The name of the Governor of Virginia at that time was Sir William Berkeley, of whom I will have more to say when I come to my story of Bacon's Rebellion. I need only tell you here that this Sir William was a fiery old Cavalier, and he resolved to send and invite young Charles II., as he called him, to Virginia. No law was passed by the Burgesses giving him authority to do so, but his design was certainly well known to the leading Virginians, among whom was Colonel Richard Lee, a planter on the Potomac, who was as strong a Cavalier as Sir William Berkeley.

Richard Lee set sail, and visited young Charles II. at a place called Breda, in Holland. Here he had a long conversation with the youth, and told him how the Virginians felt toward him. Richard Lee never wrote down an account of his interview, or the paper is now lost; but it is known that he informed the young prince that the Virginians wished to have nothing to do with the Parliament, and that if he would come over they would espouse his cause, in case there was any hope of making him king and of not destroying themselves. That this offer was made to Charles we are told by William Lee, sheriff of the city of London, and a cousin of Richard, who wrote it all down, and said he knew about the visit to Breda.

II.

Nothing came of the whole affair. Charles refused to come over to Virginia, and I think he showed more sense by doing so than people gave him credit for. The attempt to make him king in Virginia would, no doubt, have failed, and he declined to accept the offer. But he sent back to Sir William Berkeley a new commission—at this time or afterward—as Governor of Virginia, signed by himself as King of England; and this the Virginians looked on as a real commission from a real king.

Richard Lee had to come back without succeeding in his business; and the English Parliament soon showed that they were not to be trifled with. They were much too powerful and determined to allow themselves to be defied by a small colony like Virginia. There was no one in England who was fearless enough to declare openly that he was in favor of Charles II., and yet here was Sir William Berkeley and the House of Burgesses of Virginia proclaiming that he was their king.

Oliver Cromwell and the Parliament resolved to put an end to the whole matter at once. In 1652 an English fleet was sent across the water, and a part of it sailed up the river to Jamestown.

It seemed quite absurd to suppose that Virginia could resist the Parliament, and the strong force sent over, which was quite sufficient to crush her. Certainly the English commander had cannon enough to blow Jamestown to pieces. But in spite of this, Berkeley and the rest resolved to fight. Now was the time, if ever, to show that they were in earnest when they said they would fight the

Parliament, and preparations were at once made for battle. The Virginians had flocked to Jamestown, on hearing that ships of war were coming up the river, and were now furnished with muskets and ammunition. Cannon were posted to rake the river below the place, and some Dutch ships were also made use of as a sort of fort. These were merchant ships which had brought cargoes of goods to Jamestown; and as England and Holland were then at war, the Dutchmen were afraid of losing their goods. These were quickly moved on shore; then cannon were placed in the vessels, and they were drawn up in a line ready to open fire as soon as the enemy approached.

They came in sight at last, and it seemed certain that a battle would take place. But none followed. A boat came to shore, and a message was brought to Governor Berkeley. This was a summons to surrender to the authority of Parliament; and a promise was made, if they consented to do so, that they should not be interfered with in any way. At this a long consultation was held, some being in favor of it and others against it. But at last it was decided that the terms offered should be accepted, and a paper was drawn up in which Virginia agreed to submit. This paper is quite remarkable under all the circumstances. The Virginians made their terms as if they were one nation treating with another which they were not at all afraid of. There is no cringing anywhere about this paper, which is still in existence. Its tone is proud and resolute. The Virginians declared in it that they were not "forced nor constrained by a conquest of the country" to surrender, but did so of their own accord. But they would not be oppressed. They intended to enjoy every privilege belonging to English people. No man was to be punished for anything he had said or done in favor of the king. Virginia was to have the right of trading freely with all nations. Governor Berkeley was not to be interfered with, or his property touched; and they were to have the right to use the Episcopal Prayer-book in church, which at that time the Parliament party hated as bitterly as they hated the king.

These were a few of the terms, and none of them were objected to. There is very little doubt that this was in

THE KING AT BOSCOBEL.

consequence of orders from Cromwell. He was a very great statesman, and knew how desirable it was for the English colonies to remain on good terms with the Mother Country, as England was called. Destroying them would only have weakened the power of England; and I suppose he thought the Cavalier feeling in Virginia could do no great harm. Still there was danger in humoring it, too, as Charles II. might come over, and his friends might then rise in England. So Cromwell is entitled to all the credit he deserves for acting like a great ruler and a man of sense.

The Virginians thus gave up to the Parliament, and Sir William Berkeley retired to his plantation. The Burgesses then went on making laws and governing the colony to suit themselves, just as if they were an independent nation belonging to nobody, and Parliament did not interfere with them. At last a great change came, and the English people resolved to place young Charles II. on the throne. Two years before this was done, William Lee says that the Virginians proclaimed Charles II. King of England and Virginia, though nothing is found to prove this in the laws passed by the Burgesses. It is not very important. The people wished to, if they did not do so; for in March, 1660, the Burgesses re-elected old Sir William Berkeley "Governor and Captain-general of Virginia," who certainly proclaimed him. And as it was not until April of the same year that Charles was made King of England, he was *King of Virginia* first, you see, after all.

It is said that at his coronation—that is, when the crown was placed upon his head—he wore a robe of Virginia silk, to show his gratitude for all this; and after that time the kings of England looked with great favor on Virginia. It was proclaimed on coins, that is, pieces of money, that the English kingdom should thenceforward consist of "England, Scotland, Ireland, *and Virginia;*" and on these coins was the inscription, "*En dat Virginia quartam,*" which are Latin words, signifying "See, Virginia makes *the fourth.*" One of these coins is said to be in the Massachusetts Historical Society's collection. This was considered a high honor for the little colony, to rank her with such great countries as England, Scotland, and Ireland: but her course in favor of Charles, when he had scarcely a friend in the world, showed that her people were brave and devoted. She was therefore generally spoken of as the "Old Dominion," where Charles II. was first proclaimed king after the execution of his father, and where he had *dominion*—that is, "sovereign authority"—when he had none anywhere else.

The Virginians, in fact, whether they were right or wrong, had very little opinion of the way things went on under the Parliament; and the English people, you see, soon came to be of the same way of thinking. Charles II. was made king, and Virginia became quiet once more. She asked no favors, and received none. She had acted on principle, and that was enough; and you will soon see that when she was not pleased with Sir William Berkeley, the king's governor, the "Old Dominion" took up arms against him, as she had taken them up against the Parliament.

THE GREAT REBELLION IN VIRGINIA.

I.

Just one hundred years before the American Revolution, a rebellion or revolution took place in Virginia, which resembled it in the most striking manner. The Virginians, as you will see, made war on the English governor just as the Americans afterward made war on the King of England. They were led, too, by a man whose character was very much like Washington's; and I shall now describe this remarkable struggle, and how it ended.

The "Great Rebellion," as it was called, broke out in the year 1676, about seventy years after the landing at Jamestown. At this time Virginia had become a considerable colony. Only about one hundred persons, you remember, had come over at first; but others followed them, and in three years there were five hundred, and the colony went on increasing and prospering. There were times of distress, when the people nearly starved, and the Indians continued to give them great trouble. At one time Opechancanough, Smith's old enemy, fell upon them, and nearly all of them were put to death. But this did not discourage people. More settlers came to make their homes in the country. The number of people grew larger and larger, and the rich lands were settled farther and farther up the rivers. Strong settlers went to work in the woods, and cut down the oaks and pines, with which they built houses for their families. They then ploughed the ground and sowed wheat, and planted corn and tobacco, keeping a good lookout all the time for Indians. And so the country gradually grew in the number of settlers, whose houses were seen peeping everywhere from the trees; until, in the year 1676, there were no less than forty thousand people in Virginia, of whom eight thousand were servants—two thousand black and six thousand white.

Several governors had been sent, one after another, to rule over Virginia. When Bacon's Rebellion, of which I am going to tell you, broke out, the English governor was Sir William Berkeley—the same who had sent Richard Lee to invite Charles II. to Virginia. He was a high-tempered old ruler, not altogether bad, by any means, but very cruel and revengeful in his disposition, and so devoted to the King of England, as I have shown you, that he was always thinking how he could please him. He seemed to like the Virginians, and they liked him, but they were not much pleased at his high-handed manner of making them obey every order that came across the ocean. They did not mind old Sir William's living easily and in luxury at his estate, called "Green Spring," not far from Jamestown, where he had fine horses and carriages, and large numbers of servants, and ate his dinner off silver plate, and was a sort of king in a small way. The Virginians themselves were fond of that style of living, and may have liked old Sir William all the better for inviting guests to his house and entertaining them well. But what they did not like was his habit of deciding everything in favor of England and against Virginia. They also complained that he would not protect the families living up the rivers toward the mountains from the savages. The Indians were not yet entirely subdued, and would make sudden attacks on the women and children, and put them to death; and as Sir William Berkeley seemed resolved to do nothing for the people, they at last determined to take the matter into their own hands.

An opportunity for this soon came, and the Virginians found a leader who just suited them. His name was Nathaniel Bacon; and as I have given you some idea of the character of Governor Berkeley, I will now say a few words of the man who was going to give him so much trouble. Bacon was born in England, like many other persons who lived in Virginia, and had come over to the

JAMESTOWN ISLAND.

colony only a short time before. Here he owned a considerable quantity of land and a number of servants, and ranked very high among the planters, as they were called. He was about forty-five, and in many ways quite a remarkable man. As you will soon see, he was extremely brave and determined; but besides this, he seems to have been a very fine public speaker, and very popular with his friends and neighbors, from his polite and cordial manners.

Although he was a new-comer, as it was called, he was made a member of the "King's Council;" and as only the oldest and ablest planters were generally appointed to this council, this was a high compliment to Bacon. No doubt old Sir William thought he was an Englishman in his feelings, and would support him in his doings against the Virginians. But he was very much mistaken. Bacon determined to oppose him, and take the Virginia side; and his friends, who saw how brave he was, resolved to have him for their leader.

Trouble soon began. Rebellions or revolutions generally begin with some small matter; and so it was on this occasion. Bacon had a plantation near the Falls in James River, where the city of Richmond now stands, and one day he heard that the Indians had attacked the plantation, and killed his overseer and one of his servants. This highly excited him, and he resolved to act at once. He sent word to his neighbors to meet him and march on the Indians; and on the day appointed a large number of them assembled.

Bacon then addressed them, and spoke of the wrongs done them by the governor. He was an enemy of the Virginians, he said, and would not protect them from the Indians. These barbarous savages were killing the women and children, and yet the governor would not fight them; but if he would not, he, Nathaniel Bacon, would. Then he asked his neighbors if they were ready to march with him, and, if so, whom they would choose for their leader.

At this they uttered a shout, and declared that they were ready. He should be their leader, they declared, and Bacon accepted the command. First, however, he resolved to send to Sir William Berkeley to obtain his leave, and one of the men was sent to ask the governor for a commission, as it was called. This the governor refused, and the messenger came back without it. Bacon, no doubt, expected this, and had made up his mind. He told his friends that as to himself he was ready to march without any commission. He would take all the risk, and any who wished to go with him could do so.

This was followed by another shout, and the men mounted their horses. Bacon took command, and the whole body set forward. They marched up James River, and into the woods near the Falls, and here they found the Indians and attacked them. The result was a complete victory over them. They were all killed or driven off. And then Bacon and his men marched back homeward in triumph.

But while they were fighting up the river a great excitement had taken place at Jamestown. Governor Berkeley was enraged when he heard that Bacon had marched in defiance of him. So he issued a proclamation that Bacon and his men were all traitors, and got together a body of troops to attack them. Nothing occurred, however. Sir William set out, but found that there was trouble behind him. The Virginians everywhere sympathized with Bacon, and were ready to rise in arms; so the old governor changed his mind, and marched back again with his forces to Jamestown.

II.

This was a great triumph for Bacon, and all Virginia nearly was in his favor. The old governor was obliged to submit, and said he had no objection to what the people demanded. They might make any new laws they wished, as far as he was concerned; and so a new House of Burgesses was at once elected.

Bacon was chosen one of the members, as he was now extremely popular, and set out down James River in his sail-boat for Jamestown. But the governor was ready. As soon as he arrived he had him arrested and brought into the State-house. Here Sir William and the king's council were waiting to receive him, and a stormy interview followed. We know how high-tempered the old governor was, and he received Bacon fiercely. But that had no effect upon him. He was too cool a man to cower before Sir William's anger, and discussed the whole matter with him in a very plain manner. He knew that he had acted illegally, he said, in fighting without the commission, and was ready to say so, if the commission was now given to him. To this the governor at last agreed; but he did not keep his word, and Bacon determined that he would force him to do so.

He accordingly left Jamestown, and went home and told his neighbors how matters stood. He was resolved to have the commission, he said, and they said they would assist him. In a short time about four hundred planters assembled, and at the head of them Bacon marched toward Jamestown. As soon as he arrived he drew up his forces on the State-house green, and then sent word to Sir William Berkeley that he had come for his commission.

This greatly enraged the old governor. He was quite as brave as Bacon, and rushed out in front of the men. Tearing open his ruffled shirt so as to leave his breast naked, he exclaimed, violently,

"Here, shoot me—'fore God, a fair mark!—shoot!"

But Bacon had no intention of hurting the governor. He advanced toward him and bowed, and said,

"No, may it please your Honor, we will not hurt a hair of your head or any other man's. We have come for a commission to save our lives from the Indians, which you have so often promised, and now we will have it before we go."

There was then great confusion, and an angry scene followed. But Bacon stood firm, and declared that he would not go without the paper; so the governor was obliged at last to submit. He consented to what Bacon demanded, and he received his commission, when he mounted his horse again and marched his men out of Jamestown.

III.

This act of Bacon's was open defiance, you see, of the king's authority, for Sir William was his representative in the colony. The governor was a brave old fellow, and resolved to fight; so he suddenly left Jamestown, and crossed York River to Gloucester, where he raised his flag, and called on his friends to assemble.

But Bacon was quite as resolute as he was. He was not afraid to make war on the king himself, though he risked his head in doing so; and at once set out with a small army to fight Sir William. When the governor heard of this he fled across Chesapeake Bay to Accomac, and Bacon was in possession of the whole country.

He and his men then acted like true patriots. A new House of Burgesses was ordered to assemble, and in the mean while they pledged themselves not to lay down their arms. As Sir William had sent to England for soldiers to fight for him, they bound themselves to fight these soldiers, as they had fought the governor; and they signed a paper to this effect, whose date was August, 1676. This was just one hundred years before the American declaration of Independence, you see, and there is not much difference between the two papers.

In the midst of all this, Bacon heard that the Indians were making trouble again, so he resolved to march at once and put an end to them. The tribes which murdered the settlers lived in the neighborhood of the present city of Richmond, and Bacon soon reached the spot and prepared to attack them.

They had built a strong stockade, or fort, on a lofty hill east of the city, and in this they had placed their women and children, and were ready to fight. Their bravest warriors were in the log-fort, and they knew that the battle would decide everything. It was a very strong position, with a steep descent in front; but Bacon rushed up at the head of his men, and a desperate fight followed. The In-

INDIANS FIGHTING.

dians did their best, but the Virginians were too strong for them. They captured the fort, and either killed or made prisoners of all the Indians who did not fly. It was a bloody affair, and blood ran down the hill, it is said, into a small stream at the foot, which is called "Bloody Run" to this day.

This was the last of the Indian troubles in Eastern Virginia. They never fought again, and Bacon was looked upon as the deliverer of the country. But a new enemy was waiting for him, to strike him in the rear. Sir William

BLOODY RUN.

Berkeley had collected troops in the lower counties, and Bacon now heard that he was again in possession of Jamestown, with eighteen ships in the river, and an army of about eight hundred men.

IV.

Bacon lost no time. He had resolved to fight the old governor until one or the other got the best of it, and he set out at once for Jamestown.

On the way he did what he had no right to do. A number of prominent men had sided with Sir William, and Bacon stopped at their plantations, and took their wives prisoners. They were, no doubt, permitted to ride in their carriages, as the men moved on, but their arrest was a very unjustifiable proceeding. Bacon sent word to their husbands at Jamestown that he had taken the ladies prisoners, and would hold them as hostages for the good behavior of the gentlemen. This was quite unworthy of a high-toned man like Bacon, but he certainly did it; and as I am telling you a true story, I have no intention of omitting the incident.

He marched on steadily, with his lady-prisoners, and soon found that Sir William Berkeley was ready for him. The old governor was in high spirits, for he was brave and determined. Two friends of Bacon, named Bland and Carver, had attempted to cross to Accomac and capture him; but he had caught and hung them, and hoped soon to catch and hang Bacon himself. His ships, armed with cannon, were in the river near the town; his soldiers were drawn up in Jamestown ready to fight; and it was plain that a battle would soon take place.

The sun was just setting when Bacon and his men arrived. It was the month of September, when the leaves of the trees are just beginning to turn red and yellow, and the moon was shining. Bacon lost no time, but went to work at once. A long ditch was dug, and the earth thrown up in front so as to form a breastwork. Trees were then cut down, and laid one on the other so as to strengthen the works against cannon balls, and the whole was soon finished. While the men were working, the governor did not fire his cannon at them from Jamestown or from the ships. He was afraid he would kill the ladies whom Bacon had taken prisoners, and a very discreditable story is told of their treatment. It is said that they were placed in front of the men while they were building the earthwork; and if so, Bacon acted in a manner unworthy of him. No civilized nation makes war on women any more than on children, and to endanger these ladies' lives was not like a soldier. They were not to blame because their husbands had sided with Sir William Berkeley, and perhaps the story was made up by Bacon's enemies. I hope it was untrue, and that the ladies were soon sent back home, and that the men were allowed to fight the matter out among themselves.

The night passed quietly, but in the morning old Sir William marched out to attack Bacon. He had about eight hundred men, and Bacon's numbers were probably about the same. The battle began at once, and it must have been a hard fight. There is no full account of it; but we know enough about it to feel certain that some historians are very foolish in saying that Sir William's men were "degraded" people who would not fight, while Bacon's men were the "very chivalry of Virginia," and rode right over their enemies. The fact was that a large number of the bravest gentlemen of the colony had sided with Sir William, because they thought it wrong to take up arms against the king's authority; and they no doubt fought just as bravely as their opponents. It is true, however, that Bacon won the victory. After fighting hard, old Sir William found that Bacon was too strong for him, and he retreated from the field, on which many of his soldiers lay dead or groaning from their wounds.

There was no course left for him now but to fly. This was, no doubt, "gall and wormwood" to him, but there was no help for it. There was danger that he would fall into the "rebel" Bacon's hands, when every one would laugh at him; so he hastened to take refuge on board his ships. His troops hurried after him, in the midst of the cheers of the "rebels;" and then the ships set sail down the river, followed by cannon balls which Bacon fired at them from the hills near Jamestown.

V.

The capital of Virginia was now in Bacon's hands, and he set it on fire and burned it to ashes.

Why this was done it is hard to say. They probably

meant to show that they had conquered Sir William Berkeley, or it may have been done to prevent him from ever returning to it as governor. It was a great pity to thus burn the old town which John Smith and the early settlers had built; but fire was set to it, and no one made the least objection. Two gentlemen in Bacon's army, named Lawrence and Drummond, had houses in the place, but they set fire to them with their own hands; and soon the famous old place was nothing but a heap of ashes.

All now seemed over with Governor Berkeley and his people, but new enemies suddenly made their appearance. An army of a thousand men was marching from toward the Rappahannock against Bacon, and he set forward, without loss of time, to meet them. But no battle took place. Instead of fighting, the men of the two armies shook hands. The up-country men then returned to their homes, and Bacon led his army back toward James River.

He was now master of Virginia, and might easily have declared himself governor. His men would have made him their ruler at a single word, but he had too much respect for the law to agree to that; and if he had been elected he would never have been governor. His life was near its end, and he was destined to die in the very hour of his triumph.

He had caught a fever while directing the men how to work in the trenches at Jamestown; and at last he grew so ill that he saw his last hour was approaching. He had gone to Gloucester County, probably to pursue Sir William Berkeley; and here he grew worse and worse, and at last expired.

This was a terrible blow to his followers. They feared that old Sir William would now win back all he had lost, and even dig up Bacon's body and hang it upon the gallows. They therefore resolved to conceal his grave. He was buried by night, in a lonely spot; and although we have no description of the scene which took place, we may imagine it. His friends, no doubt, dug a grave secretly with their own hands, and then, when it was dark, placed the dead man's body in a wagon, and took it to the spot and buried it. If it was by moonlight, or even if the stars were shining, it must have been a strange and solemn sight. No doubt some clergyman was present and read prayers over the grave when the body was lowered into it, while his friends stood around with their hats off and their heads bent down in sorrow. Large stones were then laid on the coffin, the grave was filled up, and the grass was smoothed down in order to conceal it.

This was done so carefully that Bacon's grave was never discovered, and the wrath of Sir William Berkeley was not expended upon his enemy. He had the living to take revenge on, as I will show you in ending my story; but Bacon he could not reach. The body of that brave soldier was sleeping in the woods of Gloucester, and the great trees guarded the secret of his resting-place.

VI.

The "Great Rebellion," as Sir William Berkeley called it, was now over. When a famous leader dies, it is hard to find any one to take his place; and as soon as news came that Bacon was dead, his men returned to their homes in despair. A few kept up a show of resistance, but they soon gave way like the rest, and Sir William Berkeley marched back in triumph.

I have told you the character of this fiery old ruler. He was brave and determined, and had some other good qualities; but he was narrow-minded and cruel, and hated the "rebels" bitterly for defeating him; so he resolved to take a bloody revenge upon them.

. Every friend of Bacon's whom he could lay his hands on was put to death. Thomas Hansford, a brave young planter, was one of these. He was captured, and, after a pretended trial, was at once hung, although he begged them to shoot him. Another was Captain Wilford, who fought hard not to be taken prisoner, and had one of his eyes put out by a bullet. When some one spoke of this he said it was no matter, as Sir William Berkeley would *have him led* to the gallows; and he too was soon hung. Another was Major Cheeseman, whose wife knelt before Sir William and begged her husband's life, telling him that *she* had persuaded him to join Bacon. In reply to all her tears and prayers, the governor, it is said, offered her a vulgar insult, instead of pitying her; and Major Cheeseman soon afterward died in prison. A more important prisoner still was William Drummond, one of Bacon's warmest friends. Sir William Berkeley hated him, and felt a cruel triumph when he was brought before him.

"Mr. Drummond," said the governor, in a sneering voice, "you are very welcome! I am more glad to see you than any man in Virginia! Mr. Drummond, you shall be hanged in half an hour!"

Drummond was tried at once; and as there was no trouble in proving that he had been one of the leaders of the "rebels," he was found guilty and at once hung. The governor hated him more than all the rest, and his property was at once seized; but the King of England, as soon as he heard of this, ordered it to be restored to Mrs. Drummond, his widow.

These were a few of the victims of Sir William's cruelty. Altogether more than twenty persons were hung; and Charles II. exclaimed when he heard of it,

"That old fool has hanged more men in that naked country than I did for the murder of my father!"

All the changes in the laws made by Bacon were now repealed, and Governor Berkeley found no enemies to oppose him. But he felt ill at ease. The people of Virginia hated him for his cruelty, and he had scarcely a friend in the whole colony. He therefore resolved to visit England, fearing, it seems, that he had as few friends there, and thinking that it would be better to go and defend himself. He therefore sailed for England, and his departure was a joyful event. The Virginians fired cannon and illuminated their houses, and he never afterward returned to the colony. When he got to England the king refused to see him, and this filled him with so much mortification that he soon afterward died. And that was the end of old Sir William Berkeley.

He and Bacon were two remarkable men, but Bacon was by far the greater. He was a fearless soldier, and a true lover of his country. He had nothing to win by fighting and everything to lose, for the governor would have hung him and seized upon all his property if he had defeated him. But his duty was plain to him. The Virginians were oppressed, and he meant to risk his life against their oppressor.

This was acting precisely as George Washington did a hundred years afterward. One succeeded, the other failed; but the man who does his duty is as great in failure as in success. Nathaniel Bacon did his, and has left a noble name in history.

THE KNIGHTS OF THE GOLDEN HORSESHOE.

I.

I WILL now relate a romantic little incident which occurred in the summer of 1714, about thirty years after Bacon's death. This was the ride beyond the mountains of the "Horseshoe Knights," as they were afterward called; and I will give you, in the first place, a short account of the man who led them.

He was Alexander Spotswood, Governor of Virginia at the time, and his life had been adventurous. He was born on board a ship, in the Mediterranean Sea, in 1676, and it is not known how this singular event happened. But there seems to be no doubt about the truth of the statement, and he may have sailed about with his father, who probably commanded the ship, and thus acquired while he was young his love of adventure. As soon as he was old enough, he became a soldier in the English army under Marlborough, who was then fighting the French; and at a great battle, called Blenheim, he distinguished himself by his bravery, and was wounded by a cannon-ball. This occurred when he was about twenty-eight years of age; and as he was sent over to be Governor of Virginia when he was only thirty-four, you will see that he must have shown that he was a man of strong sense and firm character. He looked older than he really was, for that matter. His portrait is still to be seen in an old country-house in Virginia, with a picture of the field of Blenheim in the background; and this portrait shows that he was a tall, strong man, with many wrinkles in his forehead, and a determined expression of countenance, which expressed his character.

As soon as Spotswood reached Virginia, he set to work to improve everything, and make the country as prosperous as possible. He had a curiously shaped magazine built in Williamsburg, the capital of the colony, to hold gunpowder to use in case of war; and this is still standing. He then built a good house for the governors to live in, and sent word to the few Indian tribes left that they might bring their boys to the college of "William and Mary," at Williamsburg, if they wished, where they would be educated free of expense. He next set about making iron for the use of the Virginia people.

This was very important. Iron, you know, is a metal that no one can do without, as axes, ploughs, and hundreds of other useful implements are made of it. The Virginians, like everybody else, required it, but they were obliged to send to England for it; and as England always aimed to make as much as she could out of her colonies, they had to pay a very high price for all that they bought. You now see why Governor Spotswood was anxious to show them how they might make iron for themselves, and not send to England and pay so much for it. When iron is in the ground it is mixed with earth and stones; and before it is of any use it is necessary to cleanse it, which is done by melting it in large furnaces built for the purpose. Spotswood knew that there was an abundance of iron in the soil of the colony, and built the furnaces, which proved perfectly successful. They were the first ever seen in America, and made him quite famous; and the people gave him the name of the "Tubal-cain of Virginia," an explanation of which will be found in the Book of Genesis.

These exertions for the good of the country made Governor Spotswood very popular. He was a determined ruler, and had more than one quarrel with the House of Burgesses, who were as hard-headed as himself. But he was very much respected, for the Virginians saw plainly that he was resolved to put down evil-doers and have the laws obeyed; as he showed, among other things, by his treatment of a bloody marauder named Blackbeard.

Blackbeard was a pirate who sailed along the shores of the Carolinas and Virginia, attacking any ships he met, and killing all who were on board of them; after which

BLACKBEARD, THE PIRATE.

the goods in them were seized and the ships were burned. This had gone on for some time, and at last Spotswood grew tired of it. He therefore sent a ship-of-war to attack Blackbeard, or John Theach, as his real name was, and the two vessels came in sight of each other off the coast. Blackbeard now saw what was before him. He knew he must fight, and that if he was captured he would be hung in chains to a gallows; he therefore determined to die first. He ordered one of his men to stand with a lighted match near the magazine of powder in the ship; and if the Virginians boarded them and got the better in the fight, he was to set fire to the powder and blow up all together. The fight then began. The two vessels came up side by side, and the Virginians leaped on board the pirate ship, armed with their cutlasses. Blackbeard and his men met them and fought desperately, but in vain. He himself was in front, but his foot slipped in the blood on the deck, and as he staggered, one of his enemies cut him down and struck off his head. At this the rest lost heart and surrendered. Blackbeard's head was stuck on the bowsprit of the Virginia vessel, and it returned home in triumph, where the rest of the pirates who had been captured were soon afterward executed.

This is only one instance of Governor Spotswood's way of dealing with people who would not respect the laws and defied his authority. I might tell you other incidents of the same sort, but this must suffice. I will now come to the expedition beyond the Blue Ridge Mountains, which conferred on him and his friends the name of "Sir Knights of the Golden Horseshoe."

II.

It may surprise you to hear that at that time people thought that the Mississippi River rose in the Blue Ridge. In fact, nothing was known certainly about the great country beyond the mountains. They called it "Orange County;" and it was a very large county indeed, you see, as it extended from the Blue Ridge to the Pacific Ocean.

There were only vague rumors about it—that it was filled with great forests and lofty mountains; that the valleys were green and fertile, and traversed by beautiful rivers; and perhaps the ignorant still believed that the famous "Fountain of Youth" might be found somewhere there. Now and then some hunter would wander off into this unknown country, and when he returned would tell his friends that nothing was like it. It was filled, these men declared, with Indians and wild animals, and altogether was the most remarkable country that the sun ever shone upon.

All this highly excited Alexander Spotswood. He was a man, as I have told you, of adventurous character, and he longed to explore this splendid land. It was his duty, he felt, as Governor of Virginia, to discover whether the land was so rich, in order to settle it; and at last he resolved that he would set out and visit it himself, and find whether the reports about it were true.

He might easily have sent a party, with some intelligent man at the head of it, to report to him all about it. But this did not suit him. He resolved to go in person, as I have said, and to make a holiday excursion of the expedition. He was well acquainted with the planters, old and young, and he now sent them word that he was going to march to the mountains: if any one wished to go with him he would be welcome, and the governor would be glad to have the pleasure of his company.

This excited the young Virginians and filled them with delight. They were fond of horseback exercise and hunting, and a number sent word that they would be ready at the time appointed. A day in August (1714) was fixed by Spotswood, and the party assembled at Williamsburg, prepared for their long ride. Every arrangement had been made. Mules were ready, with pack-saddles strapped upon their backs, in which were baskets of provisions and bottles of wine and other liquors. These were to follow them in charge of servants; and all was now ready, when they suddenly discovered that they had forgotten a very important matter.

This was *to shoe the horses*. You may think it somewhat strange that such a thing had been lost sight of, but at that time it was the fashion generally to ride horses *barefooted*, as it is called. One reason for this was probably the scarcity and high price of iron, which people could not afford to use for shoeing horses; and there was another reason still. The roads of Lower Virginia were soft and sandy at that time, as they are now, and often you might ride for miles without seeing a single stone. There was nothing, therefore, to make shoeing really necessary, as the soft sand did not hurt the horses' feet: but now, when Spotswood and his friends intended to cross the mountains by pathways full of rocks, it became necessary to have their riding-horses shod. This was at once done; and the little incident was the explanation, as you will see, of the name of the Knights of the *Golden Horseshoe*.

We can imagine what an interesting sight the party of horsemen presented as they rode along "Duke of Gloucester Street," as the main street of Williamsburg was called, with men, women, and children flocking to the doors and windows, and waving handkerchiefs as they passed by. They were all mounted on spirited horses, and carried their guns, as they expected to hunt on the way; and behind followed the mules with their packs, in charge of the servants.

Spotswood rode at the head of the party, with his erect military bearing, learned in the wars, and clad, like the rest, in the fine costume of that time, when people dressed far more picturesquely than now; and there is very little doubt that he was in as high spirits as the rest of the party. He was in the bloom of life, for he was only about thirty-eight, enjoyed excellent health, and saw the prospect before him of an adventurous march into an unexplored wilderness, which just suited him. We need not be surprised, therefore, to be told by one of the party, who afterward wrote an account of the expedition, that Spots-

A RIVER VIEW.

wood was bright, and pleased with everything from first to last, on the whole long ride.

As the little band rode on, they were joined here and there by others, who had also determined to go on the expedition. The party thus increased in numbers as it moved on, like a snowball rolled in the snow, and they at last came to a place called Germanna, on the Rapid Ann

River, on the edge of what is now known as the "Spotsylvania Wilderness."

Here the governor had established a colony of Germans to work his iron furnaces, and had built a house for himself and his family to live in during the summer months, when the lower country was unhealthy. I would like to give you a full account, if I had time, of a visit made to this little village of Germanna by a famous old planter of James River, named Colonel William Byrd. He tells all about the place, and the governor's house, where a tame deer, on seeing him, leaped against a fine tall mirror in the drawing-room, thinking it was a window, and smashed it to pieces. But what he said of Spotswood himself was more interesting than what happened to the mirror, and shows that the brave soldier was a kind-hearted man.

He and Colonel Byrd had known each other well before Spotswood was married, as he was at this time; and it seems that the governor had then laughed at people who showed too great fondness for their wives and children. Now he was just as bad, or rather as *good*, as the rest. He never spoke to his wife or children without smiling and using some fond expression; and Colonel Byrd said, with a laugh, that he must have changed his opinion on this subject since he was married. To this Spotswood replied that he thought it was his duty to be as kind as possible to his wife, as he had brought her so far from all her friends into such a wilderness. And this shows, as I have said, that he was a warm-hearted man, however stern and determined he was as a soldier and a ruler.

III.

After resting at Germanna, the party of horsemen again set out, and rode on in the direction of the Blue Ridge Mountains.

Every one seemed to enjoy himself. The season of the year was delightful, for August in Virginia is a month when the air is pleasant, and the blue sky is filled with white clouds, drifting on before the wind like ships with all sails set. The woods were in full leaf; the streams were laughing and the birds singing; and in the midst of all these beautiful sights and sounds, the horsemen wound their way along, laughing and talking with each other. In the middle of the day they would stop in some green glade of the woods, to rest and pasture their horses; and then the baskets on the pack-mules would be unstrapped by the servants, the contents spread on the grass, and everybody would gather around and eat their dinner with an appetite sharpened by their long ride since morning.

Frequently, while on the march, some one of the party would ride into the woods, and the rest would lose sight of him. But soon they would hear him fire his gun, and he would come back, holding in his hand a fat pheasant or some other game, which he would hand to the servants for supper. At night the party would halt in some favorable spot, and hobble their horses by tying their legs together with ropes, after which they would turn them loose to graze, certain that the hobbles would prevent them from wandering off very far. Then supper would be spread on the grass, everybody would sup heartily, and, wrapping their cloaks around them, Spotswood and his friends would stretch themselves on the ground, and sleep as soundly and sweetly as if they were at home in their beds. Some of these times you will read all about this in the account given by one of the party; but I have here told you pretty much all that he says of the manner in which the Knights of the Golden Horseshoe passed their time on the expedition.

At last they reached the Blue Ridge Mountains, and toiled on up the steep sides, covered with forest-trees, to the top. It is not known precisely where they ascended the mountains, but it is supposed that the spot was near what is called Rockfish Gap, where the Chesapeake and Ohio Railroad now passes through. Some persons assert that the party went on and crossed the Alleghany Mountains also; but there is no proof of this, and no reason to believe it, as they never said that they crossed *two* ranges of mountains, and would not have forgotten the Blue Ridge, which they must have reached first. From the summit, which they now stood upon, they saw beneath them a wild and lovely landscape, through which wound the Shenandoah, whose name signifies, in the Indian language, "The Daughter of the Stars." To the right and left the Blue Ridge extended far out of sight, clothed with oaks, pines, and other forest-trees; while in front, across the valley, was seen the long blue line of the Alleghanies, like a wave of the ocean.

The sight before them must have filled Spotswood and his friends with delight; and they carved their names on the rocks, to mark the spot to which they had ascended. There were two peaks of the mountain near, and one of these was named "Mount George," in honor of the King of England, and the other "Mount Alexander," in honor of Spotswood. The party then drank the king's health, and rode down the western side of the mountain into the Shenandoah Valley.

They did not meet with any romantic incidents—fights with Indians or bears, or anything of the sort. The wild animals seen were chiefly deer; or a herd of huge elks, such as then lived in the region, may have galloped off into the thick woods as the hoofs of the horses clattered on the rocky paths. No adventures befell them in the valley; and after enjoying a sight of its fertile lands, the party recrossed the Blue Ridge, entered the low country, and, going joyously on their way, as before, reached their homes on tidewater.

IV.

This little expedition pleased every one who took part in it, and the discovery of so fine a country was very important. Spotswood therefore resolved to commemorate his long ride by establishing what is called an Order of Knighthood.

You probably know what this means. Knights in former times were brave men who went about seeking adventures, and they belonged to various "orders," which were regarded with great respect. Governor Spotswood therefore determined to form a Virginia Order of Knighthood; but he must have been puzzled at first to find a name for it. At last, however, he decided what this name should be. He remembered the shoeing of the horses at Williamsburg before the party set out, and thought the best name for them would be "Sir Knights of the Golden Horseshoe." He therefore fixed upon that title, and sent to England for a number of small golden horseshoes, one of which he presented to each of his companions. There was a motto, in Latin, cut upon them—"*Sic jurat transcendere montes*," signifying, "Thus we swear to cross the mountains;" and one of them, set with garnets, a species of jewel, is still to be seen, it is said, somewhere in Virginia.

When the King of England heard of Spotswood's expedition, he made him Sir Alexander Spotswood; but I am sorry to say the governor was obliged to pay for the golden horseshoes out of his own pocket. He requested the king to see that the shoes were paid for in London, but not the least notice was taken of this. It may have been that the king thought it rather presumptuous in him to be establishing an order of knighthood without permission; or he may have grudged the money, of which kings, even, are often much in want. However that may be, he refused to pay; so Sir Alexander did so, and was thus the real founder of the "Order."

Spotswood never returned to England. Besides his house at Germanna, he had another near Yorktown, which was called "Temple Farm;" and here he spent his last days in quiet, with his wife and children. You will remember how Colonel Byrd laughed at him for treating his wife with so much tenderness; but it was a good-natured laugh, and the old "Master of Westover," as Byrd was called, must have respected him all the more for it. The Virginia people had a very high opinion of Spotswood, for during the thirteen years in which he had been governor he had showed that the good of the country was nearest to his heart.

He died at "Temple Farm," where his old house is still standing; but for a long time it was not known where he was buried. At last, nearly a hundred years afterward, some broken stones in an old enclosure near the house were removed, and on these stones were found letters which showed that the little enclosure was once a graveyard. The pieces were put together, and at last something was made of them:

"SIR ALEXANDER SPOTSWOOD,
17—."

This much was read upon the fragments of stone; and it thus became plain that the small enclosure was the burial-place of the brave Spotswood. He was one of the best governors that Virginia ever had, and his bones were laid, you see, in the land he loved so well.

GEORGE WASHINGTON, THE YOUNG SURVEYOR.

I.

My stories are not only meant to inform and interest you, but to show you how the great men of Virginia did their duty always, and especially how their characters came to be shaped.

There is one of these men who rises above all the rest, and is looked upon as one of the greatest human beings who have lived in this world. I mean George Washington, who is called the "Father of his Country;" and it is extremely interesting to see how he passed his boyhood and early manhood. He was no better than other people in many things. He had quick and excitable passions, which he soon found he had to control, or they would control him. But he had the highest sense of duty, and determined to make a good and useful man of himself; and in this story I mean to show you how he set about it.

He was the son of a farmer who lived in Westmoreland County, Virginia, and was born on the twenty-second of February, 1732. His father, Augustine Washington, had large landed possessions on the banks of the Potomac, and was well to do in the world; but as often happened at that time, when people did not think so much of show, he lived in a small plain house, and here George was born. While he was still a child his father moved to another house in Stafford County, on the Rappahan-

YOUNG WASHINGTON'S MILITARY ASPIRATIONS.

nock River, where he sent George to what is called an "old field-school"—a sort of log-house, generally with only one room, where children were taught to read and write and cipher. While he was at school, George is said to have been very fond of playing at soldiering with the rest of the boys, which he probably gained a liking for from listening to the talk of his elder brother Lawrence, who had been a soldier in the West Indies.

When his father died, which he did at the age of forty-nine, George was left to the care of his mother. But he could not have had a better person to look after him. "Mary, the Mother of Washington," as she is called, was a lady of the highest character, with a very strong mind, and as pious as she was intelligent. She determined to make her boy a good man, and taught him to love God, and kneel beside her and say his prayers night and morning. She also taught him always to tell the truth and do his duty in everything. These lessons of his mother while he was still a small boy were the main cause of his becoming afterward so great a man.

He was very fond of out-door pleasure, riding and hunting, and games that require skill and bodily strength. These made him grow tall and strong. It is said that he once threw a stone across the Rappahannock River, at the city of Fredericksburg; and there are very few men who could do as much. He did not, however, neglect improving his mind, and learning everything that would prove useful to him in his after-life. He kept a book in which he wrote down wise maxims and rules to follow: he also taught himself how to keep accounts, and all about surveying land, which, as you will see, soon became of the greatest use to him, and had a very important influence upon his career in life.

When George was fourteen years of age he was a tall,

robust boy, and longed to lead the life of a soldier or sailor. He thought that he would like being a sailor the better of the two; and as his brother Lawrence was rich and influential, he had not much trouble in having George appointed a midshipman in the English navy. But his poor mother grieved at the thought that she was going to be separated from her boy, and might never see him again. He had persuaded her to let him go, and she had consented; but she could not conceal her tears when the time ar-

RESIDENCE OF THE WASHINGTON FAMILY.

rived. When George came, in his fine new uniform of a midshipman, to tell her good-bye, she covered her face with her hands and cried; and at this the boy gave way. He could not bear to distress his mother, and at once gave up the idea of leaving her. He took off his fine uniform, resigned his commission as a midshipman, and stayed at home to take care of his mother.

Instead of going away as a brave young sailor, George went back to school, and the time passed on until he was sixteen years of age. He often went to see his brother Lawrence at his house, called "Mount Vernon," on the Potomac River, and was a great favorite with everybody there. Lawrence had married a daughter of Mr. William Fairfax, a rich Englishman, who lived at a place called "Belvoir," not far from Mount Vernon; and here the boy met with an old English lord of singular character, named Thomas, Lord Fairfax, a cousin of William Fairfax.

Lord Fairfax was a very curious old man, and his life had been an interesting one. He was born in England, and when he was a young man, went up from his home in the country to live in the great city of London, where he moved in the highest society, and was one of the finest dressed young men of his day. He did not pass all his time, however, in idleness and visits to ladies. He became acquainted with many authors, and among the rest, with a famous one named Addison, who wrote a number of papers under the title of the *Spectator*. These papers were very much admired at the time, and are admired still for the beautiful style in which they are written. Young Fairfax offered to help Addison, and wrote some of the *Spectator* papers for him. And now one of the main things that people remember the rich, finely dressed young lord by, is that he assisted the poor, shabbily dressed Mr. Addison in writing his *Spectator*.

Lord Fairfax soon met with a lady who pleased him, and they were at last engaged to be married. But the lady treated him very badly. She saw that another person of higher rank was ready to marry her, and refused to keep her word with young Fairfax. This distressed him deeply, and he went back to his home in the country, resolved never to marry anybody, which he never did. And I will now tell you what brought him to Virginia.

His mother was a daughter of Lord Culpeper, who had been at one time Governor of Virginia. While he was living in Virginia, Lord Culpeper found how rich the land was between the Potomac and Rappahannock rivers; and when he returned to England he asked the king to give him all this land, which was then only partly inhabited—promising that he would have it settled and cultivated. To this the king consented, and Culpeper received what was called a patent for the whole country —which did not at all please the Virginians, and was one of the great causes of complaint leading to Bacon's Rebellion, about which I have told you. When Lord Culpeper died, his daughter inherited the land; and as Lord Fairfax was her son, he became the owner of it after her death. His cousin, William Fairfax, of Belvoir, had managed his great property for some time, but at last Lord Fairfax determined to cross the ocean to look after it himself. He did so; and this accounts for his living with his cousin at Belvoir, where young George Washington made his acquaintance.

I have told you this story of Lord Fairfax because he had a great deal to do with the fortunes of the youth who afterward made so great a name for himself. If he had not met with Lord Fairfax, Washington's whole life would probably have been different. The old Englishman put him in the way of making a man of himself, and gaining the reputation which led to his being appointed commander-in-chief of the American armies in the Revolution. And I will now tell you how he did so.

Belvoir was a pleasant house to visit at; and as Mrs. Lawrence Washington was a daughter of William Fairfax, you know, the two families were on the most intimate terms. When George was at Mount Vernon he often went to Belvoir, as I have said, and he and Lord Fairfax soon became great friends. The old Englishman, who was a tall, gaunt, near-sighted man, was very fond of hunting, and liked to have George go with him. So they often rode out fox-hunting together, and Lord Fairfax came to like the boy very much. He saw that he was a stout, manly, intelligent young fellow, with a great desire to make himself useful in some way; and this gave him the idea of appointing George to survey his wild lands beyond the Blue Ridge Mountains.

These lands were of very great extent, as they reached as far up as the head-waters of one branch of the Potomac River; but large as they were, they were of no great value unless they were surveyed and laid off to be sold or rented to such people as wished to settle on them. Perhaps you do not know exactly what is meant by *surveying*. It means measuring land, which is generally done by means of a chain, and laying it off into tracts, which are then marked by cutting gashes in the bark of certain trees, or describing other trees or prominent objects as landmarks in a book carried for the purpose. When you grow older you will understand the use of the compass and the calculation of angles in surveying; but this is all I can say of it at present.

Lord Fairfax wished very much to have his lands in the Valley of Virginia thus surveyed, and proposed to young George Washington that he should undertake the work. The boy at once consented. Nothing could have pleased him better than an occupation of this sort. He loved the open air and horseback riding; he would have an opportunity to explore a picturesque and beautiful country, full of Indians and wild animals; and he set about at once making preparations for his expedition.

II.

It was a fine day in early spring of the year 1748 when George set out on his ride to the valley. He had a companion, George William Fairfax, a son of William of Belvoir, who was about twenty-two years of age, and they rode along in high spirits toward the mountains.

George was at an age when the world seems full of enjoyment. He was just sixteen, and in high health, and no doubt felt delighted, as boys will, at the thought of being his own master and meeting with all sorts of adventures. He had brought his gun with him to hunt, and his surveyor's instruments were packed in a leather valise

GREENWAY COURT.

behind his saddle. I have myself seen these instruments, which his family still have; and it was interesting to look at them, and remember that they were used by so great a man when he was young and unknown to the world.

The two friends crossed the Blue Ridge at Ashby's Gap, and forded the bright waters of the river Shenandoah. They then turned a little to the left, and made their way toward "Greenway Court." This was a sort of lodge built by Lord Fairfax in the woods, and afterward his place of residence. It was a house with broad stone gables, and a roof sloping down over a long porch in front. On the top of the roof were two belfries with bells in them, which were meant, it is said, to give the alarm to all the settlers in the neighborhood when the Indians were coming to attack them. Some fast rider would bring the news; then the bells would be rung, and every man would prepare for the Indian attack. Greenway Court was thus a famous place in the eyes of every one, and business with Lord Fairfax's manager brought a great many people to the spot. To direct these visitors, a white post, with an arm pointing in the direction of the place, was set up at some distance from it. Whenever this post fell, from the wood decaying or by any accident, another was erected in its place; and one stands in the very spot to-day, in the middle of the village of White Post, which takes its name from it.

George and his friend came in sight of the white post, and soon reached Greenway Court, where they were hospitably received by Lord Fairfax's manager; and then, after a short rest, they began to survey the lands along the banks of the Shenandoah River.

This must have been a delightful employment to them. The spring was just opening, and the leaves beginning to bud in the woods. The sun was shining brightly, the birds were chirping, and on every side, as far as the eye could reach, were long blue ranges of mountains, like high walls placed there to guard the beautiful Valley of the Shenandoah. This country is very attractive now, with its green wheat-fields or waving corn, and its clumps of trees, in the midst of which are seen old houses, the abodes of happy families; but it was far more striking and picturesque at that time. Old people, whose memories went a long way back, said that in former times the land was covered with majestic forests and broad prairies. In these prairies, they said, the grass was so tall that a man on horseback could tie the heads together across the saddle in front of him, and the whole beautiful expanse, waving in the wind, was bright with flowers.

Surveying itself is hard work, but the free open-air life that surveyors lead makes it very attractive. This life was highly agreeable to George and his friend. They worked faithfully all day, and at night stopped at the rude house of some settler in the woods; or, if no house was seen, they built a fire, wrapped themselves in their cloaks, and slept in the open air. They went on in this manner until they reached the Potomac River. They then rode up the stream and over the mountains until they reached what is now called Berkeley Springs, or "Bath," where they camped out, as usual, under the stars. There were no houses there then, but a town was built in course of time, and Washington often spent a part of the summer there long years afterward with his family, to bathe in and drink the mineral waters, which are good for the sick.

George and his friend did not meet with many adventures, but they had a sight, for the first time in their lives, of the savages. They stopped at the house of a settler one day, and were soon afterward surprised by the sudden appearance of a band of Indians. They were about thirty in number, with their half-naked bodies covered with paint, which signified that they had been at war with their enemies, and one of them had a scalp hanging at his belt. Perhaps you do not know what a scalp means, so I will explain it. When the Indians killed any one, they made

INDIAN WITH SCALP.

a deep cut with a knife around the forehead and behind the head of the corpse, and then tore off the whole skin from the head, with the hair upon it. Sometimes they thus *scalped* their enemies before they were dead, and it was so painful that scarcely any one ever lived after it. The scalp was then hung to the belt; and the Indians were proud of it as a proof of victory over their enemies.

George and his friend must have been shocked at seeing the bloody scalp, but the Indians soon made them laugh. Some liquor was given them, and they executed their war-dance, as they called it. One of them stretched a deer-skin over an iron pot and drummed upon it, while another rattled a gourd with a horse's tail tied to it, in which were some shot. While this was going on, one of the savages leaped up and began to dance and turn and tumble about in the most ridiculous manner, while the rest yelled and whooped around a large fire which they had built. Altogether it was a singular sight, and the two young men must have looked on with wonder at such strange doings.

III.

Several weeks were spent by the young surveyors in this wild country, during which they were busy attending to their duties. They cooked their meat by holding it to the fire on forked sticks, and chips served for dishes. Sometimes it rained heavily, and they were drenched. At one time some straw on which they were sleeping caught fire, and they woke just in time to save themselves from being burned. Sometimes they slept in houses, but this was not much better than the open air. "I have not slept above three or four nights in a bed," George wrote to one of his friends; "but after walking a good deal all the day, I have lain down before the fire on a little straw, or fodder, or a bear-skin, whichever was to be had, with man, wife, and children, like dogs and cats; and happy is he who gets the berth nearest the fire."

In the month of April the two young men recrossed the mountains, and again reached Greenway Court. Here they found good beds and every comfort, and rested after their long ride. I have visited Greenway Court; and while walking over the green lawn under the old locust-trees in front of it, and looking at the old stone gables with the belfries on the roof, I thought of the bright boy of sixteen, with his brown curls and rosy cheeks, who once looked at the same objects and sat on the same porch there before my eyes. The old house should have been taken good care of, from these associations with the youth of Washington. But Greenway Court is gone! It was pulled down for some reason, and no human eye will ever look upon it again; so I thought I would give you this description of it, just as it looked when I saw it about ten years ago.

Soon afterward George and his friend crossed the Blue Ridge and returned home. Lord Fairfax was highly pleased with what they had done, and George was no doubt very much gratified. He was paid for his work in surveying at the rate of about three dollars and a half a day when he was only riding around, and about seven dollars a day when he was regularly engaged in surveying. This was the first money that he had ever earned in his life, and he must have enjoyed spending it, as he knew that he had worked for it. Another subject of gratification to him was the good opinion Lord Fairfax formed of him from the manner in which he had executed his duties. The old Englishman now knew how valuable his property was, and what a fine country the valley was for hunting; so he removed to Greenway Court, and spent his last years there.

I have only one other incident to relate of Lord Fairfax, which took place just before his death. He was an Englishman, and opposed to the Revolutionary war; but he continued to live in Virginia, at Greenway Court. At last the year 1781 came, and Lord Fairfax grew very ill. He was at Winchester at the time, which is not far from Greenway; and one day he heard the people shouting and cheering in the streets. He asked his old servant what it all meant, and he told him that the people were shouting because Lord Cornwallis, the great English general, had surrendered to General Washington at Yorktown. At this the old lord groaned.

"Take me to bed, Joe," he said, in a low voice; "it is time for me to die!"

And you no doubt understand what the old Englishman meant. He had been the friend of young George Washington, and brought him on in life; and now this same young fellow had defeated the great Lord Cornwallis, and compelled England to give up America. It was time for him to die, therefore, he said; and soon afterward he expired, greatly mourned, there can be no doubt, by Washington.

This was the end of old Lord Fairfax. His life was a sad one, in spite of his great wealth, for his last days were spent in the lonely forests beyond the Blue Ridge, without wife or children to cheer his declining years. I never heard that Washington visited him there in these latter years. The boy with the rosy cheeks and the curly locks, who had stopped at Greenway Court, was now the grave commander-in-chief of the American army, and had no time to spare. But he must have wished to visit the old house again, and its master, who had been the friend of his boyhood.

WASHINGTON IN THE WILDERNESS.

I.

It is so interesting to follow George Washington through these first years of his career, that I will go on now and tell you of an expedition which he made at this time into the "Great Woods," as they were called, beyond the Ohio River.

Both the English and the French claimed this country. The English, you know, had settled at Jamestown in 1607, but the French had possession of Canada long before, and it was now a question to whom the western country belonged. It was full of English and French hunters, who traded with the Indians; and it became a great point with both sides to secure the friendship of the savages, in case fighting broke out, as it probably would.

This led to the expedition I now mean to tell you about. Governor Dinwiddie of Virginia and the Governor of Canada were watching each other; and at last Dinwiddie resolved to send the French a message. This message was to the effect that the western country belonged to England, and that as the French had no right to it, they were not to build their forts on it. The person to be sent was also to make friends of the Indians; and for this important expedition Governor Dinwiddie selected young George Washington.

The events here spoken of took place in the year 1753, when Washington was twenty-one years old. It was a proof of the confidence placed in him, to choose so young a man for a mission requiring the utmost prudence and good-sense, as well as courage. But Washington was now very well known. He had not done much, but had impressed every one with a high opinion of his character. A proof of this is that at the age of nineteen, three years before this time, he had been appointed adjutant-general of one of the military districts of Virginia. In performing his duties as such, he must have shown that he was a capable person, as he was now selected by the governor to carry his important message into the wilderness.*

He set out on the very day he received his commission from the governor at Williamsburg. At Winchester his party was waiting. It consisted of three white hunters and two friendly Indians, and a Mr. Gist, who was an experienced woodsman. As the weather was very cold (the month being November), small tents were packed on horses, which were intrusted to the white men; and thus equipped the party set forward and reached the Monongahela.

The point Washington aimed for was an Indian village called Logstown, a little below where the city of Pittsburg, in Pennsylvania, at present stands. As the river flowed in that direction, it would enable him to float the tents and baggage down in canoes; so some of these were procured and the loads placed in them, in charge of some of the men, while the rest of the party followed along the bank.

They at last reached the Forks of the Ohio near Pittsburg. The weather was intensely cold, but Washington stopped to look at the position. He saw at a glance how strong it was, and that it was the very place for a fort; which was a proof of his good-sense, for Fort Duquesne was afterward erected there by the French.

At last he reached Logstown, and here he had a long talk with the "Half King" of the Indians, whose name

112 STORIES OF THE OLD DOMINION.

was Tanacharisson. The object of this talk was to persuade him to promise to have nothing to do with the French; but Tanacharisson, although he was friendly to the English, was afraid to do so, and evaded making any promises. He was full of polite speeches, after the Indian fashion; but the French commander, he said, was at

OHIO RIVER.

a fort near Lake Erie, and, if Washington wished, he would go with him to see this commandant.

Washington accepted his offer, and set out with Tanacharisson and other Indians, who guided him to a place called Venango. Here a cunning old French captain, named Joncaire, met them, and set plenty of drink before them. The object of this was to make Washington drunk, and induce him to talk freely; but the plan did not succeed, and he soon left Captain Joncaire, and pushed on with the Indians toward the fort near Lake Erie.

After a long and freezing ride he reached the fort, and was courteously received. The commandant was an old French officer, called the Chevalier de St. Pierre, with a silvery head, and clad in a fine uniform. He made the young Virginian a low bow, and invited him into the fort, and Washington then handed him a letter which he had brought from Governor Dinwiddie. This the chevalier received with another polite bow, and then he retired to read it.

Two days then passed, and, on one pretence or other, the old chevalier delayed giving an answer to the letter. Washington soon saw what this meant. The chevalier was extremely polite, but he was quite as cunning, and during all this time was endeavoring secretly to persuade Tanacharisson to remain friendly to the French. Washington found this out, and was very angry; but the smiling old Frenchman informed him that he was mistaken in supposing any such thing; and at last he gave him a reply to Governor Dinwiddie's letter. This showed that the chevalier was a good soldier as well as a diplomatist. He informed his Excellency Governor Dinwiddie that he would send his letter to the Marquis Duquesne, in Canada; but as to giving up the country, he could not and would not do so: he was ordered to hold it, and he meant to obey his orders.

This was all Washington could obtain from him, and he now prepared to set out on his return. The old Chevalier de St. Pierre was both polite and cunning to the last. He furnished Washington with plenty of canoes to carry his baggage, and a quantity of provisions, but secretly tried to persuade Tanacharisson not to return with him. But in this he failed. Tanacharisson went back with Washington in the canoes, which were rowed down French Creek. The horses followed by land. And that was the last they saw of the old Chevalier de St. Pierre.

II.

The boating expedition down French Creek was a difficult affair. It was full of floating ice, and several times the canoes were nearly staved to pieces. Now and then the men were obliged to jump into the water and drag them over shallows; and once they found that a bend in the river was so full of broken ice that they were compelled to take the canoes on their backs, and carry them a quarter of a mile before they could find open water again. At last they reached Venango, where they parted with Tanacharisson and the rest of the Indians, and Washington determined to push on, on foot, for Virginia.

He was induced to do this by the terrible condition of the roads. They were now almost impassable. The water and snow in them had frozen, and at every step the horses broke through and stumbled, and more than once fell beneath their riders. It was plain, therefore, to Washington that he would never reach Virginia if he depended upon the horses to carry him there; so he and his friend Gist strapped knapsacks on their backs to carry their provisions and papers, took their rifles, buttoned up their overcoats, and pushed into the woods, leaving the rest of the men, with the horses, to come on in the best manner they could.

The long and dangerous march of Washington and his single companion then began. The obstacles before them were enough to dishearten them. It was the depth of winter, and the weather was freezing. They were in the heart of the wilderness, which was covered with snow, and could only guess at their way; and, what was worse than all, they were surrounded by hostile Indians, the friends of the French. Perhaps in all Washington's long life he was exposed to no peril greater than on this occasion. It seemed very doubtful indeed whether he and Gist would ever return alive to Virginia.

But they pushed forward fearlessly, and Providence watched over them. They ate, when they were hungry, some of the provisions carried in their knapsacks, and at night slept by a fire in the woods. All day long the steady tramp continued through the desolate woods, and at last they reached a place bearing the gloomy name of Murdering Town, where they came upon a band of Indians. As soon as he saw these Indians, Gist, who was an old woodsman, began to suspect them. He did not like their looks, and their side glances excited his suspicion. He therefore strongly advised Washington not to stop, but to push on; and as one of the Indians offered himself as a guide, his offer was accepted, and he accompanied them.

It soon became evident that Gist was right in his suspicions. The first thing the Indian guide did was to offer to carry Washington's gun. This he was far too wise to consent to, and refused, which made the Indian sulky. He had evidently hoped to induce Washington to give up his gun, and his next attempt was to get the two men in his power. Night was coming, and they looked about for a place to build a camp-fire; but the Indian advised them against this. There were some Ottawa Indians in the woods, he said, who would certainly come upon them and murder them; but his own cabin was near, and if they would go with him they would be safe.

This was very suspicious, and they resolved to be on their guard. The good-sense of this was soon seen. They refused the Indian's offer, and went on looking for water, near which they meant to encamp. The Indian guide was walking ten or twenty yards in front of them, when, just as they came to an open space where the glare of the snow lit up the darkness, the Indian turned and levelled his gun at Washington and fired. The bullet did not strike him, and the Indian darted behind a tree. But Washington rushed upon him and seized him before he could escape.

Gist came up at once, and was eager to put the guide to death. But for some reason Washington would not consent to this. He took the Indian's gun away from him, and soon afterward they reached a small stream, where they made the guide build them a fire to camp by for the night. Gist was now very uneasy. He knew the Indians much better than Washington did, and told him that if he would not put the guide to death they must get away from him. This was agreed to, and the Indian was told he could go to his cabin, if he chose, for the night. As to themselves, they would camp in the woods, and join him there in the morning, which they could easily do by following his tracks in the snow.

The guide was glad to get away, and was soon out of sight. Gist followed him cautiously, listening to his footsteps breaking the dry twigs in the woods. As soon as he was sure that the Indian was gone, he came back to Washington and told him that if he valued his life he had better get away from this spot, as he was certain that the guide meant to bring other Indians to murder them; so they again set forward through the woods.

When they had gone about half a mile they kindled another fire, but did not lie down to sleep. The fire was only to deceive the Indians. Instead of going to sleep,

Washington and Gist set out again, and travelled all that night and the next day without stopping. They knew that their lives depended on getting away quickly from that dangerous country. And at last they reached the banks of the Alleghany, a little above the present city of Pittsburg.

III.

They had expected to cross to the eastern bank of the Alleghany on the ice, but this they now found was impossible. Instead of presenting a level floor of ice from bank to bank, the river was only frozen about fifty yards from each shore, and the channel in the middle was open and full of drifting ice. It came down in large masses, and there was no possibility of crossing; so the two travellers lay down for the night, to consider what they would do in the morning.

There seemed no hope of crossing except by means of a raft, that is, by binding logs together in some manner, and floating over upon them. This they resolved to attempt. As soon as daylight came they began the work. Gist probably had a hatchet with him, as woodmen generally carried one, and trees were cut down and tied together with grape-vines. This rough raft was then dragged to the edge of the ice, and the two men got upon it and pushed it into the water. This was done by means of long poles, which they had cut for the purpose; and soon the raft was driving on into the midst of the broken ice.

Their situation soon became dangerous. The current was strong, and in spite of all they could do to force the raft across, the ice swept it down, and they could not reach the shore. Every exertion was made to steady it, and in attempting to do so Washington met with a very dangerous accident. He was leaning on his long pole, resting on the bottom of the river, which was about ten feet deep, when the ice crashed against it, and he was thrown into the water. Few things are more perilous than this. The water was freezing cold, and he no doubt had on his heavy overcoat, and this clogged his movements and threatened to sink him with its weight. And here let me stop a moment to give you some advice which may save your life some day. Never ford a deep stream

WASHINGTON ON HIS HOMEWARD JOURNEY.

on horseback or otherwise with an overcoat on. First take it off, with your arms, if you carry any; then you may swim out if an accident happens. If you do not, you will probably be drowned.

Fortunately Washington succeeded in getting back on the raft, in which Gist no doubt assisted him. They were then swept along, and gave up all attempts to reach the shore, where they had intended at first to do. At last they saw a chance for safety. The ice drove the raft near a small island, and they managed to get upon it. The raft was then carried away, and disappeared in the floating ice, and they found themselves on firm ground again.

But their situation seemed nearly as bad as ever, if not worse. They were upon a small island which had no fuel upon it, it seems, for we are told that they could not make a fire. The shore was still at some distance, and they had no means of reaching it; and the cold was so intense that Gist had his hands and feet frozen. It was a miserable night, and they must have remembered it for years afterward. They lay down in their overcoats and shivered through the dark hours, until at last day came and they looked around.

Providence had befriended them. The floating blocks of ice had frozen together during the night, and they saw that there was a solid pathway to the shore. They reached it without trouble, though his frozen feet must have given Gist intense pain in walking; and then they set forward again with brave hearts toward the South. Soon their troubles were over. They reached without further accident the house of a trader whom they knew, on the Monongahela River, and he received them cordially and supplied all their wants.

Washington then bought a horse, as his own were far behind; and sixteen days afterward he was hundreds of miles distant, in Williamsburg, informing Governor Dinwiddie of the results of his expedition.

IV.

This adventurous journey through the Great Woods gave Washington a high reputation. It was seen that he was a man who could be depended upon, and in the next spring (1754) he was appointed one of the officers to command an expedition against the French.

I have not time to give you a full account of this expedition; but as it is well to know the main facts, I will tell you these before I finish my story of Washington's adventures in the wilderness.

The old Chevalier de St. Pierre's letter to Dinwiddie was not at all satisfactory, and the governor determined to send a body of troops and drive the French out of the country. This was approved of by everybody, and Washington was appointed to command a part of them. In April he was ready, and marched to Cumberland, then called Wills' Creek; but here he heard unwelcome news. Some Virginians had gone in front to build a fort at the forks of the Ohio, on the very spot selected, you may remember, by Washington on his way to visit the Chevalier de St. Pierre. The force sent was small, and they were suddenly attacked by several hundred French and Indians, who easily captured them. The French then set about finishing the fort for themselves, after which they marched toward Virginia, to attack the forces sent against them.

This was the news received by Washington, and, at the head of one hundred and fifty men, he advanced to meet the enemy. On the way he was joined by his old acquaintances, Gist and Tanacharisson, who told him that a large body of French and Indians were not far off. He therefore halted at a place called the Great Meadows, and threw up an earthwork. This he called Fort Necessity, and here he waited.

Tanacharisson, with some Indians, then went forward into the woods, and soon came back and reported that they had found a force of Frenchmen a few miles off.

They numbered only about fifty, he said, and Washington determined to advance quietly and take them by surprise. This was done, and a fight followed. The French were posted behind rocks, but the Virginians attacked and defeated them, killing several, among whom was their commander, De Jumonville.

All were now in high spirits, and other forces joined them. Washington had four hundred men, and he marched forward to offer the French battle. On the way, however, he received intelligence which made him hesitate. The enemy had been re-enforced heavily, and were advancing to attack *him.* He therefore retreated again to Fort Necessity, and the French and Indians, to the number of about nine hundred, soon appeared in front of it. They were commanded by an officer named De Villiers, a brother-in-law of De Jumonville's, and the fighting at once began. The Virginians fought well, but were opposed to more than double their number. They were also suffering for food, and the rain was pouring, and they could not see the French and Indians, who were concealed in the woods.

All this was very discouraging. They could not venture far into the woods for fear of being surrounded, and they could not stand a siege, as they had no provisions. After fighting for some time, the French demanded their surrender; and as the terms were favorable, Washington consulted with his officers, and resolved to accept them. He agreed to surrender, and did so on July the Fourth (1754). His men marched out of Fort Necessity, leaving their cannon behind them, and the French were thus masters of the whole country.

This was what is known in history as the "Surrender at Great Meadows." It was not a very glorious affair, as the Virginians had four hundred men, if the enemy *had* nine hundred. But I suppose Washington did what was most prudent. He certainly did not act from fear, for his whole life proves that he never had any; and the Governor and House of Burgesses approved of his course, and thanked him for what he had done.

The events here related will show you what Washington's character was, and why so much confidence was placed in him. Although quite a young man, he was cool and determined, as he clearly showed in his dealings with Joncaire and St. Pierre, and afterward in the expedition I have just spoken of. If he had been thoughtless and hot-headed, as young men are apt to be, he would have failed in everything, and perhaps shed his men's blood for nothing at Great Meadows. But he seems to have acted as coolly as he afterward did when he was a gray-haired general. He saw what was the best to do, and he did it to the best of his ability; and to say that is the same as saying that he was a great man even then.

BRADDOCK AND HIS SASH.

I.

There was one other event in the old "French War," as it was called, which I must relate. It was a remarkable incident, which many persons long remembered, and went by the name of "Braddock's Defeat."

I have told you of the surrender at Great Meadows in 1754. When the news reached England it caused great excitement. At last the long dispute between France and England had ended in fighting, and troops were sent over to make war on the Frenchmen. These troops were first to march and capture Fort Duquesne; then they were to move on and attack the other French strongholds one after another; and as no one supposed that they could be defeated, it was expected that the whole country would be in possession of the English by the end of the year.

This was a fine plan to write down upon paper, but much harder to carry out. The English soldiers knew nothing whatever about fighting in the woods, and the general who commanded them was so headstrong that he would take advice from no one. His name was General Braddock, and he was about forty years of age. He was a stout, bluff, red-faced, obstinate soldier, with the highest possible opinion of himself and his men, but very little respect for the "provincials," as he called the Americans. He did not look upon them as soldiers, and swore that his "regulars" would show them how to fight. The provincials, he said, might dodge behind trees, if they chose, but he meant to march straight forward, with his drums and trumpets sounding, and make an end of the French before the autumn. Of this there could be no doubt. Fort Duquesne would not keep him more than three or four days; then he meant to march on and attack Fort Niagara, then another fort called Frontenac. And that would be the end of the matter.

Among the persons to whom he talked in this manner was the celebrated Benjamin Franklin. He had come from Pennsylvania to see Braddock on business, and wore

BENJAMIN FRANKLIN.

a Quaker coat and hat, and was as cool and cautious as the Englishman was boastful.

"To be sure, sir," Franklin now said to Braddock, in reply, "*if you arrive well before Duquesne* with these fine troops, the fort can probably make but a short resistance."

The trouble, however, Franklin went on to say, was to get there safely. The Indians would help the French, and waylay the English in the woods probably; and if they did not look out carefully, the line of soldiers would be "cut like a thread into several pieces."

But Braddock only laughed, and sneered at the idea that a *Quaker* could tell him anything about military matters.

"These savages may be indeed a formidable enemy to *raw American militia*," he replied, "but upon *the king's regular and disciplined troops*, sir, it is impossible to make any impression!"

Braddock had intelligence enough, however, to know that it would be better to have some one with him who knew the country toward Fort Duquesne; and he was informed that a young soldier, living at a place called "Mount Vernon," was well acquainted with it. This was Washington, and Braddock sent him an invitation to come to Alexandria, where the English had landed, and see him. Washington rode over at once. Braddock offered him a place on his staff, and the young soldier accepted it, and promised to go on the expedition.

The great trouble now was to procure wagons to convey the munitions and provisions. The troops had gone forward to Fort Cumberland, but could not move, Braddock said, without wagons; and whenever he spoke of these wagons, he cursed and swore in the most violent manner. In fact, Braddock swore at everything. When he set out for Cumberland, he swore at the roads; when he spoke of the provincials, he swore at *them;* and when nothing in particular annoyed him at the moment, he swore at the country in general.

This will give you some idea of General Braddock's character. He was a brave man and a good soldier, but very high-tempered and domineering. He could not control his anger when he became excited, and, what was worst of all, he had an extravagant opinion of his own judgment. Washington observed this, and must have felt very melancholy as to the fate of the expedition. He saw that Braddock would take no advice, and that something unfortunate would probably happen. He had accepted Braddock's offer, however, to go with him, and did not mean to turn back. They set out from Alexandria, and went to Frederick, in Maryland. Then Braddock, who travelled in a fine coach, guarded by a troop of cavalry, travelled through muddy roads to Winchester, which was near Greenway Court. Whether he visited Lord Fairfax there is uncertain. But Washington did: he obtained fresh horses at Greenway, and then rejoined General Braddock, who, after a short halt at Winchester, continued his way through the mountains to Cumberland.

Here his army awaited him, and were drawn up in line to receive him. His coach, with its cavalry guard, passed rapidly along the line, in the midst of the roll of drums, and a salute of seventeen pieces of artillery was fired to welcome him.

II.

Many weeks passed at Cumberland before the little army was in order to march. It consisted of about two thousand men, and Braddock drilled it carefully and established rigid discipline. Washington saw that the general was a thorough soldier, and would be obeyed. Drunkenness was punished by close confinement, and theft by cruel whipping. Some Indians who came with their wives and daughters to the camp were ordered away at once, and Braddock's firm hand was felt everywhere.

All this proved very instructive to Washington, and he witnessed the military ceremonies which were observed with deep interest—the regular guard-mountings, the drills and reviews, and the burial of an officer one day, when a guard of honor marched beside the coffin, on which lay the dead man's sword and sash, with their guns reversed, and fired a salute over the grave.

At last the wagons, which General Braddock had sworn so often about, were obtained, and the army set out on its march. It had to penetrate the "Shades of Death," as the Great Woods were called; and this proved, as Washington had told Braddock, a "tremendous undertaking." Bodies of men had to be sent in front to cut a road for the wagons through the woods; and day after day the army toiled along, watched by parties of Indians from the

ON THE MARCH.

surrounding hills, ready to attack it on the first opportunity.

At last Washington lost his patience. It seemed utterly absurd to him that the army should be delayed by this long, cumbrous train of wagons, loaded down, for the most part, with the baggage of the English officers, which they refused to leave behind. He therefore went to General Braddock, and told him that the wagons must be left to come on, while the army marched forward. He could carry the powder and provisions on pack-horses; and if this was not done, they would not reach Fort Duquesne until the French had collected a large army to receive them.

Rash and impatient as Braddock was, he saw the goodsense of this advice. He began to understand that there were some things which the provincials could teach him, and ordered Washington's views to be carried out. Twelve hundred men and ten pieces of cannon, with the stores on pack-horses, advanced in front, commanded by Braddock, and the rest followed with the slow wagon-train under Colonel Dunbar.

The twelve hundred men now advanced steadily in the direction of Fort Duquesne. On the way an incident occurred which again showed how obstinate General Braddock was, and how little he knew about fighting in the woods. A well-known hunter and woodsman named Captain Jack, or "Black Rifle," joined the troops with some of his men, and offered Braddock his services. Captain Jack was a wild-looking hunter, with a long rifle, and dressed in deer-skin. He informed the general that he and his men were well acquainted with Indian fighting, and, if he wished, they would scout in front, and report whether they discovered any enemies.

General Braddock ought certainly to have had sense enough to accept this offer. Why he did not it is hard to say, unless he was determined to show that he did not require assistance from anybody. At all events, he received Captain Jack's offer very coldly, telling him that "there was time enough for making arrangements, and that he had experienced troops, on whom he could rely for all purposes." He then made Captain Jack and his men a bow, to show them that he had said all that he had to say, and that was the end of it. They left without further words; but if Braddock had accepted their services, it is probable that the fate of the whole expedition would have been different.

They were now approaching Fort Duquesne, and had seen few signs of Indians. Sometimes they came on a pile of black brands in the woods where some one had been, and one day a French officer was shot as he was out hunting. But the woods seemed nearly deserted, and no enemy was seen.

At last Braddock halted on the Monongahela River,

MILITARY ENCAMPMENT.

about fifteen miles from Fort Duquesne. He was on the same side of the river, but found he would have to cross it, as a steep mountain just in front of him ran down into the water, and left no road for the cannon. There was, however, a good ford near his camp, and another, he heard, about five miles farther on. By crossing at these he could advance straight on the fort; and he made all his arrangements to do so at daylight on the next morning.

6*

That was the last night on earth for many of the brave fellows in the little army. Death was coming upon them swiftly. And I will now relate what took place.

III.

At daylight the army was drawn up and ready to march. It was the morning of the 9th of July, 1755.

The force was the advance, you know, of twelve hundred men and ten pieces of artillery. They were partly English regulars and partly Virginians, and at the word they marched down to the ford and crossed without trouble. The regulars went in front, though Washington had strongly advised Braddock to allow the Virginians to go before. These "Rangers," as they were called, were far better acquainted with fighting in the woods, he said, than the English regulars. But this only irritated Braddock. He gave a very short answer, and would not make any change. And what he now did was still worse. Instead of advancing in silence, so as to surprise the enemy, as he should have done, he ordered the drums to be beaten and the fifes to be blown, as if he was anxious to inform the French that he was coming. In this manner the English marched on, in their bright red uniforms, and with their muskets glistening in the sun. The flags floated, the cannon rumbled, the drums and fifes were in full blast; and Washington afterward told his friends that it was the finest sight he had ever looked upon in his life.

They were soon at the second ford, and found that there was no trouble in crossing here either. The water was shallow, and the men waded, and were followed by the cavalry and cannon. The drums were beating still and the fifes sounding shrilly; so if the French had not known of Braddock's approach, they would have known it now.

Before them, beyond the river, they saw a plain; and as Braddock knew that he was near the enemy, he made his preparations for battle. A part of the army was to advance in front under Colonel Gage, and Braddock himself was to follow with the reserve or main body, which was to support the advance if it was attacked. Flanking parties were then sent out on both flanks of the army, which at once moved forward toward Fort Duquesne.

The name of the officer in command of the fort at this time was De Contrecœur. As the whole country was full of reports about the expedition, he knew that Braddock was coming to attack him. This he was very much afraid of. His force was not large, and he feared that he would not be able to defend the place, but be compelled to retire and give it up to the English. But this did not suit a young French officer in the fort, named De Beaujeu. He offered to take a party of French and Indians and march to meet Braddock, and to this De Contrecœur consented. De Beaujeu accordingly selected his men, and, placing himself at the head of them, set forward to meet and fight the English.

The bloody encounter followed very soon. I have mentioned the plain over which the English were marching. Beyond this plain, in front, was a rising ground, behind which were woods; and on each side of the army, as it marched up the hill, were two ravines or hollows full of bushes and trees.

Here the battle took place. Colonel Gage was marching up steadily, with his men in close order, and followed by Braddock with the reserve, when suddenly a heavy fire was opened upon him from the right, left, and front at the same moment. These were De Beaujeu's men, Frenchmen and Indians, whom he had concealed in the brushwood, and he himself leaped forward, in his fine fringed hunting-shirt, in front of all. A bullet struck him as he did so, and he fell dead; but this did not discourage his men. They poured a hotter fire still into the dense mass of redcoats on the slope of the hill, and every shot seemed to kill a man.

All was now uproar and confusion. The surprise was complete, and the English officers lost all control of the men. They were huddled up like sheep, and only fired at random; and still the fatal fire from the front and the two ravines continued to destroy them.

Braddock galloped to the front and waved his sword, ordering the men to fire and charge. His voice was loud and his face furious, but the panic-struck regulars did not seem to hear him. This sudden attack confused them so much that they seemed to have lost their wits; and Washington rode up to Braddock and said if he did not order them to scatter they would all be killed. At this Braddock grew furious.

"What!" he exclaimed, "a *Virginia colonel teach a British general* how to fight!"

Even in that perilous moment he thus showed his prejudice against the provincials. He resolved to form line of battle, and march in solid column on the enemy. And all this time the French and Indians were scattered through the woods, every man behind his tree, taking dead aim at the huddled-up regulars, and killing them one by one. They were worse than hornets, buzzing and stinging, and as difficult to get at: and the youngest boy can see that Washington's advice ought to have been followed. But Braddock would not follow it. His soldierly pride was aroused at the idea that, with his fine British regulars, he was to be stopped by a body of skirmishers or sharpshooters dodging behind trees; and he rushed around on horseback, shouting his orders, and calling for his cannon to clear the woods by firing grape-shot into them.

At last the cannon, which had been in the rear, came up with the horses at a gallop, and was unlimbered, that is, gotten ready for fighting. But it seemed useless to bring it up. The English cannoneers were no cooler than the foot-soldiers. The incessant crack of the enemy's rifles, bringing down a man at every shot, confused them and filled them with panic, and they seemed ready to desert their guns and fly.

All would have been lost now, in the very beginning of the battle, but for the Virginia rangers. They knew the Indian way of fighting, and at once scattered, and fought from behind the trees: while the regulars were firing in wild confusion, without knowing what they fired at, each of the Virginians picked out an enemy, and took good aim and put a bullet through him. George Washington, whom they looked to as their leader, did his part. I have mentioned the panic which seized upon the English cannoneers. They seemed to be stunned by the bloody sight around them and the yells of the savages, and made no effort to man the guns. Washington therefore leaped from his horse, wheeled one of the cannon with his own hands, and fired a round of grape-shot into the woods where the enemy was concealed.

Wild yells were heard, and some of the French and Indians were no doubt killed. But they continued to fire as hotly as ever. Washington and the English officers made every effort to rally the regulars, but it was impossible. The officers were on horseback, and were picked out by the Indian sharp-shooters as they galloped to and fro. Braddock was as brave as he was obstinate and impatient. When it came to fighting, he showed what a true soldier he was. He had five horses shot under him, one after another, and Washington had two killed under him also. Four bullets passed through Washington's clothes, and nothing but Providence preserved him. As he rode in front, rallying the men, he was an excellent mark; and many years afterward an old Indian said that he had done his best to kill him. He took dead aim at Washington, he said, and fired at him *fifteen* times, but he never could strike him.

The confusion and uproar went on and grew worse and worse. Nothing could be done to rally the panic-stricken English regulars. The brave English officers did all they could, but the redcoats did not seem to hear them; and one by one men and officers were killed by the hidden marksmen, who uttered wild yells as they saw them fall.

At last Braddock was shot. The bullet passed through his right arm and pierced his breast, and he would have fallen from his horse had not Captain Stewart, of the Virginia Light-horse, caught him. In his agony and mortification he uttered a deep groan, and asked them to leave him to die on the field of battle. To this, of course, they would not consent. He was hurried away, as everybody saw that the army was about to break, and they placed him in a light wagon, which was driven hastily toward the ford in their rear.

The fall of Braddock was the signal for a disorderly flight. The English regulars gave up all hope now, and broke in confusion. Men, cannon, and all rushed back toward the river, hotly pursued by the French and Indians, who fired on them, uttering loud shouts and yells. The Virginians were obliged to give way like the rest, and retreated over the battle-field, which was strewed with dead bodies. More than seven hundred of Braddock's men had been killed or wounded, and sixty-two officers out of eighty-six, of whom twenty-six had been killed on the field. This was a terrible mortality in so small a force; and the Virginians, who brought up the retreat, lost more heavily than the English. One of the companies was destroyed almost to the last man, and in another every officer was shot, down to the lowest corporal.

The only course for the remnant of the fine army to pursue now was to get away as quickly as possible. They were in the heart of the Great Woods, with a triumphant enemy in pursuit; and they rushed pell-mell toward the river, and plunged into the water. Many threw away their muskets, and this unsoldierly act seems to have preserved them from destruction. The Indians pursuing them stopped to pick up these guns, and, no doubt, also to scalp the dead, as they always did; and this gave the English a little time. Their officers acted bravely, as English officers always do. They managed to get the flying troops over the river, and restore something like order among them; and then the defeated army hurried on toward Virginia.

It was a terrible defeat; and to think of it probably gave poor Braddock worse agony than his wounds. He did not wish to give up, even after all was lost. Like the brave soldier he was, he asked his friends to take him back and let him die on the field, fighting to the last. But this was mere madness. He had no army to fight with. There was nothing left for him but to do as the rest had done—endeavor to get away in safety.

IV.

How to get the wounded general off, however, was the difficulty. He was so badly wounded that it was impossible for him to ride upon horseback. Even the jolting of the light wagon in which he had been taken across the river was more than he could bear; but at last a plan was devised for carrying him away without giving him pain. This was to employ a sash, which he wore, as a sort of hammock. At that time soldiers' sashes were made very large and strong. They were of close-woven silk, and though thin and fine in texture, would bear a great strain upon them. Braddock wore an uncommonly large one; and his friends now took it off and tied the ends to the saddles of two horses, thus forming a hammock or swinging-bed. In this the wounded soldier was placed; and as the silk was elastic, the movement of the horses as they were led along did not give him pain.

I ought to tell you, before going on, that this incident rests on tradition: but there are no good grounds for doubting it, for two reasons. One is that the men present reported that it was done, and another that the red sash is yet in existence, or was some years since. It was kept by some one, and in the year 1846 was sent to General Taylor, who was then fighting the Mexicans, to be presented to "the bravest man in his army." The old general looked at it, and saw the figures "1707" woven in the silk, and told the other generals about it. One of these, General Gaines, said it was no doubt true that Braddock had been carried off in it, as sashes were often used for that purpose in old times, and General Ripley had been laid in one when he was wounded at the battle of Lundy's Lane. I suppose this statement is true, and the tradition also, and that Braddock was thus carried along; and so I will go on and finish my story.

It was a sorrowful march through the Great Woods toward Virginia. The fine army which had advanced so bravely, with drums beating and flags flying, was now only a crowd of fugitives listening for the yells of the Indians behind them, and hurrying along to reach a place of safety. Why the French did not follow them and cut them to pieces it is hard to say. It seems that they might have done so, but for some reason they did not. This may have been for fear that the English had fresh troops, and might lay a trap for *them*. Some fresh men did come to help them from the force which had remained in rear under Colonel Dunbar. Washington galloped back and ordered up these troops, but it was too late to think of doing anything. The only thing to do was to press on and get away from the enemy, and the men hurried along in the direction of Fort Cumberland.

Poor Braddock was never to reach that place, from which he had set out with such high hopes. His wounds grew worse and worse, and his strength failed more and more, as he went on. Very few persons were with him. His regulars seemed to have forgotten all about him, thinking only of their own safety; but the English officers and the Virginia Light-horse stuck to him, resolved to fight for him to the last. The Virginians, it is stated, were "unremitting in their attentions," and proved better friends than his own men in his time of trouble. He saw how unjust he had been to them now, and told them they had fought gallantly and like true soldiers. He begged Washington's pardon for all his ill-humor, and to show his regard for him, presented him with a fine riding-horse, and an old soldier named Bishop, who had been his own body-servant.

As he went along, he kept groaning to himself:

"Who would have thought it! who would have thought it! But we shall know better how to deal with them another time."

He was not to have any more dealings with the French, or any one else. He was about to die. His wounds became more and more painful, and his strength was failing fast. Finally they reached the Great Meadows, where

Washington had surrendered, you know, to De Villiers just one year before. Here they were obliged to stop. Poor Braddock could go no farther. His life was ebbing away, and he called his friends around him and took leave of them. After this his end soon came. On the 13th of

BRADDOCK'S DEFEAT, 1755.

July, four days after the battle, his eyes closed and he expired.

A grave was dug near the fort, and in this he was buried. The ceremony took place at night, and as there was no chaplain present, Washington himself read the burial-service over the grave. Everything was done with the utmost secrecy to prevent the Indian scouts, who were no doubt lurking near, from discovering Braddock's resting-place, as they would no doubt have dug up his body to scalp it, if they had known where he was buried. The Virginians were afraid to fire a salute above the grave, which was customary, you know, at the funeral of a soldier. This would have been heard, and none was fired. Before daylight the grave was filled up, and the earth smoothed down carefully, in order to conceal it. Then the Virginians and the English officers, who had remained faithful to the last, took up their sorrowful march again through the forests toward Cumberland.

This was the famous incident known as "Braddock's Defeat." It is an interesting story, I think, and has an important moral. Poor Braddock was ruined by his refusal to take advice. He was obstinate, and had so high an opinion of his own judgment that he would not listen to Washington, who knew far more about fighting in the woods than he did. This blinded his eyes, and was the cause of his destruction. He was a brave and generous soldier, but this did not avail him. His fine army was destroyed, and his friends had even to conceal his last resting-place from his enemies.

POINT PLEASANT, AND THE DEATH OF CORNSTALK.

I.

In October, 1774, a bloody battle took place between the Indians and Virginians on the banks of the Ohio, and this was followed some time afterward by the murder of the Indian leader, whose name was Cornstalk. Of these fierce old border scenes I will now try to give you a description.

Many persons have treated the Indians with injustice— I mean, in the opinions formed and expressed of them. They have been looked upon as only blood-thirsty wild animals full of savage instincts; but this is only half the truth about them. They were blood-thirsty enough, but were men of great courage and often of generous traits. They fought for what they considered their rights,—as what man will not?—that is, for the soil on which their forefathers had lived and hunted for many generations; and it certainly is hard to find any fault with them for that. The English came to take it away from them, with no better reason for doing so than that they were a superior and stronger race, which was no reason at all, unless we say that "might is right." They attacked each other, and many cruelties were committed, in which the Indians took the lead, in accordance with their savage character. North and South, war went on with them, and the two races hated each other bitterly; but there were great and noble Indians, as there were great and noble white men.

Of one of these I mean to tell you to-day, and first of a hard-fought battle, in which he was the leader of the "Redskins."

As I have said, it was the year 1774, and war was about to begin between England and the colonies. It was believed at that time that the English governors had secret

INDIAN COUNCIL.

dealings with the Indians to make them attack the colonists, and so prevent them from fighting England. Whether this was true or not, one thing is certain, that in this autumn of 1774 the Indians collected a large number of warriors in the woods beyond the Ohio River, to make war on the Virginians, and the whites at once prepared to meet them.

The name of the English Governor of Virginia at that time was Lord Dunmore. The Virginians did not like him much, as he was not very friendly to them; and in what now took place, they said that he had a secret understanding with the Indians to make them attack white people. He, however, seemed to be doing all in his power to prevent them from injuring the Virginians. He raised an army, and marched with a part of it toward the Indian country, as if he intended to fight them; but he failed to do so, as you will see, and many people said that he never meant to do anything of the sort.

While Governor Dunmore was marching with one part of his army toward the Great Woods, where George Washington had the adventures I have told you about, another little army was getting ready to march from Lewisburg, in Western Virginia, not far from what is now the famous White Sulphur Springs. This was commanded by a brave soldier named General Andrew Lewis. He was a tall, powerful man, about forty-five years of age, with long hair, and generally wore a hunting-shirt. This was a loose sort of coat, made like a common shirt, but a belt was buckled around the waist, in which were carried a long knife, and sometimes a tomahawk, the name of a small sharp hatchet which the Indians and white hunters used in fighting. When he was dressed in his hunting-shirt and deer-skin leggings, both of which were generally ornamented with fringe, and stood, with his head up and his long rifle in his hand, Andrew Lewis was a brave-looking soldier. A tall bronze statue of him now stands in the Capitol Square at Richmond, and shows how he looked. He was born in Ireland, and all his family came from that country, to escape being punished for killing a powerful man who had acted very cruelly toward them. But Lewis was a thorough Virginian in his feelings, and when Lord Dunmore called on him to march at the head of his friends against the Indians, he set about collecting men as soon as possible for the purpose.

As everybody liked Andrew Lewis and had the highest opinion of him, his friends took down their long rifles from the pegs driven into the log-walls of their houses, and marched to Lewisburg, which was then called Camp Union, to meet him. He soon found that he had a little army

POINT PLEASANT, AND THE DEATH OF CORNSTALK. 143

IN THE MOUNTAINS.

of about eleven hundred men, and in the month of September, 1774, he set out on his march toward the Ohio River to fight the Indians.

The country through which Andrew Lewis and his men now made their way was one of the roughest in the world.

It was full of woods, and swift rivers running between rugged mountains, over which no paths had ever been cut. The men had to toil along slowly; but they were strong hunters, used to the woods, and did not mean to stop for anything. Their provisions and gunpowder were carried on pack-horses—just as Washington had advised poor General Braddock to carry *his*—for no wagon could be driven through such a country. At last, after marching one hundred and sixty miles, which took them nineteen days, the little army reached the Ohio River, at a place called Point Pleasant, where the Great Kanawha, or "River of the Woods," as the name signified in the Indian language, empties into it.

Nothing had yet been heard of Lord Dunmore. As I have told you, he was marching far off—somewhere in the direction of Fort Duquesne, or Fort Pitt, as it was now called by the English, near which Braddock had his unfortunate battle—and Andrew Lewis could hear nothing about him. He sent off "runners," as they were called—that is, hunters who knew the woods, and travelled rapidly—to look for Dunmore; and, as all of his own men had not arrived, he determined to wait at Point Pleasant until he heard from the Governor. Soon afterward he received a message from Governor Dunmore that he must cross the Ohio River and march forward, and he immediately got ready to obey the order. But the Indians were too quick for him. They had resolved to fight Lewis before he could reach Dunmore, and this brought on the bloody battle about which I am going to tell you.

It was now the month of October, which is a fine time for hunting, and one morning two of Lewis's men went up the bank of the river to shoot deer. They had gone about two miles when a large number of Indians suddenly rose up from the bushes in front and fired at them, killing one of them. The other man ran back to camp as swiftly as possible, and said he had seen Indians enough to "cover four acres of ground" packed close together. When he heard this, Lewis knew that the Indians had come to attack him, and made haste to get his little army ready to receive them (October 10th, 1774).

II.

Andrew Lewis was a brave man, as he showed on this and many other occasions. Some people grow excited when the moment of danger approaches, but this was not the case with Lewis. He took his pipe from his pocket, filled it with tobacco, lit it, and began to smoke. He then gave his orders to the men.

These orders were that they should form two lines of battle, the one on the left to be commanded by his brother, Colonel Charles Lewis, and the one on the right by Colonel William Fleming, while he himself commanded the whole. It was not very good ground to fight upon. At this spot the Ohio and Kanawha rivers form a sort of elbow, and a small stream, called Crooked Run, ran into the Kanawha on the right of the Virginians, while the broad Ohio was on their left. They were thus hemmed in with a river behind them, and there was no road to retreat if they were defeated, except across Crooked Run. Lewis would not have chosen such ground to fight upon if he had had his own way, but there was no help for it now, as the Indians, he knew, were close to him. So he ordered the men to see that their rifles were all loaded, and march forward at once to attack the savages. At this order every man advanced, keeping a keen lookout; and when they had gone about four hundred yards they suddenly found themselves face to face with about a thousand Indians.

The battle at once began. The Indians were commanded by a celebrated old chief whose name was Cornstalk, who was the "King of the Northern Confederacy," toward the Great Lakes. I will tell you more about Cornstalk before I finish my story; at present I must give you an account of the battle. The Indians rushed forward, firing and yelling. They had excellent muskets, given them either by the English or the French, and the Virginians soon saw that they knew how to use them. At the first fire Charles Lewis, the brother of the general, was killed. He fell at the foot of a tree, and soon afterward expired; and as Colonel Fleming, commanding the right, was wounded about the same time, the men lost heart, and fell back slowly toward the Kanawha, behind them.

This was a very bad beginning. Two of the bravest of the Virginia officers and some of the best men were killed, and it seemed that the day was going against them. Andrew Lewis, however, remained cool. He ordered up a fresh body of men under Colonel Field, and the firing became hotter than before. The Indians had built a log breastwork from Crooked Run to the Ohio River, and they fought from behind this and the trees in the woods. The Virginians also took to the trees, and killed a number of the savages by the following stratagem: To deceive the Indians, they would take off their hats and hold them in sight at the side of the trees. Then some Indian would take aim at the hat, supposing that it was his enemy's head, and put a bullet through it, when the hat would be dropped, as if the owner of it was killed. Then the Indian who had fired at it would rush out to scalp his enemy, when the Virginian would dart at him, and dash his brains out at one blow with his tomahawk. Several were killed in this way, but the number did not amount to much. The Indians were still firing steadily from behind their log breastwork, yelling in triumph whenever they saw any of the Virginians fall, and General Lewis saw that he would be obliged to attack them in some other way, or give up the battle.

He soon determined what he would do. I have described the small stream called Crooked Run, running across the right of the Virginians into the Kanawha. The banks were very high, and covered with weeds and bushes; and Lewis saw that if he could send a party and get in rear of the Indians in that direction, he would surprise and probably defeat them. It was necessary to do something, as night was coming, and he would be in great danger; so he determined on making this attempt, and did so at once. Three companies stole away secretly while the fighting was going on in front, and got to the Run without being seen by the Indians. They then crept along the bank under shelter of the bushes, and in this manner got in rear of the Indian breastwork.

Lewis was waiting anxiously for the signal. At last it came. A rapid fire was heard in the rear of the Indians, showing that the party sent around had attacked them; and at this sound Lewis placed himself at the head of his men and charged the breastwork. The Indians made a desperate resistance. They were cheered on by old Cornstalk, who was heard shouting, "Be strong! be strong!"—that is, "hold fast!"—and when one of his warriors exhibited cowardice he buried his tomahawk in his brains. But he could do nothing. The Virginians were fighting him in front and rear; and at this the Indians lost heart. The fighting continued until sunset, and the crack of rifles rang through the woods without ceasing for a moment; but at last the Indians gave way. They scattered in every direction, pursued by the white hunters, and, about three miles up the Ohio, crossed the river on rafts, and escaped into the Great Woods, from which they had come.

It was a bloody affair. The Virginians lost seventy-five men killed and one hundred and forty wounded. What the Indians lost was not known, as they always carried off their dead, if possible. Only thirty-three of their dead were found; but the main thing was that they were defeated and driven from the soil of Virginia.

Such was the battle of Point Pleasant. And before we leave the subject, perhaps you would like to hear some verses from a song, or "Lament," as it was called, written concerning it by one of the hunters, probably, who took part in the fighting. These verses were as follows:

> "Colonel Lewis and some noble captains
>   Did down to death like Uriah go,
> Alas! their heads, wound up in napkins,
>   Upon the banks of the Ohio.
>
> " Kings lament their mighty fallen
>   Upon the mountains of Gilboa;
> And now we mourn for brave Hugh Allen,
>   Far from the banks of the Ohio.
>
> "Oh, bless the mighty King of heaven
>   For all his wondrous works below,
> Who hath to us the victory given
>   Upon the banks of the Ohio."

These verses are rude, and not remarkable for their poetry, but they describe the feelings of the brave men who fought on that occasion, and you must not laugh at them, or find fault with the manner in which they are written. The author of them might not know much about poetry and rhyming, but you can see that he was in earnest, and that his heart was full of sorrow. This induced him to write his rude "Lament," as he called it, in honor of brave

Hugh Allen, Charles Lewis, and the rest who had fallen in defence of their country.

III.

As I have called my story "Cornstalk and the Battle of Point Pleasant," I will now tell you more about this

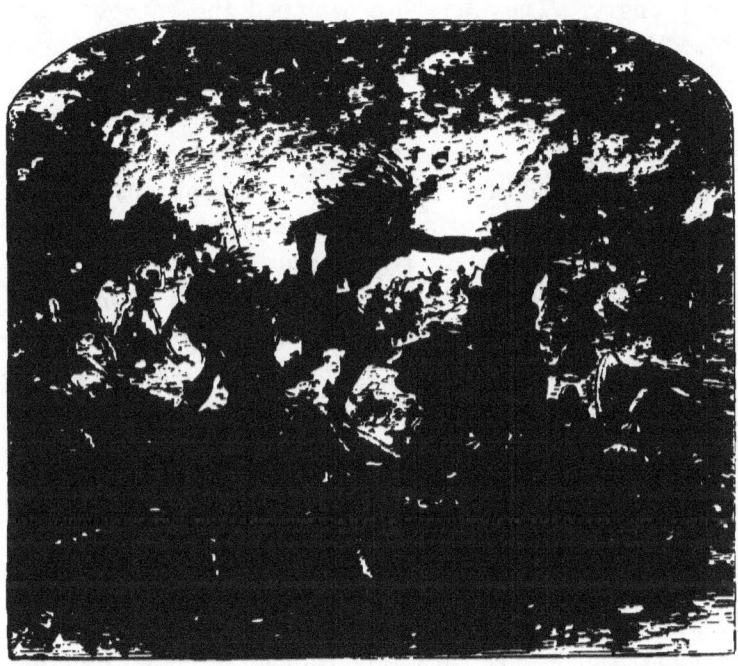

AN INDIAN ATTACK.

great Indian warrior, and how he came to his death about three years afterward.

As General Andrew Lewis had defeated the savages, and killed so many of them, he thought the best thing for him to do was to march straight on into the Indian country and make an end of the matter. His men were in the highest spirits; and as the Indians had cruelly murdered the Virginia women and children all along the border, they hated them, and determined not to give them any rest until they were all killed or driven away into the Great Woods. Lewis, therefore, set out at once; but he was surprised to meet a messenger on the way from Governor Dunmore, with an order to him to march back to the Kanawha River. This made him and his brave men very angry. They had just whipped the savages after bloody fighting, and now Lord Dunmore ordered them to go back, and not finish the work. They had heard the charges made against the governor—that he was, secretly, the friend of the Indians, and wanted them to attack the Virginians—and this made Lewis so suspicious that he refused to go back. He marched straight on, and on the way met the governor. High words took place between them, and it is said that Lord Dunmore was so angry at Lewis's disobedience of his orders, that he drew his sword and threatened to kill him. If he did so, it is not probable that a man like Lewis felt very much frightened. But Dunmore was the governor, and he could not resist. He and his men were very much enraged, but as Dunmore told them that he was going to make peace with the savages, they had nothing more to say.

The Indians were persuaded to make peace by the old warrior, Cornstalk. When Lewis drove him and his people into the woods, Cornstalk called the chiefs together to consult upon what was best to do.

"Well," said the old ruler, "what will you do next? 'The Big Knife' is coming on us now, and we shall all be killed. Now you must fight or we are all undone."

The Indian chiefs who were squatting down around him made no answer. Every one looked sulky, and did not seem to know what to do.

"Let us kill all our women and children, and go and fight till we die!" Cornstalk said.

To this the warriors made no more answer than to what he had said at first. Cornstalk looked at them one after another, waiting to hear what they had to say, but they said nothing at all.

"Well," he said, "then I'll go and make peace!"

With these words he struck his tomahawk into a post by him, while the warriors grunted "Ough! ough!" meaning that they agreed to what he had said; and a messenger was sent to Lord Dunmore to say that the Indians were ready to make peace. The governor sent back word that he would meet and talk with them, and soon afterward the Indian chiefs visited him at his camp for that purpose.

Cornstalk was at the head of them. He did not seem to be at all cast down by his misfortunes in the bloody battle, and stood up and spoke boldly. He said that the Indians were not to blame for hating the white people and making war on them; and to show how cruel the pale-faces had been to the red-skins, as the savages were then called, he mentioned what had happened to an Indian chief named Logan, whose whole family had been murdered by the white people in the spring of that year; and that was the reason why Logan was not there to talk with the rest. This was done, he said, by a Captain Cresap, of Maryland—which, however, is not true.

As Logan sent a famous answer to Governor Dunmore's invitation to him to be present on this occasion, I will here tell you what it was. When he received the invitation, he took the officer who brought it into the woods, and they sat down on a log. Logan then said, with tears in his eyes, that he could not go to meet Lord Dunmore and the rest of the white people.

"I appeal," he said, "to any white man, to say if he ever entered Logan's cabin hungry, and he gave him no meat; if he ever came cold and naked, and he clothed him not? During the course of the last long and bloody war Logan remained idle in his cabin, an advocate of peace. Such was my love for the whites that my countrymen pointed as they passed, and said, 'Logan is the friend of the white men.' I had even thought to have lived with you, but for the injuries of one man. Colonel Cresap, the last spring, in cold blood, and unprovoked, murdered all the relations of Logan, not even sparing my women and children. This called on me for revenge. I have sought it. I have killed many. I have fully glutted my vengeance. For my country, I rejoice at the beams of peace. But do not harbor a thought that mine is the joy of fear. Logan never felt fear. He will not turn on his heel to save his life. Who is there to mourn for Logan?—Not one!"

Logan made this speech, of course, in the Indian language, but the officer understood him, and when he went back to Lord Dunmore, repeated it in English, and it was printed. Everybody was very much affected by it. But if Indian women and children were murdered by the whites, the Indians had begun doing so first; and though that does not justify the whites, it shows how they came to act in so bloody and cruel a manner. Cornstalk spoke, as I have told you, of poor Logan, throwing all the blame of the hatred between the Virginians and the Indians on the white people. Other speeches were made, and the whole matter was talked over; but at last it was determined that peace should be made, and what is called a treaty was concluded between Dunmore and the savages, each side promising not to go to war any more. The Indians then went back to the woods, and Dunmore and his army marched home again.

As I shall not have any more to say of Andrew Lewis in this story, I will tell you that he afterward became a famous man, both as a soldier and statesman. He was so tall and heavy that on one occasion the Governor of New York said that the ground seemed to shake as he walked along. He never liked Lord Dunmore from the very first; and you will see, when I come to that part of my book, that when the governor was driven away from Virginia, it was Andrew Lewis who drove him.

IV.

I will now tell you more about Cornstalk, and the manner in which he and his son, Ellinipsico, were cruelly murdered by the white people.

After the battle of Point Pleasant a fort was built there, and in the fall of 1777, three years after the battle, Cornstalk and another Indian chief, named Redhawk, came to pay the soldiers at the fort a visit. Such visits were often made at that time by cunning Indians, with a bad purpose. Sometimes they came to find out how many fighting-men and cannon were in the forts, so that when they made an attack afterward they might know all about it. At other times their object was to deceive the white people, by pretending that they were friendly to them and would help them, after which they would go away and join their enemies.

Cornstalk did not make any pretences whatever on his visit to the fort. He told them that they knew he was friendly to the Americans, who by this time were at war with the English, and that his own tribe, the Shawnees, did not like the English any better than he did himself. But, he went on to say, the Indians in general looked upon the English as their friends, and he was afraid he and the Shawnees "would have to run with the stream," and make war on the Americans. He was sorry for this, but he could not help it; and he had come to tell his friends how it was, so that they might not think badly of him. He was not afraid to tell them this, he said. It might be dangerous, but he did not care for danger.

"When I was a young man and went to war," said the old chief, "I thought that might be the last time, and I would return no more. Now I am here among you; you may kill me, if you please: I can die but once, and it is all one to me, now or another time."

This showed how brave the old warrior was, and how little he cared for his life. He was in the midst of a crowd of soldiers, but he spoke fearlessly, in his firm voice. He felt that if he *was* an uneducated savage, he was the ruler of his people, and spoke and acted like a true king.

The old chief had not many more days to live. The commander of the fort told him that, as he said he would be obliged to fight for the English, he could not allow him to leave the fort. And he and Redhawk thus became prisoners. Cornstalk did not complain. Perhaps he came to the fort knowing that they would not let him go back to his tribe, by which means he would be prevented from fighting against his friends, the Americans. He did not ask them to release him, or grow angry, but remained quiet, talking over matters of one sort or another very calmly, and making no effort to escape.

The sad tragedy of his and his son's death now took place. This son's name, as I have told you, was Ellinipsico. He seems to have been a handsome, fine-looking boy, with a slender figure, and about seventeen years old. He was very fond of his father, and as Cornstalk had stayed away longer than was expected by his tribe, Ellinipsico came to find if anything had happened to him. Cornstalk was stooping down, with a piece of chalk in his hand, to draw a map of the western country on the floor, which the officers of the fort had asked him to do, when he heard a voice shouting from the opposite bank of the river. He raised his head and listened. The shout was repeated, and Cornstalk told the officers that it was his boy Ellinipsico, as he knew him by his voice. This proved to be true. The boy was hallooing for some one to come over in a canoe and bring him across. This was done, and he came up to the fort, where he clasped his arms around his father in a very affectionate manner. The old chief was quite as glad to see his son, and they went into another room, where Cornstalk slept, and were heard talking far into the night. Cornstalk was no doubt asking the news in the tribe, and Ellinipsico telling him everything, and asking why he did not return.

This was the last night the father and son passed together on earth. Early on the next morning two of the men belonging to the fort, whose names were Gilmore and Hamilton, crossed the Ohio River to hunt for deer. As there had been no trouble with Indians for some time, they thought it was safe to venture into the woods; but they soon found how much they were mistaken. A band of Indians were lying hidden in the tall weeds on the bank of the river, and as Gilmore and Hamilton passed by, one of the Indians levelled his gun and shot Gilmore; after which he rushed on him and scalped him, tearing off his whole head of hair by the roots, and the skin and flesh with it. This was the bloody manner, you know, in which the Indians treated their enemies; and as Hamilton thought that it would be his turn next, he ran back to the bank of the river and shouted to his friends that Gilmore was killed, and they must come over and help him.

The men at the fort could hear what he said, and rushed toward a canoe, which was tied to the bank not far from the fort, and leaped into it. At the head of them was Captain John Hall, a relation of Gilmore's, and he and his men were in a violent rage at hearing that their friend had been killed. The canoe shot across the river, and the men ran up the bank. The Indians were nowhere to be seen, but they found poor Gilmore's body, scalped and all bloody, and brought it to the canoe, in which they crossed back to the fort.

As they came up the bank, carrying the dead body, it was easy to see that they were full of anger at the death of their comrade. A person who saw them said that they were "pale with rage;" and with their guns in their hands they rushed forward, exclaiming,

"Let us kill the Indians in the fort!"

By this they meant Cornstalk, his son Ellinipsico, and the chief Redhawk. Captain Arbuckle and others tried to stop them; but they shouted out, as they came up the bank, that the Indians who killed Gilmore had come with Ellinipsico on the day before, and therefore he and his father should die. A woman living in the fort, who was very fond of Cornstalk, ran in and told him what the men said. Ellinipsico at once exclaimed that this was not true, and declared that no one at all had come with him. As he was only a boy, he was very much frightened and trembled all over. But Cornstalk did not show the least fear. Only an hour before he had been talking with the men in the fort, and used the words—

"I am here among you; you may kill me, if you please: I can die but once, and it is all one to me, now or another time."

He now encouraged his boy Ellinipsico, and told him not to be afraid. The pale-faces, he said, were coming to kill them, but that was all right, and the *Great Man above* —by which he meant God — had sent him there to be killed and die with his father. As Cornstalk said this the furious soldiers rushed in at the door. The old warrior, who had been quietly seated, rose to meet them, and looked them straight in the face without showing the least fear. As he did so, they levelled their guns at him and fired; and he fell and died, shot through the body with seven or eight bullets. Ellinipsico was then shot and killed, and so was the chief Redhawk, who tried to hide in a chimney. In a few minutes they were all lying dead on the floor, and that was the end of the great warrior Cornstalk, and his son and friend.

I hope I need not tell you that this was a cruel murder, as neither Cornstalk nor the others had anything to do with the death of Gilmore. Ellinipsico could not have brought the band of Indians with him, or known that they were going to kill any soldiers belonging to the fort; for he must have had sense enough to know that this would put Cornstalk's life in danger. There is no good reason to believe that he came with any other purpose than to see what had become of his father—and to kill him, and the brave old chief who was friendly to the white people, was a barbarous murder, and nothing else.

Cornstalk died, as he said he would, without fear. He stood calmly before his furious enemies, and fell dead pierced by their bullets. But, poor Indian as he was, he proved himself greater and braver than them all.

PATRICK HENRY, THE "MAN OF THE PEOPLE."

I.

WE are now nearly at the beginning of the great American Revolution. In this struggle Virginia was one of the foremost of the colonies, and her promptness was due in a large measure to the determined character of her leaders. Patrick Henry was the most famous of these, and I shall here give you an account of him: but first I ought to tell you how affairs were at the moment when he appeared.

There were many other colonies, you know, on the soil of America. Soon after the settlement at Jamestown, a party of Dutch and English established New Amsterdam (1614), now the City of New York. Then (in 1620) a number of English, who had made a bargain with the Virginia Company, in London, landed at Plymouth, in New England, and founded the Colony of Massachusetts. Soon afterward (1624) the Dutch and Swedes settled Delaware and Pennsylvania, and a party of English Catholics, under Lord Baltimore, founded Maryland (1631). And so, step by step, the whole country along the Atlantic was settled by white people, who drove back the Indians, and every year grew stronger and more prosperous.

This may not seem very interesting; but when you hear of a famous man, you like to be told when he was born, and how his early life was passed: and it is well to know the origin of nations. The United States is now the largest republic in the world, and American boys ought to know how their country had its beginning.

For about one hundred and fifty years the colonies went on prospering; and if England, to whom they be-

PORTRAIT OF PATRICK HENRY.

longed, had treated them justly, they might have remained a part of the British Empire. They were strongly attached to the "Mother Country," as they called England; but instead of returning this attachment, and taking pride in her robust children, who were growing to manhood in the New World, England seemed to have no thought in reference to them but what profit she could derive from them. She seemed to look down upon them, and treated them like inferiors. To call a man an American was the same thing with them as saying that he was rough and uncivilized; and, in part, this feeling continued almost up to the present time, when at last it seems to be changing. But, what was worse, they were resolved to make all the money they could out of the colonies, fairly or unfairly. Laws were passed taxing them heavily, although they were not represented by any of their own people in the English Parliament; and at last, in the year 1765, came the celebrated Stamp Act. This directed that no business papers of any sort should be binding on any one unless they had a certain stamp upon them, and for this stamp the Americans had to pay. A tax was laid on tea, glass, and other articles; and when intelligence came that these laws had been passed, a violent commotion took place in the colonies.

Virginia and Massachusetts were foremost in declaring that they would not submit, and I shall now tell you what sort of men led the people in Virginia. Patrick Henry was in front of all, and Thomas Jefferson followed him. I shall therefore give you an account of these two remarkable men, and endeavor to show you by what circumstances their characters were shaped, as well as what sort of persons they were.

I am particularly anxious to present this familiar view of them, as it will show you how they looked, and talked, and acted among their friends and neighbors. You will thus be able to form an idea of the men as they really were. When we look at their statues in marble or bronze they seem hard and cold. You fancy that they were always performing some grand public action. On the Capitol Square at Richmond are two tall bronze statues of Henry and Jefferson. The latter is standing, wrapped in his cloak, with a pen in his hand; and the former is holding up both arms, as if delivering a speech. The pen in Jefferson's hand means that he was the author of the Declaration of Independence, and Henry is represented as he is supposed to have looked when he exclaimed, in one of his great speeches, "Give me liberty or give me death!"

You here see the men in their public characters; and in making statues of them it is right to so represent them. But this was not all about them. If we suppose that they were always making eloquent speeches or writing great declarations, we are very greatly mistaken. They were men just like other people. When they were hungry, they liked to eat; when they were tired, they liked to sleep; and if anything amused or grieved them, they laughed and cried like everybody else. It is hard to believe this when we look at the grand statues. They appear cold and unapproachable, and a boy is apt to fancy that *he* never could be a great man. But this is all a mistake. These celebrated people had their faults and failings, and little peculiarities, like the humblest of their species. By showing you this, I may convince you that they are not so far off,

PATRICK HENRY'S STATUE.

after all; and this may give you courage, if you are ever called upon to imitate them.

I will first tell you of Patrick Henry. He was the greatest orator that Virginia every produced—I might, perhaps, say, that ever lived in America. His fearless character and wonderful genius render all about him interesting; and I shall now relate some particulars of his early life.

II.

Patrick Henry was the son of a farmer in Hanover County, and was born in May, 1736. In his boyhood and early manhood he was so idle that he was looked on as good for nothing. He spent most of his time in hunting and fishing, or playing the fiddle, instead of helping on his father's farm; and at last, as his family did not know what to do with him, he was sent to be a clerk in a small country store. Some time afterward he opened a store for himself, but soon failed. He then married a young lady of the neighborhood, whose father gave him a farm; but he failed at farming, too, and two years afterward the farm was sold. He then went back to store-keeping, and failed at that again; and now he was without the means of support for himself and his wife.

This was his own fault, as you can easily see. He would not attend to his business. He still passed his time in fishing and playing the fiddle, and the consequence was that he succeeded at nothing which he undertook. A stout, healthy young man may fail in store-keeping, but he ought not to fail on a farm. If he is industrious and follows his plough, he can always make a support for his family. But Patrick Henry was too lazy to do so. So he fell into debt, his farm had to be sold, and he found himself without a home.

Something, he now saw, had to be done. His friends

could not support him, and no doubt he was too proud to consent to that. He therefore resolved to study law, and borrowed some old law-books, which he began to read; and six weeks afterward he applied for a license to practise law. This seemed quite absurd. The old judge to whom he applied found that he knew almost nothing of law, and was unwilling to give him his license. As Patrick Henry promised him, however, that he would go on studying, he at last consented. The license was granted him, and he set up at Hanover Court-house as a lawyer.

None of his friends had the least idea that he would ever do anything in his profession. They knew how idle and ignorant he was, and no doubt supposed that the law-office would soon be shut up, just as his store had been. There was nothing about him to show that he would succeed. His appearance was as ungainly as possible. He had a stooping figure, and was awkward in all his movements. He wore faded old clothes, leather breeches, and yarn stockings, and his manner of speaking was quite as rough as his dress. As an instance of this, he pronounced "natural," "learning," and "earth"—*nait'ral, larnin'*, and *airth;* for, when he and one of his friends were disputing one day about the advantages of education, he exclaimed:

"*Nait'ral* parts are better than all the *larnin'* on *airth!*"

No one could suppose that a person who spoke in this illiterate manner would ever turn out to be a great public speaker; and his friends and neighbors had a lower opinion of him still as a lawyer. He was so ignorant that he could not write the simplest law-paper; so he got no business to attend to, and was reduced to the greatest distress. He had to help to keep a tavern belonging to his father-in-law at the court-house, to earn his daily bread; and the whole prospect before him was as gloomy as any one can imagine.

But the time was near when a great change was to take place in his fortunes, and of this I will now tell you. A lawsuit was brought by the clergymen of the Episcopal church in Hanover County to recover money which they said was due them for preaching in their parishes. When you grow older you will read all about this famous lawsuit. It turned upon the question whether the "parsons," as they were called, should be paid for their services in money or tobacco, which was then used as currency, like gold and bank-notes; and the King of England had decided in one way, and the Virginia House of Burgesses in another. As the king's decision was in favor of the parsons, they brought a lawsuit to get their pay—and there seemed nothing to do but to pay them. All the old lawyers, who examined the question, gave it up at once; when the report suddenly spread that young Patrick Henry was going to "plead against the parsons."

When this became known, everybody began to laugh. It seemed absurd that an ignorant youth should attempt to do what the old lawyers could not. He was only twenty-seven, and almost unacquainted with law. Besides this, he had never made a public speech in his life, and it was known that there would be a crowd to hear how the case would be decided. Everybody predicted that he would make a complete failure; and though the people wished him good-luck, as they were against the parsons, they expected that the whole affair would be quite ridiculous.

At last the day came, and a great crowd assembled at Hanover Court-house. The court was opened, and Patrick Henry came across the street from the tavern where he lived, and took his seat behind the bar. The sight before him was enough to frighten a young man unaccustomed to public speaking. The court-house was crowded with people, and the twelve men of the jury were ready. On a raised platform opposite sat the magistrates and a large number of the clergy, or parsons; and these were waiting, with a feeling of triumph, for the decision which they were certain would be in their favor.

All eyes were fixed on the poorly dressed young lawyer, and he hung his head and seemed confused. His friends felt as if he had placed himself in a very ridiculous position; but it was too late to think of that now, and the counsel for the clergymen opened the case. He said that there was no doubt at all about the law of the matter. His majesty the King of England had decided it, and so had the courts. All that was to be done now was for the jury to fix the amount of damages—that is to say, how much money was to be paid the clergymen. And then the speaker took his seat, and Patrick Henry rose to reply to him.

Every sound was now hushed, and every eye was fixed upon the young man. He seemed to feel this, and to be almost too much confused to utter a word. His voice could scarcely be heard, and his head hung down as though he were ashamed of himself and his presumption. His friends felt for him, and were almost tempted to leave the court-house, in order not to be present and witness his humiliation.

Very soon, however, a change took place in Patrick Henry's whole appearance. He seemed gradually to become accustomed to the sound of his own voice, and his tones grew firmer and louder. As he went on, he became more and more excited, and soon his eyes began to flash, and his voice to fill the whole court-house. He seemed scarcely to be the same man, and carried every listener along with him; and they saw, from his treatment of the case, that he knew just what he was about. He scarcely touched the question of the law, as he knew that it was against him. He addressed himself to the jury, and told them they had to decide between the King of England and the Virginia House of Burgesses. The Burgesses were their own people, and the king a stranger to them. He had no right to issue his orders to them—

Here the old lawyer who was for the clergy started up, exclaiming,

"The gentleman has spoken treason!"

But Patrick Henry did not stop. It never did any good, as people afterward found, to try to frighten him. The interruption only made him more violent in his denunciation. He repeated what he had said, and declared that the parsons were no better than the king. Men who led such lives as they did had no right to be demanding the people's money: and his expressions grew so violent at last that the clergy rose in a body and indignantly left the court-room.

Henry then ended his speech in the midst of great excitement, and soon afterward the jury retired to consult upon their verdict. This was awaited with breathless interest. The law was wholly in favor of the parsons, as the king's order could not be disobeyed; but the jury could fix any amount of damages they chose—or at least they did so, as everybody soon perceived. They came back at length and gave in their verdict. It was *one penny damages*—about two cents; and no sooner had the crowd heard this than they uttered a shout of delight. All was uproar and confusion. The old lawyer who represented the clergy rose and exclaimed that the verdict was against the law, and demanded that the jury should be sent back. But his voice could scarcely be heard. The crowd was shouting, and gathering with delight around Patrick Henry. At last they caught him up and placed him on their shoulders, and bore him out. And in this way he was carried in triumph around the grounds of the old court-house, the crowd cheering and shouting in his honor.

The scene of this great event remains almost unchanged to this day. The old court-house is still standing in its grassy yard; and I have visited it, and looked with deep interest at the old colonial building where the voice of young Patrick was first raised against England.

This was the beginning of his great career. On the day before he was almost unknown, but now he was famous. There is no doubt that everything happened just as I have related. His friends and neighbors wondered at his genius and eloquence; and when they wished to pay a compliment to any public speaker afterward, exclaimed, "He was *almost* equal to Patrick Henry when he *pled* against the parsons!"

HANOVER COURT-HOUSE.

Henry soon obtained a plenty of law practice. His dark days had passed, and two years afterward he was elected to the Burgesses. Here he made his great speech against the Stamp Act, and "started the ball of revolution."

III.

As the scene which took place on this occasion was quite a remarkable one, I will describe it.

You will remember what I said about the English law called the "Stamp Act," which ordered that the Americans should not transact business unless all the papers had a certain stamp upon them. As you have been told, this produced a great excitement in the colonies. It was regarded as an open attempt to make them the slaves of England, as they were not represented by any of their own people in the Parliament which made the law; and when the stamps came over, they were so angry that they seized upon them in many parts of the country, and burned them.

In Virginia the excitement about the stamps was very great. Some people said that as the colonies belonged to England, and the king had authority over them, they ought not to refuse to obey the law, but to write a petition asking the king to change it, and that this petition should be as respectful as possible. But others said that such petitions would be of no use. They had been tried over and over, and the best thing to do now was to tell the king plainly that no one on earth had the right to tax Virginians except the Virginia House of Burgesses.

The Burgesses soon met at Williamsburg. It was in the year 1765, two years after Patrick Henry's great speech against the parsons; and, as I have told you, he was a member of the House. Everybody soon saw that there would be an excited time. The people everywhere were talking about the Stamp Act, and the Burgesses knew that something would have to be done. They were generally rich men, with large farms, and lived in great style. They loved England, for the Virginia people had never forgotten that their fathers and grandfathers were Englishmen; and they were proud of their blood. They were quite willing that the King of England should continue to reign over them, if they were treated like the rest of his subjects who lived in England. If they were not, they meant to resist, but not to act in a passion. It

STAMP ACT RIOTS.

would be far better, they thought, to petition the king to do them justice, than to tell him in plain words that they would not obey him.

When Patrick Henry reached Williamsburg he found that this was the general way of thinking. Scarcely a single member of the Burgesses was ready to act promptly. They still hoped for a "redress of grievances," as it was called, by sending a petition to the king; but Patrick Henry had made up his mind that this would do no good. He therefore determined to act boldly, and soon after the House assembled he rose to address them.

They were a grave and imposing body, very different from the plain countrymen whom he was accustomed to in Hanover. Their dress and appearance indicated their rank in society. On all sides were powdered heads and ruffled shirts, and faces full of dignity. They were almost all large landholders, accustomed to be treated with the highest respect; and the contrast between them and Patrick Henry was very striking. He was as rough-looking as ever. His hair was unpowdered, and he wore a faded old coat, leather breeches, and yarn stockings. In short, he was exactly the same awkward-looking countryman as before.

As he rose in his place, the Burgesses turned their heads and looked at him. They scarcely knew his name, and no doubt thought it presumptuous in this plainly dressed young man to be taking the lead, and telling older persons what was best to be done. But Patrick Henry paid no attention to their looks of surprise. He had made up his mind to say what he had to say, and give his own opinion at least on the subject of the Stamp Act. He spoke in a quiet tone, and was listened to in deep silence. The Stamp Act was illegal, and oppressive to Virginia, he said; and he therefore moved that the House of Burgesses should pass the resolutions he was about to read to them. He then read the resolutions, which he had written on a blank leaf torn out of an old law-book. The tone of them was respectful, but there was no doubt what they meant, as the last of them declared that no one had the right to tax Virginia but the Virginia Burgesses.

The resolutions were looked upon as violent and very imprudent. They, in fact, asserted that the king had no right to levy taxes in Virginia, which was very much like rebellion; and several speakers at once rose, and denounced them as highly injudicious. There was a violent excitement, as one after another spoke against the resolutions, and then Patrick Henry rose to defend them.

His whole appearance had changed, and the Burgesses soon found that the poorly clad young countryman was a matchless speaker, and superior to all of them. His head was carried erect, and his stooping figure grew as straight as an arrow. His eye flashed, and his voice rolled through the hall like thunder. He was fully aroused, and denounced England in terms of the bitterest insult. Why were English people better than Virginians? he asked. What right had the Parliament to tyrannize over the colonies? And as to the King of England, he had better look to his life.

"Cæsar had his Brutus," he exclaimed, "Charles the First his Cromwell, and George the Third—"

"Treason!" came from every part of the hall; but Henry did not shrink.

"And George the Third may profit by their example!" he added. "If this be treason, make the most of it!"

He took his seat after uttering these brave words, in the midst of great excitement. It was plain that his speech had made a strong impression. Speech after speech was made—some in favor of, and some opposed to the resolutions; but at last, it was seen that Henry's wonderful eloquence had swept away everything. When the House was called upon to say whether the resolutions should pass or not, they were passed—the last and most important of them, by a single vote.

The Burgesses then adjourned in the midst of general excitement. One of them rushed out, declaring that he would have given five hundred guineas for a single vote, in order to defeat the resolutions. But the people were delighted to hear that they had passed. As Henry pushed through the crowd, a plain countryman slapped him on the shoulder, and exclaimed,

"Stick to us, old fellow, or we are gone!"

IV.

I ought not to leave the subject of the life of Patrick Henry without saying a few words of what was looked upon as the greatest of all his speeches. This was made at St. John's Church, in the city of Richmond, and rang like the blast of a trumpet through all the colonies, summoning them to resistance.

It was now the spring of 1775, and the whole country was drifting toward revolution. What Patrick Henry had said against the Stamp Act proved like seed sown in the ground. It lay there for ten years, but at last it began to sprout, and now, in the year 1775, it appeared above the ground. England seemed determined to make the colonies submit to her. Soldiers were sent to Boston, and as Virginia took part with Massachusetts, the governor drove the Burgesses away from Williamsburg. To this they paid no attention, however. As they could not meet there, they determined to assemble in Richmond. A convention of the Virginia leaders was accordingly elected; and in March, 1775, they met to consult on the state of the country.

The old church of St. John's, in which they assembled, is still standing. It is a plain old building, crowning a hill not far from Bloody Run, where Bacon defeated the Indians, and in sight of Powhatan, where the old Indian

ST. JOHN'S CHURCH.

emperor was visited by Captain Smith. In front is James River, winding away below the falls and green islands with their dipping foliage, and all around the ancient church are old tombstones crumbling away in the grass.

Here the convention assembled, and it embraced some of the bravest and wisest men in Virginia. The president was Edmund Pendleton, who was celebrated for his powers of public speaking and for his ready and vigorous intellect. Thomas Jefferson said of him, "Taken all in all, he was the ablest man in debate I have ever met with;" and his voice was so sweet and "silvery" in its tones that it was delightful to hear him speak. Many other distinguished men were present, and among the rest Patrick Henry. He was looked upon by this time as the leader of the Revolution in Virginia, and soon showed that he deserved the name which had been given him— the "Man of the People."

As soon as the convention took their seats, he rose and moved that Virginia "be immediately put in a state of defence." This was coming to the heart of the matter in a very few words. He meant that the time for discussion had passed, and the time for action come. If the Americans intended to submit, then they could go on offering petitions; but if they meant to fight England, it was time to get ready.

As had happened to him in the old House of Burgesses, his proposition met with strong opposition. There were many good patriots who still thought that peace could be made with England. They dreaded going to war and shedding blood if they could avoid it: they therefore spoke against Henry's resolution, and declared that it ought not to pass. The scene was exciting, and Henry listened in silence. When they had finished, he again rose, and his face showed that he was fully aroused. His speech surpassed all others which he had ever delivered, and the whole man seemed to be on fire as his voice echoed from the old walls of the church. They must *fight!* he exclaimed; there was no longer any hope but in a reliance on God and their own strong arms. It might be said that they were weak and unable to oppose England;

but God would fight for them and protect them in the great struggle. They must fight!—and even if they were not willing, they would be obliged to. No choice was left them.

"There is no retreat," he exclaimed, "but in submission and slavery! Our chains are forged—their clanking may be heard on the plains of Boston. The war is inevitable, and let it come! I repeat it, sir, let it come! It is in vain, sir, to extenuate the matter. Gentlemen may cry 'Peace, peace!' but there is no peace. The war is actually begun. The next gale that sweeps from the north will bring to our ears the clash of resounding arms. Our brethren are already in the field. What is it that gentlemen wish? What would they have? Is life so dear, or peace so sweet, as to be purchased at the price of chains and slavery? Forbid it, Almighty God! I know not what course others may take, but as for me, give me liberty, or give me death!"

As Patrick Henry uttered these words, with both arms raised and eyes on fire with excitement, it is said that a thrill ran through the whole assembly. They were ready to start from their seats and shout, "To arms!" No further opposition was made. The voice of Henry had swept it away. His resolutions were passed by a large majority, and Virginia thus announced to the world that she was ready to fight.

All things considered, this speech was one of the greatest ever delivered; and Patrick Henry seemed to be almost a prophet. It was made in the month of March, and in April the fighting began. General Gage attacked the people in Massachusetts; and if Virginia had not been so distant, the sound of his cannon might have been heard upon the wind from the north, and the "clash of resounding arms" at Lexington and Concord.

"GIVE ME LIBERTY, OR GIVE ME DEATH!"

This is all I can say to-day of Patrick Henry. He was a remarkable man, and suited to the times in which he lived. Nothing could shake his resolution, and his wonderful eloquence astonished the greatest men who listened to him. Thomas Jefferson said of him:

"It is not easy to say what we would have done without Patrick Henry. He was far before us all in maintaining the spirit of the Revolution. His eloquence was peculiar—if, indeed, it should be called eloquence, for it was impressive and sublime beyond what can be imagined. After all, it must be allowed that he was our leader. He left us all far behind."

These were strong words to apply to the plain country lawyer who had failed at store-keeping and nearly everything else which he had attempted. But they were true. Patrick Henry found at last what his true business in life was, and his name is now one of the greatest in the history of America.

THOMAS JEFFERSON, THE "PEN OF THE REVOLUTION."

I.

On the day when Patrick Henry made his great speech against the Stamp Act, a number of students from William and Mary College were standing at the door listen-

THOMAS JEFFERSON.

ing. Among these was a young man of twenty-two, who drank in every word. When he was afterward asked about the debate, he said it was "most bloody." He was unknown at the time, but was destined to become as famous as Henry himself; for the name of this youth was Thomas Jefferson.

I have told you that I meant to try and give you some idea of these men of the Revolution as they appeared every day to their friends and those who knew them best. This I can do in the easiest way by giving you anecdotes and familiar details of them, from which you will see how they passed their time, and what their real characters were. Jefferson has told us himself, in his letters, about his youthful days; and as these were very different from his after-life as a famous statesman and ruler, I will tell you about them, to show you what a gay youth this great man was.

He was the son of a wealthy farmer in Albemarle County, Virginia, and was born in the month of April, 1743. As was then the fashion, he was sent to William and Mary College at Williamsburg, and here for a part of his time he studied very hard. While not thus engaged he was visiting young ladies, and from all accounts he was very much liked by them. He was tall and not very graceful, and had sandy hair; but he was full of wit and fun, and fond of dancing and other amusements. There is no reason to believe that he neglected his studies for the society of young ladies, but he certainly had his share of the fun and frolic around him. He tells us so himself. He had a friend named John Page, who was afterward Governor of Virginia, and wrote him a number of letters, which were published. In these he gave an account of his daily doings, and it is amusing to read them. In one, he describes a night which he spent at an old country house, where the rain leaked upon his watch, and the rats ate up his pocket-book and garters, which were then worn by men; and in another he speaks of "dancing with Belinda in the 'Apollo,'" and tells his friend how happy he felt while doing so.

The "Apollo" was a large room in the old Raleigh Tavern at Williamsburg, and became famous afterward,

RALEIGH TAVERN.

like Faneuil Hall in Boston, as the place of meeting of the patriots. At that early day, however, it was only used as a ball-room, and the "Belinda" the young man speaks of was a young lady with whom he had fallen in love. His letters are full of her; and it is amusing to find a person who afterward became the grave President of the United States breaking forth into exclamations at the delight he felt in dancing with her. They were never married, and young Jefferson either was, or pretended to be, very disconsolate. He meant to rig out a boat, he said, and sail to Europe, and remain absent two years; but this was probably a jest, and he turned his attention elsewhere.

Soon afterward he left college and began the practice of law, and it was not till he was nearly thirty that he was married. On this occasion an interesting little scene occurred; and as it gives us a good idea of his light-hearted disposition, I will relate it.

His bride was a beautiful young widow of Charles City County, named Mrs. Skelton. She was about twenty-three, and lived at a place called "The Forest;" and, as she was very wealthy, she had a number of admirers. Of these she preferred Mr. Thomas Jefferson, and in January, 1772, they were married at "The Forest." It was an old Virginia party, with crowds of friends and relatives, huge roaring fires, and music and dancing, which was kept up throughout the night. On the next morning the bride and groom set out in their carriage, drawn by four horses, for the mountains, where Jefferson lived, and then their troubles began.

It was the depth of winter, and a snow-storm began to fall. They stopped at "Blenheim," the residence of Colonel Carter, not far from the end of their journey; but as the family were not at home, they determined to push on

MONTICELLO.

and reach "Monticello," the name of Jefferson's place, before night. They therefore continued their way, but it proved a terrible undertaking. The snow was falling steadily, and the mountain roads were full of drifts, through which they could scarcely force their way. The horses plunged and snorted, and the coach rolled from side to side, and it seemed probable that they would be compelled to spend the night in the fields or forests, without fire or food. It must have tried the young lady's courage, but she laughed and kept up her good spirits, and at last the coach plunged through and ascended the winding road to "Monticello."

The sight before them was dreary enough. The hill was covered with snow, and not a light or a fire was to be seen. But this did not affect the young married couple. Jefferson opened a small pavilion, and led his bride in. He then kindled a fire, and brought out a bottle of wine and some biscuits from behind the books on the shelves, and they supped, and laughed, and sang, and were as gay as if they had been two children enjoying a frolic.

This is one of the small incidents which I set out with the intention of relating. They are not very important in themselves, but they afford us an idea of the persons who figured in them, and that is precisely what we wish to obtain. Jefferson's good-humor on this occasion shows one trait in his character which many persons gave him no credit for; and I have always thought of this little incident with pleasure. The snow was falling and the wind blowing outside the mountain pavilion, but within all was warmth and laughter. They were happy, for they loved each other, and did not mind the snow. None of us mind it in youth, when those we love are beside us. As we grow old they leave us sometimes, and the snow settles in our hearts—when we have a dreary time enough.

II.

In the spring of 1773, which was the year after his marriage, Thomas Jefferson took his seat in the House of

Burgesses. He was only about thirty, and therefore quite a young man still, but it soon became plain that he would be one of the greatest leaders of the Revolution. He was a very poor speaker, and it is doubtful whether he ever made a regular speech in his life; but he was an excellent writer, and this was the foundation of his fame. He wrote a pamphlet on the subject of the quarrel between England and America, which was so defiant that he was declared a traitor by the English government. But this had no effect upon him. He said what he thought, and men like himself are always ready to support their opinions. He was heart and soul for resistance to England, and now became the author of one of the greatest of all plans for uniting the colonies. This was a "Committee of Correspondence," whose duty it was to write to similar committees to be formed in other parts of the country, by which means each colony would know what the rest were ready to do. Jefferson proposed this, and the committee was appointed. The effect was soon seen. From the North to the South the scattered colonies formed one country in their resistance to oppression; and through their committees they made an arrangement to meet in Congress at Philadelphia.

In these movements at Williamsburg Patrick Henry and Thomas Jefferson were the great leaders. Each had his peculiar gift. Jefferson could not speak, but was a powerful writer. Henry could not write, but was a wonderful orator. Thus each did his part, and urged resistance as the only course now left. The Burgesses followed their suggestions, and the English governor dissolved them, as it was called; but they determined to meet at the Raleigh Tavern, in the "Apollo Room," and did so. Here they consulted as to the next step. Jefferson was among them. He must have looked around him, and remembered the days of his youth, when he was so well acquainted with the old apartment. He had danced many a set with "Belinda" and other young ladies in this very room when he was a thoughtless young man; and now

THE APOLLO ROOM.

he was a grave statesman, organizing revolution on the same floor which he had danced upon. He must have closed his eyes sometimes, and fancied he heard the music again; for even the busiest men find time to go back in this way often, and return in memory to the happy days of their youth.

I have mentioned the General Congress of the colonies which met at Philadelphia. Jefferson was one of the delegates to it, and in the year 1776 he became immortal in American history as the author of the Declaration of Independence. In May of that year, Virginia suggested that this declaration should be made, and directed Richard Henry Lee, one of her most distinguished patriots, to move the resolution. He did so, and Congress resolved that the declaration should be made; after which they looked about for a person to write it.

The choice fell upon Jefferson. He had scarcely risen in Congress since he had been a delegate, for he was nothing of a public speaker, as I have said, and left debating to others. But his powers as a writer were well known. His style was plain, vigorous, and went straight to the point. What he had to say he said clearly always, and he knew well what to say. The colonies meant in this great paper to declare themselves independent, and give the reasons for doing so; and, sitting down in an old house in Philadelphia, Jefferson wrote the Declaration.

It was then offered to Congress, and a hot debate took place upon it. Jefferson had no share in this; he left the struggle to the great John Adams and other friends, who fought like giants for it. Many were opposed to it, and did all they could to defeat it, but failed. The time had come to declare that the colonies were independent, and Congress resolved that this declaration should be made in the terms used by Jefferson. It was passed with a few changes which did not alter the meaning, and was the crown of Jefferson's fame as a statesman.

It was natural that he should be proud of it, and he seems to have been so. By his own request, the words "Author of the Declaration of American Independence" were cut upon his tombstone.

III.

I cannot tell you, in this short story, of Jefferson's long and famous career as a statesman and ruler. He became President of the United States, and the head of a great party; and his fame as an upholder of democracy extended throughout the world. For good or evil—and there are different opinions as to that—he left a powerful impress on the country; and his name will probably last as long as its history.

All this you will read of some day. I cannot speak of it here. With a glance at Jefferson as an old man, I will proceed to other stories.

He passed his last days at "Monticello," where he and his bride had spent that snowy night so long before. He was old, but still active. The University of Virginia was established by him, and he spared no exertions in these his last years to make a great institution of it, in which he succeeded. He wrote many letters, and still watched political affairs keenly; but his chief sources of happiness were literature and the society of his family.

He was happy in his home. His family loved him tenderly, for he was kindly and affectionate. His neighbors liked him, for he was extremely hospitable and cordial whenever they came to see him, and he entertained so many visitors that it nearly ruined him. These came to see him from all parts of the world, and especially from France, where he had been minister and was exceedingly popular. One and all were met with a warm welcome and smiles; and they went away and said that the "Sage of Monticello" was one of the most agreeable as well as one of the greatest men in the world.

He still remained busy. Such a man, with a mind so keen and active, never rests. He labored to establish firmly the great University of Virginia. He wrote thousands of letters to people on politics or other subjects. He read and studied, and wrote for many hours every day, and took a very deep interest in everything relating to Virginia. He had himself, you know, played a great part in her history. He and Edmund Pendleton had rewritten the laws, and Jefferson had overturned with his own hand the old order of things, and made all new. He had put everybody on a level. The old religious intolerance was swept away by his exertions, and, in spite of Edmund Pendleton's opposition, he had destroyed the old system of giving the land to the eldest son, which kept up distinctions in society. This quite altered the State, and he was

UNIVERSITY OF VIRGINIA.

not much liked by the old planters for it; but the people in general were delighted, and said he was the defender of the "rights of man."

He was very fond of farming operations, and would go into the harvest-field in the hottest part of the day to see his cradlers cut the wheat. He also took a deep interest in stock, and raised blooded horses and fine breeds of cattle. He was an excellent rider. Even when he was an old man and very feeble, he would mount the most spirited horses, and control them with ease. To the last his seat in the saddle was erect and firm, and he continued to ride out on his high-mettled horses when his servants had to lead them up to the porch for him to mount them.

These little details will give you an idea how Thomas Jefferson passed the evening of his life at "Monticello." His sun was setting gradually, and all eyes were fixed upon it as it sank. At last it began to descend below the horizon, as

THOMAS JEFFERSON'S STATUE.

you may have seen the large red orb of the real sun touch the blue mountains in the west and slowly disappear. In the year 1826, he was taken sick and went to bed. His family and friends gathered around him, and were deeply distressed, but he himself was entirely resigned. He did not seem afraid to die. But he gradually sank; and on the night of the third of July, those at his bedside saw that he was dying. Very singularly, the famous John Adams, who had been his friend and supporter in the great struggle over the Declaration of Independence, was dying at the very same time, far off in Massachusetts. He remembered his old friend in Virginia, and was heard to say to himself,

"Thomas Jefferson still lives!"

Just as midnight struck, Jefferson roused himself, and his lips moved. Those beside him bent over him, and heard him murmur, in a low voice,

"This is the fourth of July!"

He lived until twelve o'clock in the day. He then said, in a feeble voice,

"I resign myself to my God, and my child to my country!"

After uttering these words, he expired; and John Adams died on the same evening. Fifty years before, almost hour for hour, these two great men had placed their names to the Declaration of Independence in Philadelphia.

A BALL AT THE CAPITOL.

I.

On the 27th of May, 1774, the Virginia Burgesses gave a ball to the English governor, Lord Dunmore, and his family at the Capitol in Williamsburg. This ball was quite remarkable from the circumstances connected with it; and before relating some important events which followed, I will give you an account of it.

Lord Dunmore had come to Virginia in the year 1772. He soon became unpopular. He was a man of bad disposition, and seems to have looked upon the Virginians as his enemies.

THE OLD CAPITOL.

The rising spirit of rebellion excited his anger, and he shut himself up in his "Palace," as it was called, for the greater part of the time, watching the House of Burgesses.

This Palace was a large and fine building near Gloucester Street, in the middle of the capital. It was seventy-four feet long, and nearly as deep, and stood in a beautiful park of three hundred and seventy acres. The grounds were full of walks and carriage-drives, and had a bowling-alley in them. Fine old trees were seen everywhere, and on these colored lanterns were hung, when balls were given at the Palace, to light the guests on their way to the house. All about the place was fine and imposing. There was a guard-house at the large gateway for the governor's guard, and a porter's-lodge. A broad walk led up to the Palace, and within it was decorated with carved wood-work, and well furnished. Two portraits of the King and Queen of England hung opposite each other in the main apartment, and in this room the royal governors received their visitors.

Governor Dunmore did not entertain much. As I have said, he had no great opinion of the Virginians, and seldom offered them any courtesies or received any. They were probably doubtful whether he cared to have any such compliments paid him; but at last an opportunity came to give him an example of Virginia hospitality.

REMAINS OF GUARD-HOUSE.

Lord Dunmore had left his family behind him in New York; but they now joined him in Virginia, and the Burgesses resolved to give them a warm reception. From all accounts, they deserved this. They were very different from the governor, and ready to respond to any attentions they received, with pleasure. One who knew them wrote: "Lady Dunmore is here—a very elegant woman. Her daughters are fine, sprightly, sweet girls. Goodness of heart flashes from them in every look. How is it possible my Lord Dunmore could so long deprive himself of those pleasures he must enjoy in such a family?"

But here they were at last—Lady Dunmore and her sons, and three handsome daughters, Catherine, Augusta, and Susan. The windows were illuminated as they drove into the capital in their coach, and then the House of Burgesses set about arranging for a ball in their honor.

A BALL AT THE CAPITOL.

On the very day before that on which the ball was to take place, a remarkable scene took place at the Capitol. To understand this scene, I must tell you what had just happened. You have heard how the English tea was thrown overboard from the ships in Boston Harbor by the Americans, to show that they did not mean to use it if they had to pay the tax upon it. As soon as they heard of this in England, it caused general excitement; and a law was passed which ordered that the port of Boston should be closed—that is, that no ship should sail from it —by way of punishment. This aroused the Virginians, and they determined to show their displeasure at the law. The port was to be closed on the first day of June in this year, and the Burgesses recommended that this day should be passed by the Virginians in fasting and prayer, to show that they were mourning over the destruction of American liberty.

I wish you to observe particularly what now took place. The Burgesses passed their law, about the fasting and praying, on the 24th of May. On the 26th, two days afterward, the scene occurred which I will now describe.

In order to show you just what happened, let us fancy that we are living in Williamsburg at the moment, and endeavor to see with our own eyes all that took place. It was more than a hundred years ago, but there was an old newspaper published at that time which gave an account of everything, and this informs us accurately in regard to the whole affair.

It is the morning of May 26th, 1774. The old city of Williamsburg is in commotion. To and fro along Gloucester Street roll the coaches of the planters, drawn by their four glossy horses, with their liveried drivers; and men on horseback, and country people in carts, are arriving at every moment. It is reported that something interesting is going to take place to-day, and at last Lord Dunmore is seen passing in his fine coach from his palace to the Capitol. The crowd follows and gathers around the portico, where a marble statue stands of good Lord Botetourt, the former governor. Lord Dunmore then gets out of his coach and goes up-stairs to his council-chamber, and the crowd flock in and fill the gallery of the House of Burgesses, which is in session.

Let us follow them, and see what is going on. We find seats in the gallery at last, and look down on the large apartment, which is crowded with the members of the Burgesses. On a raised platform opposite sits the Speaker, or presiding officer. He is seated in a tall-backed chair, which is still used for the same purpose in Richmond, and behind him is a large red curtain, held up by a gilded rod. Below him sits the clerk, with the mace, a sort of heavy weapon, lying before him on his table. This is in imitation of the old practice in the House of Commons in England, and means that the Burgesses are in full session, and that no one must disturb them.

Let us look attentively at this distinguished body of men. You may see at a single glance that they are the "men for the times." They are richly clad, and present an imposing appearance. They wear coats with heavy sleeves, long waistcoats covered with embroidery, ruffled shirts, silk stockings, buckled shoes, and their hair is covered with white powder. They are grave and dignified; bold-looking, but cautious too, for the times are dangerous. They are the greatest men of Virginia, to whom the people have left the decision of everything; and before we see what takes place, it is worth while to look carefully at a few of the most famous men of the assembly.

II.

You no doubt recognize that plain-looking man yonder in the old faded coat. His dress and general appearance, you see, are not at all like those of the rest. His hair is unpowdered, and he wears leather breeches and yarn stockings. His face is grim and determined, and his keen eyes flash under his bushy eyebrows.

He has just risen to speak, and every eye is fixed upon him. Nobody seems to think of his shabby coat and plain appearance. They listen, for they know what is coming. His voice is low, you observe, at first, and his manner quiet. He speaks deliberately, and pronounces some of his words in a very singular manner. He calls earth *airth*, and seems to be uneducated; but no one takes any notice of this. Now his voice is growing louder and his appearance more animated. His stooping shoulders grow straight, his eyes are full of fire, and at last his voice begins to thunder above the heads of his listeners. The fire of the man seems to burn them. Their faces flush, and they lean forward in their seats, with their eyes fixed upon him. His voice grows louder and more passionate: he pours a flood of denunciation upon England and everything English. The time has come to act, he tells them, or they and their children will be slaves; and, with both arms raised and his hands clinched, he ends his speech, and takes his seat in the midst of murmurs of approval.

I need not say who this is. You know Patrick Henry. He is at his post in front, but has followers as brave and resolute, if not as fiery, as himself. There is one of them not far from him. He is tall and distinguished-looking. His forehead is lofty, his eyes are blue, and as he rises to address the Burgesses, you can see that he is an orator. His voice is sweet and silvery, and falls on the ear like music. But those who listen to him know that his mind is as powerful as his voice and gestures are attractive. That is Edmund Pendleton, of "Edmundsbury," in Caroline, the leader of the party in the Burgesses which is in favor of calm and deliberate action. He is deeply attached to England, like almost every one in the assembly. He loves the Episcopal Church, of which he is a member, and the old English law that the eldest son in a family should inherit the land and keep up the name; he is proud that he has English blood in his veins, that Virginia is a part of the famous old land, and hopes still that there will be no war, and that they will all live in peace together. He sees no good that can come from a new state of things; but he is as determined as Patrick Henry that the rights of Virginia shall not be trampled upon. And this is known to everybody. The utmost confidence is placed in him. He will hereafter become the head of the Virginia Committee of Safety, the president of her great conventions, and the chief judge of her Supreme Court. He shares the counsels of the leaders, and is one of the most distinguished of them, and will rank in future years as one of the greatest men of her history.

Not far from Henry and Pendleton sits a person of about thirty, with sandy hair, a square face, and a quiet expression of the eyes, who does not speak, but seems to listen to every one and to be waiting. His manner is so unpretending that you would not suppose that he was one of the greatest of the leaders in the Burgesses. But this quiet-looking man is Thomas Jefferson, who uses his pen as vigorously as Patrick Henry uses his tongue. Calm as he seems, he is full of fire, and resolved to stop at nothing. He has no fondness for England. He laughs quietly at kings and noblemen, and the idea that they have a right to rule over anybody. He wishes to overthrow them all, and thinks it is necessary to act at once. He is ready to fight, in order to sweep away every landmark of the past—rank in society, the English Church, and every trace of monarchy. He is for levelling everybody, and setting up a republic, where all are equal; and is one of the greatest political overturners of the age.

III.

These men are the leaders of the two great parties in the Burgesses—one in favor of deliberate action, the other for revolution at once.

But there are other celebrated men before us at whom we ought to glance before passing on. Yonder is one of the most remarkable of them. You see the portly figure, the swarthy face, bronzed by the sun, and the dark, stern eyes, both sad and severe in their expression. He leans back, with his right hand buried in the ruffles under his gold-laced waistcoat, and in every eye fixed upon him you may see the regard and respect that is felt for him. He is George Mason, of "Gunston Hall," on the Potomac. His family supported Charles I., and were obliged to fly to Virginia; but George Mason is a determined patriot, and ready to oppose George III. He is an admirable writer, and will soon distinguish himself as such. The "Bill of Rights of the People of Virginia" will proceed from his pen, and make him famous before long; and he will write to his son in France that he hopes to see him again as a free man, or not at all; and that if he only has "a crust of bread and liberty," he will be ready to die.

Not far from him is a tall gentleman, with a noble Roman head, bent forward courteously. His right hand is covered with a bandage, as he shot himself one day while hunting swans on the Potomac. But his gestures in speaking are so graceful that people say he practised them before a looking-glass. That is Richard Henry Lee, of "Chantilly," in Westmoreland, called the "gentleman with the silver hand," as Pendleton is spoken of as the "silver-

RICHARD HENRY LEE.

voiced." He is a remarkable orator, and a man of the highest character. Two years from this time he will make a great name for himself, by moving in the General Congress that the Americans shall declare themselves independent.

Yonder is a person worth our attention—the man of small stature and long hair, with the piercing eyes. That is Archibald Cary, of "Ampthill," in Chesterfield. He is descended from Lord Falkland, who fell in the English revolution, and is heir-apparent to the English barony of Hunsdon. People call him "Old Iron," either because he has an iron-foundry on his farm, or is as firm as iron in character. He will show hereafter that he is a determined man. When people speak of making Patrick Henry dictator of Virginia, Archibald Cary will say to a halfbrother of Henry, "Sir, I am told that your brother wishes to be dictator. Tell him from me that the day of his appointment shall be the day of his death, for he shall find my dagger in his heart before the sunset of that day!"

There are many other striking figures, you perceive, in the assemblage, as we look down upon them from the crowded gallery. Notice that calm-looking gentleman with the erect head and lofty forehead. That is Thomas Nelson, of York, hereafter to be Governor of Virginia, who will spend his whole estate to fit out soldiers, and never be repaid. At the siege of Yorktown he will cannonade his own house, and there is no truer patriot in the Burgesses. Many others are worthy of attention. Yonder is George Bland, of Prince George, called the "Virginia Antiquary," old and nearly blind; and Edmund and Peyton Randolph—one to serve in the cabinet, and the other to be president of the first Congress. There is Robert Carter Nicholas, the sound financier, and Benjamin Harrison, of "Berkeley," who is said to be descended from the regicide, Colonel Harrison, who signed the warrant for the execution of Charles I.

PEYTON RANDOLPH.

Last of all, see that man of tall stature, with the erect head and the military bearing. He is in the midst of Patrick Henry, Thomas Jefferson, and the other patriots, as you will see him in bronze one day, on his horse, in the Virginia monument to him. That is Colonel George Washington, of "Mount Vernon," on the Potomac. The old wars on the border are over, and he is a planter now. He is married, and represents the county of Fairfax in the Burgesses; but, as you know, he is soon to be called to a greater stage of action. His appearance is imposing, and there is something calm and majestic about him. His glance is clear and steady; you see he is the man of action. The time is not far off when the country will call him. He will take command of the American army, and die the founder of the American republic.

IV.

As we look at these distinguished men, grouped upon the floor of the old House of Burgesses, a stir takes place at the door, and a messenger enters and delivers a paper to the Speaker.

It is an order from Lord Dunmore to attend upon him in a body, in his council-chamber, to receive a communication which he has to make to them. The Speaker rises, and informs the House of the order received. Nothing is said: the members leave their seats; the Speaker, followed by the sergeant-at-arms carrying the mace, goes in front; and the Burgesses repair in a body to the council-chamber.

They enter, and are received with stiff courtesy by Lord Dunmore. He is seated at the head of a large table, with the members of his council around him. He is richly clad, and resembles a monarch receiving the homage of his subjects.

"Mr. Speaker, and gentlemen of the House of Burgesses," he says, "I have in my hand a paper published by order of your House, conceived in such terms as reflect highly upon his Majesty and the Parliament of Great Britain, which makes it necessary to dissolve you, and you are dissolved accordingly."

The governor then bows stiffly again, and the Burgesses return the bow; then they leave the council-chamber and go back to the hall, when they at once adjourn.

But they do not mean to return to their homes without further consultation. The Capitol is closed to them, and the House of Burgesses dissolved; but they are free to go elsewhere and consult with each other, if not act as a legal body. They therefore repair to the old Raleigh Tavern in Gloucester Street, where they hold a meeting in the "Apollo Room," and discuss the state of affairs. The meeting is an excited one. They declare themselves a "convention," and draw up a paper addressed to the people, in which they say that the attack on Massachusetts is precisely the same as an attack on Virginia. The time has come, they declare, for action, and to that end they recommend that a General Congress shall be held to consult how to oppose the tyranny of England. They resolve to observe the 1st of June as a day of fasting and prayer, in spite of Lord Dunmore; and then, after calling a convention of the people in August, this remarkable meeting in the "Apollo Room" adjourns.

V.

Night has come at last on this famous 27th of May, 1774. It is the night of the ball to be given to Lord Dunmore and his wife and daughters. Will the Virginians feel in a mood to assemble? They have just been dismissed, like a party of school-boys, by the governor, who has told them that their action deserves punishment, and that he inflicts the punishment. Will the ball follow?

The question is soon decided. As night comes the windows of the Capitol blaze with lights. In front of the portico is a great crowd watching coach after coach as they stop, and ladies and gentlemen, in full-dress, descend and enter. The array of silks and satins and embroidered coats is dazzling. All the grace and beauty of Williamsburg and the surrounding country has assembled to do honor to the governor and his family.

Let us go up the steps and enter with the rest. The hall of the Burgesses is the ball-room. The chairs are removed, and the whole apartment blazes with lights. It is crowded with beautiful women and stately gentlemen, among whom are Washington and a large number of other Burgesses.

Then a stir is heard at the door; the crowd divides, and Lord Dunmore, superbly dressed, enters with his wife and family. They are received with profound bows and cordial courtesy. The governor's manner is not very encouraging, but Lady Dunmore and her "fine sprightly girls" make up for that by their bright smiles. And so the famous ball goes on its way with music and dancing, and the hall which has just echoed to the voices of Henry and Pendleton is full of gay accents and mirth and laughter.

It was a singular affair—was it not?—this ball at the Capitol in May, 1774. At least the Virginians showed their gallantry, and acted with true courtesy. Whatever they thought of Lord Dunmore, it did not prevent them from welcoming the ladies. From all accounts, these enjoyed themselves highly, and were gratified at the respect paid them; and the ball was long spoken of as one of the finest that had ever taken place in Williamsburg.

LORD DUNMORE AND THE GUNPOWDER.

I.

I WILL now tell you how Lord Dunmore attempted to disarm the Virginians by seizing their gunpowder, and how they drove him from Virginia forever.

In spite of the fine entertainment given in his honor, the governor did not seem to like the people any better than before. He was a man of harsh character, and was charged with being underhanded and treacherous. I have told you of his expedition against the Indians in the fall of this same year, 1774. He was charged, you remember, by Andrew Lewis and his men, with secretly stirring up the savages, and persuading them to attack the border people. Was this true, or only the result of the dislike felt for him by the Virginians? I do not know, but appearances were against him, and in the next spring he did commit this great crime. A man named Connolly was employed by him as his agent, and this man was captured on his way to the Ohio. As people suspected him, he was searched, and hidden beneath his saddle were found a number of papers. These left no doubt of anything. They were signed by Lord Dunmore, and proved clearly that Connolly was sent to stir up the Indians against the Virginians, and that when he was caught he was on his way to do so.

The fact is that no one could trust Lord Dunmore. His word could not be relied upon, as what I am about to tell you will show. You will see that he told the Virginians that he was anxious to protect them from an insurrection of their slaves, and immediately afterward called on the black people to rise and fight them. Of this fact there is no doubt, and it will enable you to form your own opinion of Lord Dunmore.

We have now come to the spring of 1775, just one year after the ball at the Capitol. In these twelve months the spirit of resistance to England had gone on growing more determined. The General Congress which the Virginians

INDEPENDENCE HALL, PHILADELPHIA.

had recommended in their meeting at the Raleigh Tavern was agreed to at once. Six days afterward Massachusetts had suggested it also, probably before the news of it reached them from Virginia. The other colonies were as prompt, and the Congress met in the autumn at Philadelphia, where the greatest men of all the sections consulted together. "Carpenter's Hall" was the first place of meeting, but "Independence Hall" was afterward chosen, and this is still standing.

As the spring of 1775 opened, there was excitement

everywhere. People felt that great events would soon take place, and all were ready. There never was a people more ready to resist. The very women and children were determined not to submit to English misrule. As the tax on tea remained in force, the ladies would not purchase any. They even resolved that they would not use what they had already, and sealed it up in canisters and put it away. The boys were quite as rebellious. In Massachusetts a party of them, who were sliding on the snow, got into a quarrel with the English soldiers, and defied them, and in Virginia they formed companies to fight the English when they came.

I will tell you an anecdote of one of these small boy-companies. On one occasion Lady Nelson was riding out, when she met with one of them. They had guns, and a flag, and a drum, which they were beating; and when Lady Nelson stopped to look at them, she saw that two of her own boys were in the company. The young soldiers knew her carriage, and drew up by the side of the road to salute her. They were going to fight the British, they said, but this seemed quite absurd in such mere urchins. Lady Nelson therefore called to her two boys to get into the coach, and they did so, crying from mortification—which will show how much in earnest these youthful patriots were.

In the month of April the storm burst forth. The British government had determined to get possession of all the arms and gunpowder in the colonies, and sent word to the various governors to seize these stores on a day fixed for the purpose. The orders were first sent to General Gage, who commanded the English troops in Boston; and they were then transmitted to Lord Dunmore, in Virginia, through the same Connolly who was his agent in stirring up the Indians.

These orders were now obeyed. Gage marched from Boston to the village of Concord, to seize the powder in Massachusetts; and the people assembled, and a battle was fought, which resulted in the retreat of the English back to Boston. This was on the 19th of April, and on the very next day (April 20th, 1775) Lord Dunmore seized the powder belonging to Virginia.

For this all had been arranged. Several English ships-of-war had been sent to Virginia, and one of these quietly sailed up York River, and anchored not far from Williamsburg. This ship was named the *Magdalen*, and was commanded by a Captain Collins. On the day before the scene which I will now describe, Lord Dunmore sent word to Captain Collins that the time had come. He

MINUTE-MAN.

was to march after dark with a party of soldiers to Williamsburg, and seize the powder in the magazine. And this order the English captain obeyed. About midnight he marched silently into the town to the magazine. He had the key, and opened it quietly, and took possession of the powder, which was in half-barrels. He then retired as he came; and all had been done in such silence that the people did not hear of the affair until the next morning.

As soon as the news spread it excited general indignation. The town was in commotion, and the people resolved to seize the governor and make him answer for his act. But they were persuaded not to use violence, and

THE OLD MAGAZINE.

sent to demand the return of the powder. To this Lord Dunmore made an evasive and untruthful reply. He had only taken the powder, he said, to use in case there was an insurrection of the slaves in a neighboring county, of which he had heard something. He would soon return it; there need be no trouble whatever about it. All of which was wholly untrue, as there was no such report. The people then retired to their homes and waited.

But the news soon spread through the length and

breadth of Virginia. The people rushed to arms, and seven hundred men assembled at Fredericksburg, and sent word that they were ready to march on Williamsburg.

CULPEPER FLAG.

Among these were the famous Culpeper "minute-men," ready to march at a minute's warning. They wore green hunting-shirts, and had knives and tomahawks in their belts. On their breasts were Patrick Henry's words, in white letters, "Liberty or Death!" and their flag bore the picture of a coiled rattlesnake, with "Don't tread on me!" beneath it.

But Patrick Henry had already taken the matter into his own hands. As soon as he heard that Dunmore had robbed the people of their powder, he sent word to his friends to meet him at a place called New Castle, fully armed and ready to fight. Everybody hastened to obey his call, and with one hundred and fifty men under him, Henry set out at once to go and attack the governor.

You see he was not a man to trifle about anything. He had told everybody that he was ready to fight England, and he now showed that he meant what he said. He marched without delay on Williamsburg, and no doubt a battle would have taken place in Virginia, as in Massachusetts, if Governor Dunmore had not become frightened. He sent one of his friends to say that he was ready to pay for the powder, and Patrick Henry determined to take the money. It was three hundred and thirty pounds sterling (about sixteen hundred dollars), and this was paid to him at a place called Doncastle's Ordinary, or tavern, where he had stopped to rest his men.

It is more than probable that Henry was sorry at having the money paid to him. He saw that the very best thing that could happen now was a fight with Lord Dunmore, which would excite the whole country, and bring on war before a large army of English were sent to America. But he was afraid of putting himself in the wrong by refusing to take the money; so he took it, and then marched back home with his friends.

II.

Lord Dunmore was now in a great rage. His authority was in danger, and his person not safe. He therefore issued a proclamation against Henry and his followers, declaring that they were traitors, and sent to the *Magdalen* for English troops, which he posted in his palace. Rows of arms were laid on the floor, ready to be used at a moment's warning; and the redcoats swaggered about the streets, scowling at the people, who scowled back at them.

Things were ready, you see, for an outbreak, and it soon came. Some arms were supposed to be still in the magazine, and a party of young men forced open the door to secure them. A startling incident followed. No sooner had they done so than a loud explosion took place, and one of them staggered back wounded. Lord Dunmore or some one had set a spring-gun behind the door of the magazine. The opening of the door discharged this, and one of the party was shot.

At this the people assembled, uttering shouts of indignation. They broke into the magazine, and seized all the arms they found, and made a discovery which raised their excitement to the highest pitch. Several barrels of gunpowder were found buried beneath the floor of the magazine, ready to blow up any one who entered the building. These, they knew, must have been placed there by Lord Dunmore, as no other person had control of the magazine, and it put the finishing touch to everything.

At the same moment the report spread that English troops from the *Magdalen* were marching on Williamsburg; so the people rushed to arms, and determined to seize the governor, fight the troops, and settle the whole affair at once.

This brought out Lord Dunmore in his true character. He was not even brave. He ought to have stayed and fought, if he thought that he was in the right. He had the means of doing so, for there were the English troops; but he lost heart at the idea of fighting, and fled with his family on board the English ships. After this he never again showed his face in the town of Williamsburg.

The Virginians, you see, were more lucky than the people of Massachusetts. They had succeeded in driving away the governor and his English soldiers, and everything was now in their own hands. But they were not yet entirely rid of Lord Dunmore, who was full of spite and hatred at being obliged to fly from his palace. He got together some ships-of-war which were lying in Chesapeake Bay, and sailed for Norfolk, a Virginia town of about six thousand inhabitants at that time, where he sent word to all the negroes in the surrounding country to rise and help him. This showed exactly how he felt toward the Virginians, and how little trust could be placed in what he said. When he seized their powder, he told them that he intended to use it to *prevent* a rising of the negroes. Now he called on them to rise and fight for him.

Many of the slaves and lower class of white people joined him, and he soon showed the Virginians how he meant to treat them. He seized the printing-presses in Norfolk, and plundered the whole country; and by his orders his motley army of negroes and others committed many acts of violence.

Virginia was now thoroughly aroused, and a "Committee of Safety" was appointed. Troops were hastening from every direction to attack Dunmore's men, and as fast as these arrived they were sent toward Norfolk. It was not easy to fight Governor Dunmore, as he was most of the time in his ships, prowling around more like a pirate than the commander of regular troops. Some time thus passed, but finally a fight took place. Dunmore had

VIEW OF GREAT BRIDGE.

landed his troops at Norfolk, and hearing that the Virginians were near, resolved to send a force to attack them.

They awaited the English attack at a place called Great Bridge (December 9th, 1775). This was a common wooden bridge over a stream, approached on both sides by a causeway, or road made by throwing up earth. On this causeway, at one end of the bridge, the Virginians had thrown up a breastwork, and behind this they lay ready to receive the British assault.

It soon came, and the attack was a determined one. It was made by a force of English grenadiers, led by two captains, named Leslie and Fordyce, who proved themselves brave men. Cannon were posted across the bridge, and opened fire on the Virginians, after which Fordyce rushed forward at the head of his grenadiers, crossed the bridge, and charged the breastwork.

The Virginians did not fire until the enemy were within fifty yards of them. The order was then given, and the crack of rifles ran along the whole breastwork, staggering the grenadiers, and throwing them into confusion. Captain Fordyce was at the head of his men, waving his hat and shouting, "The day is ours!" Suddenly he fell, but instantly leaped up, brushing his knee, as if he had only stumbled. But he had been mortally wounded. Fourteen bullets had passed through his body, and, staggering a few steps forward, he fell dead.

At this the grenadiers gave way, and retreated in disorder. They hastened back across the bridge and along the causeway on the other side, leaving the ground strewed with their dead. The Virginians leaped over the earthworks and pursued them, firing upon them as they fled; and the pursuit was not stopped until the grenadiers were safe back in Norfolk.

III.

Lord Dunmore was now furious. He had fully expected to defeat the Virginians in the battle, and was so much enraged at his failure that he threatened to hang a boy who brought him the news. This would have done him no good, however, and he hastened to look after his own safety. He at once left Norfolk, and took refuge in his ships, and then the Virginians marched in and took possession.

Fire was opened upon the ships, and a furious cannonade followed. At this Dunmore sent word that if it did not stop he would destroy the town with hot shot. He was told by the Virginian commander that he might do his worst, and he at once opened fire on the place. It was very soon in flames, and for three days the fire raged in all directions. The weather was intensely cold, for it was in the month of January, and the women and children were obliged to fly from the burning houses, and take refuge where they could. Not content with burning their houses, Lord Dunmore sent troops on shore to fire on the Virginians; and all the horrors of war were thus visited on the once peaceful place. At last the flames died down. Norfolk was completely destroyed. The town, of six thou-

GWYN'S ISLAND.

sand inhabitants, was a mass of smouldering embers; and having glutted his revenge, Lord Dunmore sailed away in triumph.

From this time forward he resembled a pirate more than ever. He landed, and plundered the shores of Chesapeake Bay in every direction. But his end was coming. At last he anchored at a place called Gwyn's Island, on the western shore of the bay, and here he threw up a fort, in which he placed a part of his forces, consisting largely of negroes and low white people. His intention, no doubt, was to await re-enforcements from England, and then march on Williamsburg and hang all his enemies. But this plan was never carried out. The Virginians resolved to attack him, and the affair was intrusted to General Lewis, the very Andrew Lewis who commanded the hunters at Point Pleasant. Lewis marched at once. He soon reached the shore just opposite Gwyn's Island, where he planted his cannon, and opened fire on the fort and the ships.

The affair did not take long. Lewis fired the first gun with his own hands at the ships. The ball passed through the *Dunmore*, on which the governor was at the time; and the second ball also struck the ship, and cut one of his men in two. The third smashed the governor's cups and saucers, and a splinter of wood wounded him in the leg. At this he lost heart, and gave up the idea of fighting, and his ships were seen scattering, like white-winged sea-fowl, in every direction.

Still no sign of surrender was made, and the Virginia fire continued. It went on all day, and at night they had seen no white flag. What was Lord Dunmore doing? If he was beaten, why did he not surrender? The Virginians resolved to discover what was going on, and at daylight two hundred men were sent over in boats to attack the island.

Then the whole truth was discovered. Lord Dunmore was preparing to fly. He had gotten everything of value on board the ships; and as the Virginians approached on one side, they saw a great commotion going on on the other side. English soldiers hurried on board the vessels, the anchors were raised, and as the boats touched the shore, the whole fleet rapidly sailed away.

When the Virginians landed on the island it presented a horrible sight. Dead bodies of men were lying all around, and many wounded persons, black and white, were groaning and begging for water to drink. Graves were all over the island, and these were so shallow and hastily dug that the dead men were only half covered. Many were found burned to death in the brush huts, which had been set on fire by the cannon-shot, and altogether the sight was a sickening one. While they were looking at it, a bright light suddenly burst out on the waters of the bay, not far off, and they soon saw what this meant. Some of Lord Dunmore's ships had run aground in the sand, and as he could not get them off, he had. ordered them to be set on fire, to prevent them from falling into the hands of his enemies. The flames soon caught the masts and riggings, which blazed up, presenting a fine spectacle. Then the hulls were seen to be on fire, and burned down to the edge of the water, when the ships sunk and disappeared from sight.

This was the last of Lord Dunmore. He seemed fond of fire, as he had tried to blow up the magazine at Williamsburg and burned the town of Norfolk, and now his burning ships lit him on his way. For some time he prowled about, plundering the houses along the shore, and once sailed up the Potomac to "Mount Vernon," to capture Washington, if possible. But he failed to do so, and at last resolved to depart. His ships, with the plunder which he had secured, and about one thousand slaves whom he had carried off from the Virginia plantations, sailed for the West Indies, and he himself went to New York, and thence to England.

The Virginians were thus rid of him, and must have rejoiced at the fact. They had had some bad governors, but Lord Dunmore was the very worst of them. He had been, from the time of his arrival, their secret enemy, and had done all he could, at all times, to injure them; and thus his disappearance excited general joy.

The great year 1776 had now arrived, and the first thing the Virginians did was to elect a Republican governor. Their choice fell on Patrick Henry, who had marched against Lord Dunmore; and the new governor went to live in the very "Palace" at Williamsburg from which Dunmore had issued the proclamation declaring him a traitor.

ELIZABETH ZANE: THE STORY OF A BRAVE GIRL.

I.

WE have now reached the period of the American Revolution; but before I speak of some great events which took place in Eastern Virginia, I have two or three remarkable stories to tell you of fighting in the woods of the West.

In this country, along the Ohio, everything was quite different. In Lower Virginia the people were generally large landholders, who lived in comfort, if not in luxury. Their houses were excellent, and they had servants to wait on them, and travelled in coaches, and wore rich clothes, and altogether led very agreeable lives. Their wives and daughters were tenderly cared for, and the boys were not brought up to work with their own hands: life was passed in peace and enjoyment, and the laws protected every one from injury. If a robbery or murder was committed, there was the constable to arrest the criminal, and the whipping-post or gallows to punish him. On Sunday the families went to church in their carriages; the young men rode fine horses and visited the young ladies; entertainments were often given, at which the ladies and gentlemen dressed in silks and velvets; and altogether the old-time Virginians of the Tidewater region, as it was called, led as pleasant lives, perhaps, as any people ever did in this world.

Over the mountains toward the Ohio things were very different, as I have told you. The country was thinly settled, and covered with great woods, from which peeped up, here and there, the few log-forts of the settlers, built to defend them from the savages, who were lurking in the forests around. The men who lived in these log-houses or forts were brave fellows from Lower Virginia, or Maryland, or Pennsylvania, and they dressed in hunting-shirts, and had no servants to wait on them. As there was no law to protect them, they had to protect themselves and their families; and this they did with their knives and rifles. They supported their families by hunting, and tilling the soil with their own hands, and were not able to educate their children or afford them luxuries. This probably did the young people good, however, as they learned to take care of themselves. They were happy and contented, if the Indians would only let them alone. Thus they grew up to be brave and independent. And there never was a finer race of men than these hunters of the border. The very women and children were cool and determined, as they showed on a hundred occasions; and in the story I shall now tell you, I will relate a brave action performed by a border girl, whose name deserves to be recorded in history.

Before telling you this remarkable story, however, I will say a few words of the border boys. They were as brave as their fathers, and not only worked for the family, but took part in fighting the Indians when they came to attack them. The name of one of these boys was Lewis Wetzel. His father lived near Wheeling, on the Ohio River, and Lewis soon learned to use his rifle, and hunt like a man. As he thought it might be useful to him some day, he taught himself to load his gun while he was running. He did this with an eye to the Indians. The borderers often had to run from them, and Lewis learned this trick, so that when the Indians pursued him he might fire back at them, and then load again without stopping.

One day, when Lewis was about thirteen years old, he and his younger brother, Jacob, who was about eleven, went off into the woods to hunt. Here they came upon some Indians, and, of course, ran as soon as they saw them; but the Indians fired upon the boys, and wounded Lewis in the breast, and captured them both. They then took them along with them into the great woods beyond the Ohio, and marched for two days. At last the second night came, and the Indians lay down to sleep. As they considered the boys mere children, they did not tie them or watch them very closely, and Lewis determined to attempt to escape. He therefore waited until the Indians were asleep, and then whispered to his little brother that he must get up and go back home with him. At first little Jacob was afraid, but Lewis persuaded him to try, and they stole off quietly until they were a hundred yards in the woods. Lewis then sat down on a log and said to Jacob,

"Well, we can't go home barefooted. I will go back and get a pair of moccasins for each of us"—moccasins, you know, being a sort of Indian shoes made of deer-skin.

Lewis stole back to the place where the savages were still asleep, and got two pair of moccasins, and with these he returned to his brother. They put them on, and Lewis next said,

"Now I will go back and get father's gun, and then we'll start."

He stole off again, creeping along the ground and listening until he got to the savages; and there, lying by them, was his father's gun, which he caught up and brought back with him. The boys then started at once for home; but they had not gone far before they heard the Indians running after them. They began to run themselves, but they heard the Indians coming nearer and nearer. As it was a bright moonlight night, Lewis knew that they would be seen very soon, so he told his little brother what he must do. Their only chance, he said, was to hide until the Indians went by, and this they did. Lewis pulled Jacob into some bushes, and they crouched down and waited. They soon saw the Indians running past them, as they did not know that the boys had stopped to hide; and then Lewis told his brother to come on—they must follow behind the Indians. They did this at some distance, but soon heard the Indians coming back. They then hid again, and waited until the savages had passed; and then Lewis and little Jacob hurried on, and safely reached home, after dodging two of the savages who followed them on horseback, in the same manner as before.

This was a brave adventure for mere boys, and what made it nobler still, in the case of young Lewis, was his dangerous wound. Of this he made no complaint to his little brother; but when they crossed the Ohio River on a raft which they made, and got back home, the boy was nearly dead. He recovered, however, and became a great Indian fighter; and you will some day read the stories about him and others, and see what hard lives they led, and how fearless they were.

I might tell you a number of these stories of bloody fighting, but I doubt if it is well to fill the minds of boys with such things. It is apt to excite them and make them wish to do likewise, for which there is now no necessity. What I have told you was to show the courage of the border boys, which ought to be known; and these anecdotes will give you an idea of the times. The old histories are full of fighting, but I cannot stop to tell you of all the instances of Indian cruelty. One related in these old books will give you a good idea of them.

"An Indian seized Mrs. Scott," the book says, "and ordered her to a particular spot, and not to move; others stabbed and cut the throats of the three smaller children in their bed, and afterward lifting them up, dashed them upon the floor near their mother: the eldest, a beautiful girl of eight years old, awoke, escaped out of the bed, ran to her parent, and, with the most plaintive accents, cried, 'Oh, mamma! mamma!—save me!' The mother, in the deepest anguish of spirit, and with a flood of tears, entreated the savages to spare her child; but, with a brutal fierceness, they tomahawked and stabbed her in her mother's arms."

If you will try to think how you would have felt if this little girl had been your sister, you will understand the feeling of the border people toward the savages. They hated them bitterly, and never saw an Indian without longing to put a bullet through him, as if he had been a venomous reptile. They and the redskins hunted each other, and every fight was a life and death affair. The hunters knew that they would be scalped, and the Indians that they would have their brains dashed out if they were overcome; and this made the fights on the border so desperate.

II.

I will come now to the particular incident which I set out to relate—the attack on Wheeling fort, and the fearless act of a young girl on that occasion.

This took place in 1777, which was called the "year of the three sevens," and was one of the darkest hours of the Revolution. The English and Americans were at war, and the struggle had become bitter. The British forces were more numerous than those of the Americans; and to make matters worse, the English had persuaded the Indians to join with them and attack the frontier settlements. They supplied them with muskets, and paid them, and even offered a certain sum of money, it is said, for every white man's scalp.

Such was the state of affairs at the time when the incident I will now relate took place. The English had a number of forts toward Canada, on the lakes, and Fort Detroit was one of the most important of these. It was commanded by Colonel Hamilton, Governor of Canada, and he was the chief agent of the British in stirring up the Indians. I will have more to say of him hereafter; at present I will tell you of his scheme to get possession of Fort Henry, at Wheeling, in north-western Virginia.

This was an important border fort, and a small village of about twenty-five log-houses had sprung up around it. These were occupied by the settlers when times were quiet; but as soon as a report came that the Indians were approaching, the settlers hastened into the fort with their wives and children, and prepared to fight. It was quite a good place of refuge. It was built of logs, in the shape of a long square, and had block-houses, as they were called, at the four corners; in these the men fought, firing through holes in the logs. There were, besides, a number of cabins for the women and children, a good well to supply water, and a magazine to hold the arms and gunpowder. The main entrance was by a gate which was on the east side, toward the village; and you now have a tolerably good idea, I hope, of Fort Henry, as it was called, in honor of Patrick Henry.

In the autumn of 1777 Colonel Hamilton resolved to attack Wheeling. For this purpose he employed a man named Simon Girty. He was a white man, who had been captured, when he was a boy, by the Indians, and joined their tribes, and became one of them. He was a very great rascal, and for some reason hated the Americans. The attack on Wheeling was therefore intrusted to him, and collecting together about five hundred Indians, he marched southward from the Great Lakes toward Kentucky. This was meant to deceive the whites. The route taken by Girty was not in the direction of Wheeling. But when he reached the Ohio River, a little above Cincinnati, he turned to the left, and hurried up the river to surprise Fort Henry.

In this he did not succeed. The woods were full of hunters at that time, who kept their eyes on the Indians, and the people at Wheeling were promptly informed that the enemy was coming to attack them. At this all was commotion. The women and children left their homes in the village and hastened into the fort. The men followed them, and closed the gates; and this was no sooner done than Girty and the savages made their appearance.

Every one knew now that a desperate fight would take place, and there seemed very little probability that the whites would be able to hold out against their assailants. They had only forty-two fighting-men, even counting old men and boys, and the Indian force was about five hundred. What was worst of all was the small supply of gunpowder in the fort. A keg containing the main supply had been left by accident in one of the houses of the village; and this, as you will see, gave rise to the brave action which I will now relate.

The whites were commanded by Colonel Shepherd, who seems to have been a cool and determined man. He kept a keen lookout for the Indians, who were known to be in the woods near the fort, and an incident at once took place which showed that they were ready to attack him. Two men, one of them white and the other a black man, were

10*

sent out on some errand. They left the fort, and were passing through a field of corn, when suddenly a large Indian started up from the midst of the corn and knocked the white man down with the butt of his musket. The negro at once turned back and ran for his life, and as soon as he reached the fort, told Colonel Shepherd what had happened.

Everybody knew now that the Indians were upon them, and Colonel Shepherd determined to send out a party and attack them. This was done. Captain Samuel Mason, with fourteen men, marched out of the fort and into the cornfield, but the Indians were nowhere to be seen. This was, however, only a proof of their cunning. They saw Captain Mason and his men as they passed through the cornfield, and when they had gone some distance, closed in on their rear and thus cut them off from the fort.

A desperate fight followed. The Indians started up from the brushwood in all directions, and opened fire on the party. The hunters did not flinch. They returned the fire, and then clubbing their rifles, rushed on the swarm of savages to break through them and regain the fort. They knocked down and killed a number of them, and made a brave resistance; but the Indians were too many for them—they had at least thirty to their one—and the desperate struggle was soon over. Captain Mason was wounded, and almost all his men killed. The few remaining fought on, but they saw that there was no hope for them. Mason was shot a second time, but turned on the Indian who was close to him, and knocked him down with his gun. He then ran into the brushwood, and crawled into a pile of logs, where he concealed himself, and remained safe until the end of the battle. Two of his men did the same; and these three were all that escaped with their lives.

This was followed by another incident equally unfortunate. A party of thirteen men had rushed out to help their friends, but these also fell into a trap, and eight of them were killed. The Indians then came out of the woods and advanced on the fort.

III.

The Indians advanced in two ranks, in "open order," dodging behind the trees, and ready to begin the attack.

Girty was at the head of them; but he first resolved to summon the place to surrender. He therefore went into a log-cabin which was not far from the gate of the fort, and, opening a small window, waved a white flag, which meant that he had something to say. At this the whites ceased firing, as they had begun to do, and listened, and Girty read a paper to them. This was a proclamation from Colonel Hamilton, ordering them to lay down their arms and surrender. If they did so, he promised that no harm should happen to them; but if they refused, the fort would be attacked, and the Indians would put them all to death.

Girty read to the end of the paper, and then asked what they meant to do. The reply was prompt. Colonel Shepherd called out from the fort that they never meant to surrender to a rascal like *him*, and that he would never get possession of the fort until he had killed the last man in it. At this the people in the fort cheered, to show their approval of his reply, and a young man fired at Girty, who slammed to the window and disappeared.

The fighting at once began. It was a beautiful September morning, and the red and yellow foliage of the woods shone in the sunshine. The Indians advanced with loud yells, firing as they came; and the fire was returned from the fort, where each one picked out his man and took dead aim, in order not to waste powder. A number of the savages were killed, and they saw that nothing could be done by fighting in that manner. A party of them, therefore, rushed up close to the fort, and endeavored to thrust their guns through holes in the logs and fire at the whites. But this was an unfortunate attempt. The whites killed nearly all of the attacking party, and then the whole army of Indians fell back, yelling, into the woods.

The men in the fort now held a consultation. They knew too much about Indians to believe that they were going to give up the struggle. Their retreat into the woods, they felt sure, was only make-believe, and they would probably make another attack very soon. They therefore prepared for this, but found to their great dismay that scarcely any gunpowder was left in the fort. They had forgotten the keg of powder in one of the houses near, as I have told you, and now they found they had scarcely any. What was to be done? They must have more powder or they could not fight, and they and the women and children would all be murdered. The only thing to do was to try and get the keg which had been left behind; but this would be almost certain death to anybody who attempted it. The house in which the keg was, stood only about sixty yards from the gate of the fort; but they knew that although they could not see the Indians, they were on the watch. As soon as a man left the fort, he would probably be killed before he had gone ten yards; but they had to have the powder, and somebody must run the risk.

Colonel Shepherd told his men exactly how the matter was. He would not *order* any man to go and get the powder, he said, as the Indians were almost sure to kill him; but if any one chose to volunteer, that is, offer to go himself, he would accept his offer. At this three or four young men and boys stepped forward, and said they were willing to go. But the colonel replied that he could not spare three or four men—there were too few in the fort. One would do, and they must agree among themselves which one it was to be. This caused quite a dispute. One said *he* would go, but another said *he* would; and they went on disputing and losing time, until there was danger that the Indians would renew the attack before they came to any arrangement.

At this moment a young lady among the women in the fort came forward and said *she* was ready to go. Her name was Elizabeth Zane, and she had just come home from boarding-school in Philadelphia, where she had gone to be educated. This made her brave offer all the more remarkable, as she had not been trained up in the fearless life of the border; so you will see that she must have been a noble girl. Of course the men would not hear of such a thing. It was their place, they said, to expose their lives, not the place of women or girls; but Elizabeth went on urging that she ought to be allowed to go. She was told that she would almost certainly be killed, and therefore a man ought to go for the powder. But this, she said, was the very reason why she offered herself. They could not spare *a man*, as they had so few, and the loss of a girl would not amount to much. And so, at length, they reluctantly agreed that she should go for the keg of gunpowder.

The house containing it stood, as I have said, about sixty yards from the fort, and Elizabeth hoped to run and bring the powder back in a very few minutes. She said she was ready, and then the gate of the fort was opened, and she passed through, running like a deer toward the house.

IV.

As I have told you, Girty had ordered the Indians to fall back into the woods to protect themselves from the bullets of the whites; and this they had done, yelling as they went off, carrying upon their shoulders the dead bodies of their warriors who had been shot. And here I will tell you, for fear of forgetting it, that this was always the custom with the Indians. They were strange people, and had their own ideas of what was proper and dignified. To be able to say that they had conquered their enemies was a great thing with them, and they were just as much mortified when the whites could say they had conquered *them*. So, whenever their warriors were killed, they would not leave them on the battle-field for their enemies to count, and boast of the number they had killed. They always carefully bore off the dead bodies; and this they did on the present occasion, as they fell back into the woods.

When Elizabeth Zane ran out from the fort, however, a few straggling Indians were observed dodging about among the log-houses of the town, which stood about three or four hundred yards east of Fort Henry. They saw the girl, for the people in the stockade observed them looking at her; but for some reason they did not fire at her. Why they did not it is difficult to say. They may have supposed that she was only running to the house to get her clothes, or a hair-brush, or some other article which girls like to have; and as the Indians loved fun under all their cruelty, they may have laughed to see the young lady running, with her skirts flying behind her, toward the house. It is just as likely, however, that they thought it would only be throwing away a load of gunpowder to fire at a girl, who was of no use to anybody. As they felt certain that they would take the fort, they could easily kill her afterward by dashing her brains out with a tomahawk. So they quietly looked at her as she ran across to the house, and not a shot was fired at her.

As they were so anxious to capture Fort Henry, it would have been better for them to have killed that girl, for she was destined to save it. She hastened into the house, found the keg of gunpowder, which was probably small, and, holding her precious load with both arms close to her breast, darted out again, and ran with it in the direction of the fort. As she ran the Indians saw her, and understood what she had come for. Uttering a wild yell they levelled their guns and sent a shower of bullets at her, but all flew wide of the mark; they whistled to the right and left, but did not strike her; and, with the keg still hugged close to her bosom, she reached the fort, and the gate closed as the bullets of the Indians buried themselves in the thick panels behind her.

A weak girl had thus saved a dozen men and their wives and children. It was a brave act, and Americans should never forget to honor the name of Elizabeth Zane.

V.

I must not finish my story without telling you what took place next, and how the siege ended, as well as how a brave man made a wonderful leap, on horseback, and saved his life in the most remarkable manner.

Soon after Elizabeth's return with the keg of powder the Indians once more rushed from all sides against the fort, and the fighting became more obstinate and bloody than before. But the whites kept cool. Every one continued to pick out his man and take sure aim at him, and the ground was soon strewed with dead Indians on every side. Toward evening about eighteen or twenty savages made a rush from the house which Elizabeth had visited in the morning, toward the gate of the fort. They were armed with heavy rails and logs, and tried to force in the gate. In this they failed. The whites shot down five or six of them, and the rest then ran back.

About nightfall they made one more attempt to force their way in. They had found an old maple log, which was hollow, and in one end of this they drove a plug of wood, so as to close it tightly; they then wrapped around it some heavy chains, which they had found in a blacksmith's shop in the town, and loaded it with a full charge of gunpowder, on which they rammed stones, and slugs, and pieces of broken iron, until it was full to the muzzle. This strange sort of cannon was then lugged forward to within about sixty yards of the gate of the fort, and pointed at it. As a touchhole had been made, the maple-log cannon was then fired, and went off with a tremendous explosion, in the midst of loud yells. These yells were not, however, shouts of triumph. The old log had burst into a hundred pieces, and the splinters and broken iron killed many of the Indians who were standing around. This so much discouraged them that they fell back to the woods, and the whites had a short time to breathe after their long day's work. They had fought steadily from daylight till dark; and we are told that their rifles became so hot by such constant firing, that they were forced to lay them aside to allow them to cool.

By this time the news had reached other settlements near Wheeling that the Indians were attacking the place. The hunters, therefore, seized their rifles, and hastened to help their friends. Some were shot as they arrived, but others fought their way in; and about daybreak next morning Major Samuel M'Culloch, from a place called Short Creek, arrived with forty men to assist the whites.

As soon as the people in the fort saw them the gate was opened, and the men hastened in. The Indians had seen them, and were rushing after them and firing upon them; but all of them succeeded in entering the fort, except Major M'Culloch himself. Like a good soldier, he was behind, facing the enemy, and determined to be the last man to enter the gate. All were safely in now, and M'Culloch spurred his spirited horse after them. But the Indians rushed between, and he found himself completely cut off.

He looked around him, and saw that he could never force his way to the gate. He tried to do so more than once, but a swarm of Indians were in front, and he knew that his only hope was to escape in some other way. He therefore struck the spurs into his fine horse, and set off at full speed in the direction of Wheeling Hill, pursued by the Indians. They could easily have killed him, but did not wish to do so. He was a famous Indian fighter, and they knew him at once. As they hated him bitterly, they did not wish him to die by a death so easy as shooting. What they desired was to take him prisoner, when they intended to burn him to death, sticking splinters in full blaze into his naked body while he was burning, in order to glut their revenge upon him for killing so many of their warriors.

M'Culloch knew this, and he resolved to die rather than be taken prisoner. There seemed no hope at all for him. He had reached Wheeling Hill, beneath which ran the creek, and the Indians had hemmed him in on every other side. Before him was a precipice of about one hundred and fifty feet, at the bottom of which ran the waters of Wheeling Creek. To attempt to leap from this precipice was almost certain death, but M'Culloch saw that it was his only hope of escape. The Indians were now close upon him, and there was no time to lose. He accordingly took his rifle in his left hand, gathered up his reins in his right, and dug spurs into his horse, who leaped forward with his rider from the brink of the precipice. Strangely enough, they were neither of them killed. Horse and rider fell into the water of the creek below, and plunging into the woods, with a shower of bullets whistling around him, the brave M'Culloch succeeded in making his escape.

Altogether, this was one of the most remarkable incidents in the history of the border. The leap was certainly made, and the hill is there still to show how dangerous it was; and one of the advantages in visiting such scenes is that they bring back old times, when men seemed not to know what fear meant. M'Culloch was one of this class of men, and we are now enjoying quietly what they fought so hard for and suffered so much to win for us. In this wild western land of woods and rivers, which once swarmed with savages, great cities now stand, and railways are laid, and happy families of women and children live, without fear of having their brains dashed out by Indians. It was the hardy borderers, like M'Culloch and the rest, who laid the foundation for all this peace and happiness; and, in praising the men, we must not forget the women and boys and girls. They were as brave and true as the rest; and I have shown you how one of these girls proved that she had as much courage as the coolest Indian fighter of them all.

The attack on Fort Henry soon ended. Girty saw that the attempt to capture the place was hopeless, and, after burning the village, disappeared with his Indian army in the woods.

On his return to Detroit he probably informed Colonel Hamilton that the fort was heavily garrisoned, and defended by regular troops with cannon. If he did so, you know whether it was true or not. *Twelve men and boys had held it against him and his five hundred Indians;* and if I knew their names I would write them down, in order that they might be remembered.

THE FATE OF COLONEL ROGERS.

I.

Would you like to hear another interesting border story about these old times? I found it out myself, and perhaps you would like to know how this happened.

One day I was looking over some old papers in the Capitol at Richmond, and found a bundle which seemed to have been there for a very long time. It was covered with dust, and when I opened it, I found the writing on the papers so much faded that I could scarcely read some parts of it. As the papers did not seem to be very interesting, I was about to tie them up again, when some words caught my eye here and there which attracted my attention. Somebody or other was mentioned who had "a beautiful silver-hilted sword and excellent gold-laced hat;" and this somebody, whoever he was, had "landed at the mouth of the Ozark, now the Arkansaw River," where he was received by somebody else "with three discharges of heavy ordnance"—that is, cannon—when the first somebody raised the American flag, which was "the first Thirteen Stripes ever seen on that ground." As I read farther on I found, also, that somebody had been "surrounded almost immediately and overpowered by numbers;" then, that he "remained in the woods during the night of the battle, in extreme pain and utterly past recovery;" and then, that this somebody was "never afterward seen or heard of."

All this excited my curiosity, and made me anxious to

find what the papers were about. I sat down, therefore, and read them over carefully. They proved to be a highly interesting account of an expedition undertaken by a brave soldier of Maryland or Virginia to the lower Mississippi, and of a fight in which he was engaged with the Indians. I had never seen an account of this battle in any book, nor have I met with any since, so I wrote down the main incidents, and these I now intend to relate. There is no doubt of their truth. The papers were all sworn to by the brave fellows who signed them—Douglas Baker, James Paule, and Basil Brown by name. They were "bounty-land papers," as it is called, to secure the land which the law gave to old soldiers of the Revolution; and as the statements were under oath, I thought, and still think, them as good authority as what passes for such in the big histories.

The incident took place in the year 1778, during the Revolutionary War, and not very long after the Indian attack on Wheeling. Things looked gloomy for the Americans at the time, as they were in want of everything nearly, especially of arms and ammunition to carry on the war; and it was to obtain a supply of these that the expedition I shall now tell you of was undertaken.

The leader of it was Colonel David Rogers, who lived on the border, and was either a Marylander or a Virginian—I do not know which. This is not important, however, as the two names amount to pretty much the same thing; and, as you will see, the events took place along the Ohio, which then belonged to Virginia.

Colonel Rogers was at home at this time, on leave of absence, probably, from the army, but was ready, as you will soon see, to do anything in his power to help the American cause. One morning a letter was brought to him from the American officer commanding at Fort Pitt, which was the name now given to old Fort Duquesne, near which Braddock had been defeated. In this letter the officer asked Colonel Rogers if he would like to take command of an expedition down the Ohio and Mississippi rivers, to bring back some ammunition which the Americans had purchased from the Spaniards or French there; if so, he would be furnished with boats and men, and the expedition would be ready to set out at once.

Colonel Rogers at once accepted the offer. He was "a brave and energetic man, highly respected" by everybody, as his friends testified, and he mounted his horse and rode to Fort Pitt, where every arrangement was soon made. He was to have forty men for the purpose, and the boats were ready at Red Stone Old Fort, on the Monongahela, above. Rogers rode thither without delay; found the men were waiting; they all embarked on the boats, and were soon descending the river. Before long they passed Fort Pitt and entered the Ohio, making their way toward New Orleans, where they expected to find the "munitions" awaiting them.

II.

The little party were now on the bosom of "La Belle Rivière," as the French called the Ohio in old times, and looked forward in high spirits to the pleasant journey before them. The weather was beautiful, for the season was summer, and the banks of the "Beautiful River" were green with trees in full foliage. The skies were blue and the air delightful; and the rough woodmen bent to their oars, passing the time in talk, or singing old songs of the border, like that I have told you of about Lewis and his men at Point Pleasant.

They knew that the woods along the river were full of Indians, but their rifles lay beside them, and they were ready to fight if they were attacked. All day long they rowed on, taking their meals on the boats, and probably sleeping upon them at night; and thus the brave Colonel Rogers and his men descended the Ohio, and turned into the Mississippi toward New Orleans.

Here they ran some danger from the snags in the river, that is, large logs with one end buried in the mud of the bottom, while the other end swayed about near the sur-

SPANISH FORT.

face. The boatmen avoided these, and went on safely, and at last reached the mouth of the Arkansas River, then called the Ozark.

Here stood a Spanish fort. Colonel Rogers had been told of it, and was directed to stop when he came to it, and see the officer commanding at the fort; and this he now did. To give notice of his arrival, he ordered his men to fire thirteen guns, by way of saluting the Spaniards, and the woods echoed with the discharge. The Spaniards in the fort fired three of their cannon in reply, and then Colonel Rogers landed. Unfurling the American flag of the Stars and Stripes, which no one, we are told, had ever before seen in that country, he marched at the

AMERICAN FLAG.

head of his men up to the fort, and was received with great politeness by the Spanish commandant, named Devilie, who came to meet him, with his own troops drawn up behind him. They made low bows to each other, and then the Spaniard invited Rogers to go inside the fort. Soon afterward the Spanish soldiers were ordered to go through a parade on the ground near the fort, for the pleasure of the Americans, and they were put through all the military movements—Colonel Rogers, with his gold-laced hat and silver-hilted sword, standing beside Commandant Devilie, and all looking on

The colonel told Devilic what he came for—to procure the "munitions" which the Americans had purchased at New Orleans. But he now heard that these munitions had been removed higher up the Mississippi, to a fort near where the city of St. Louis stands at present, in the State of Missouri. As Colonel Rogers, however, had been ordered to go to New Orleans, he thought it would be better to obey his orders, and get a paper from the authorities there to the officer at St. Louis, directing him to let him have the ammunition, so he determined to do so.

It was a dangerous attempt to go down the river to New Orleans. The English had a fort on the river, at a place called Natchez; and Colonel Rogers knew that if they saw his boats passing they would fire at them, and probably sink them, with all the men in them. He therefore resolved to take only six or seven men with him, while the rest stayed behind at the Spanish fort, and steal by, in a single pirogue (a sort of canoe), during the night, when no one could see him. This was successfully done. The pirogue glided quietly by the fort in the darkness without being discovered, and Rogers and his men safely reached New Orleans.

Here he found there was no trouble in getting the order for the ammunition at St. Louis. It was at once handed to him, and without loss of time he set out on his return to the Spanish fort. This was both a difficult and dangerous undertaking. He could not go back in his pirogue, as the current of the river was too strong to row against; so he was obliged to travel by land, and make his way in the best manner he could. It was hard work. The banks of the Mississippi are often overgrown with canebrakes, and woods so thick that a pathway can scarcely be forced through them; and in addition to this, Rogers and his six or seven men were in danger of being seen and taken prisoners or killed by the English. They nevertheless toiled on, and were fortunate enough to pass by the fort at Natchez without being seen, and at length reached the Spanish fort on the Ozark.

There was nothing further to detain them here, and Rogers set out in his boats for St. Louis. Here they found the munitions, and the officer at once delivered them. They were stowed in the boats, the men again embarked, and the little fleet at last turned toward home.

III.

By this time it was autumn. The journey down the Ohio and Mississippi had been slow; and the visit to New Orleans, and afterward to St. Louis, had been a tedious affair. It was thus the month of October when Colonel Rogers and his men once more found themselves on the bosom of the Ohio, going in the direction of home.

This is the most beautiful season of the year, and the party probably enjoyed it to the utmost. They had fully succeeded in their expedition, and no doubt looked forward with delight to seeing their wives and children again after their long and toilsome journey. If they sung before, they probably sung even more gayly now as they rowed on up the broad river, thinking that all their toil and trouble was nearly over.

But there was to be a bloody ending to all this hope and joy, and I will now go on and tell you what a sorrowful tragedy took place. The boats had gone on up the Ohio until they reached a point in the river, near where the city of Cincinnati now stands, when the men saw a small party of Indians crossing the river in a boat in front of them. To understand what the Americans now did, we must remember the feeling of the whites at that time toward the Indians. The savages had burned their houses, and dashed out the brains of their wives and children with their tomahawks, and the very first thing which the old hunters thought of when they saw an Indian was to send a bullet through his heart. As soon, therefore, as Rogers and his men observed the party of Indians cross the river in front of them in the canoe, they determined to pursue them and kill them.

The boats at once pushed toward the mouth of Licking River, which here empties into the Ohio, and, gliding under the boughs of the trees, reached shore. Rogers gave his orders to the men, and, marching at the head of them, went up the bank to look for the Indians.

But he had made a terrible mistake in supposing that he would meet with only a small party of savages. A large band were hidden in the undergrowth on the bank, and it is not improbable that the few seen crossing in the canoe had done so as a decoy, to make the whites land and attack them. If so, they succeeded, and the whites fell into the trap. Colonel Rogers had no sooner landed and marched up the bank than the woods in front of him suddenly swarmed with Indians, and a hot fire was opened upon the whites.

It was a complete surprise, and enough to test the courage of the bravest men. The whites returned the fire, and rushed upon the Indians, and an obstinate hand-to-hand struggle took place. The woods were full of smoke and the crack of rifles, mixed with shouts and yells, as the whites and savages closed in on each other. Colonel Rogers was in front, sword in hand, cheering on his men, and as long as they saw his tall figure leading them, they fought on, without regarding the disproportion in numbers.

At last Rogers was shot and fell, and at this his men lost all hope. They broke and fled into the woods, pursued by the Indians. The ground was covered with their dead, and out of the forty men of the expedition only thirteen escaped.

In this bloody manner did the expedition end. It was a tragic affair, and the lot of brave Colonel Rogers was sorrowful indeed. Little was known of his fate after he was shot, except that one of his men reported that he "remained in the woods during the night of the battle, in extreme pain and utterly past recovery." The man who made this statement was obliged to leave him, to save his own life, and says that "Colonel Rogers was never afterward seen or heard of."

The thirteen men who escaped reached the Kanawha River, in Virginia, after wandering through the woods for nineteen days. And that was the last of this sorrowful affair.

I have related it to give you one more illustration of those troubled times, and to show you what men had to pass through in former days. Great cities are to be seen, now, throughout all that "Dark and Bloody Ground," as it was called. But for the brave old race to which Rogers and his men belonged, they would never have been built.

THE CAPTURE OF VINCENNES.

I.

I HAVE one more story to tell you of border fighting, from which you will see that the brave and hardy frontiersmen of that time allowed nothing to stop them.

The leader in the famous expedition you will now be told of was named George Rogers Clarke. He was born in Albemarle County, Virginia, and was at this time a little more than twenty-six years old; so you see he became celebrated at an early age, like John Smith and others whom I have mentioned. He first followed the business of a surveyor, like young George Washington, and was captain of a company in 1774, when Lewis and Dunmore marched to the Ohio. This gave him a great fondness for life in the woods, and we soon find him paddling down the Ohio River, exploring Kentucky and all the great region around.

This country, as I have told you, belonged at that time to Virginia. You may not understand this, but it is easily explained, and you ought to know all about it. The boundaries of each of the old colonies were fixed by the laws of England; and in 1609, two years after Smith landed at Jamestown, a law was passed that what was called the Virginia or "London Company" should have all the land two hundred miles north and two hundred miles south of the mouth of James River, where Fortress Monroe now stands, as far back as the Pacific Ocean. This was a very great country, for Virginia thus reached nearly to the city of New York on the north, and to Charleston, South

Carolina, on the south, and over all the Great West as far as what is now California, which belonged to her, like the rest. Afterward a part of this country was cut up into the colonies of Maryland, Pennsylvania, and others on the sea-coast; but Virginia was still the owner of the Great West, as you will see when I tell you that as late as the year 1786 the State of Kentucky was a county of Virginia, governed by laws passed in Richmond. This will explain

GEORGE ROGERS CLARKE.

what I meant by saying that this fine country, now forming Kentucky, Ohio, Indiana, Illinois, and other great States, was at that time a part of the "Old Dominion." I will only add here that in January, 1781, while the Revolutionary War was still going on, Virginia voluntarily gave up her title to this large tract of country, making a present of it to the other colonies; and now it is one of the richest and most prosperous parts of the American Union.

In 1778, however, this had not been done; and when the

English and Indians attacked the settlers, Virginia sent soldiers to protect them. Among these, as you will see, was George Rogers Clarke, and a better man could not have been chosen for the work. He was not only a fearless soldier, but, what was more important, had a very fine mind, and knew how valuable this great country in course of time would be. He saw that the land was rich, and that some day it would be filled with people, who would build great cities there. He accordingly determined to settle in it himself, and do all in his power to prevent the English from seizing upon it.

A few words taken from an account of Clarke will show you what people thought of him. This account says: "His mind was clear and comprehensive; his personal courage of the truest stamp; his energies, physical and mental, always vigorous; and he soon became an oracle with the backwoodsmen." As you may not understand some of these words, I will tell you that they meant that Clarke was a strong man in body and mind, and that the hunters of the western woods believed everything he told them. He soon became a great man in the country, and before long began to think whether he could not drive the English out of their forts in the region.

The most important of these forts was at the spot where the city of Detroit now stands, and this was commanded by Colonel Hamilton, Governor of Canada, as I have told you, in relating the attack by Simon Girty on Wheeling. There were others at Kaskaskia, in Illinois, and Vincennes, in Indiana, but all were under Colonel Hamilton, who was the great man of the country.

II.

Well, now I will come to Colonel Clarke, as he was called, and tell you what he resolved to do. In the winter of 1777 he visited Eastern Virginia, and had a long talk with Patrick Henry, who had just been made governor. He told Henry that the English forts ought certainly to be attacked, and if they would let him try it, he thought he could capture them. This highly pleased Patrick Henry and the other Virginia leaders. They wrote an order that he was to "proceed to the defence of Kentucky;" but they told him privately what this meant—he was to attack Kaskaskia. Then they furnished him with twelve hundred pounds sterling in money, and four companies of men; and in the spring of the next year (1778) all was ready for the march on Kaskaskia.

This was quite an old place, and had belonged to the French, who first settled the country, but was given up to the English in 1763, after the "French war," in which Braddock lost his life, you know. There were only about one hundred families living there besides the English soldiers in the fort, and Clarke thought he could easily take the place if he surprised it. He accordingly set out with his men in boats on the Ohio, and floated down to Paducah. Then he went on and landed on the Illinois shore; and then he and his men hid the boats, and set off through the woods in the direction of Kaskaskia. On the way they nearly starved, and were obliged to live on roots; but at last they reached the place (July 4th, 1778).

The men concealed themselves in the woods until night came, and then rushed in and captured the English soldiers almost without a struggle. Rocheblane, the commandant, was caught in bed and made prisoner; and then the Americans began to rummage for his papers, to find what the English were going to do. But they did not discover many, in consequence of their politeness. Most of the papers were in Madame Rocheblane's chamber, which was separate from his own, and this brave lady no sooner heard that the place was captured than she set about burning them. The Americans might have prevented this by rushing into her room; but they had too much respect for ladies to do that. So Madame Rocheblane went on burning the documents, and soon they were nothing but a pile of cinders. Some were found, however, but these only showed them what they knew very well before—that is, that the English were all the time exciting the Indians to attack the borderers. The commandant, Rocheblane, and his papers were then sent off, under guard, to the Virginia authorities at Williamsburg; and I hope, if Madame Rocheblane went with him, as she no doubt did, that they treated her well on the way.

The capture of Kaskaskia was soon followed by that of other places, and at last of Fort Vincennes, where Father Gibault, a French priest, persuaded the people to submit to the Americans. The American flag was raised, and floated proudly in the wind, and Colonel Clarke now found himself master of the whole country.

He soon afterward sent word to the Indians that he wished to see them; and when they came he talked to them, and told them that there was no reason why they should fight for the English. Some of them seemed to be persuaded, and all listened to him with the deepest respect, for they knew what a determined man he was. Of this I will give you an instance, and it will show you why the Indians respected and were afraid of him. At a place called Fort Washington once he met three hundred Indian warriors to talk about making peace. Clarke had only seventy men with him, and the Indians thought he would be afraid of their number.

One of the warriors then made a speech in a loud and threatening voice, while Clarke, who was sitting by a table, with his elbow leaning upon it, listened without saying a word. There were only two or three other persons with him, but the whole three hundred Indians had gathered around to listen to the speech made by their chief. This speech, as I have said, was noisy and threatening. The chief spoke as if he had only to give the word, and Clarke and his men would be tomahawked in a moment. He came to the end of it at last, and threw upon the table two belts of wampum, one black and the other white —meaning that he was ready for peace or war—when the savages uttered a wild yell, and the chief looked frowningly at Clarke. The first thing Clarke did showed the Indians that he was not a man to be easily frightened. He had a small rattan cane in his hand, and with this he carelessly pushed the wampum, or "speech-belts," off the table on the floor, which was a sign of the greatest contempt. He then rose, frowning, to his feet, put his heel on the belts, and, turning to the Indians, ordered them, in a commanding voice, to leave the room. One look at him showed them that they could not frighten him. They obeyed his orders without saying a word, and on the next day came back humbly, and said they were ready to make peace.

This adventure of Clarke's did not occur, however, at the time I am now telling you of, and I must come back to my story. Having arranged everything at Vincennes, Colonel Clarke went back to Kentucky; but in the winter exciting news was brought to him. Colonel Hamilton, the English commander at Detroit, had marched down to Vincennes, driven away the American garrison, and placed his own men in the fort. Clarke also heard that Hamilton meant to march and retake Kaskaskia, and then to come and attack Kentucky; and as soon as he heard this, Clarke determined to be beforehand with him. In other words, he resolved to march and attack Vincennes, in spite of the fearful weather, and so nip the whole British plan in the very bud.

III.

It was a tremendous undertaking. The march was so hard that it afterward gave Clarke the name of the "Hannibal of the West," in allusion to a great Carthagenian general, who underwent terrible trials in crossing some high mountains to invade Italy. Clarke had no mountains to climb over, but the obstacles in his way were even more difficult to overcome. He had to march nearly one hundred miles through the wilderness in the depths of winter, and traverse what were called the "drowned lands" of the Wabash River, of which I will tell you more directly; and, at the end of this terrible march, he expected to find Colonel Hamilton and his English soldiers ready to receive him.

All these difficulties, however, did not make him change his mind or give up his design. He collected a force of one hundred and fifty of his bravest men, and in February, 1779, set out on his perilous expedition. Every man was clad in his hunting-shirt, and carried his knapsack, long rifle, and horn of powder. They wore fur hats, ornamented with the tails of bucks or raccoons, and were the very sort of soldiers for the work. They had, besides, the very highest confidence in their leader, and began their march with a feeling which goes a great way to make men succeed in anything in this world—the feeling that they would meet with success.

I will now go on and tell you what followed. Clarke sent one of his captains, named Rogers, with forty men and two small cannon, in a boat up the Wabash River, with orders to stop at a point where White River empties into it, about fifteen or twenty miles south of Vincennes.

And here I will say that you ought always to look at a map when you are reading about historic events. This will show you just where every place is, and one glance at the map will often give you a better idea of things than whole pages of explanation.

Having sent Captain Rogers ahead with the forty men, Colonel Clarke followed with the rest. They had a terrible time. As I have told you, it was in the depth of winter, and the weather was intensely cold. The hunters had to struggle on, with their long rifles in their hands and the packs containing provisions on their backs, through thick woods, day after day, and, what was worse still, plunge on through what were called the "drowned lands" of Illinois. These were low grounds, which the river had overflowed to the depth of many feet; and as the water was now nearly frozen, it was a fearful attempt to force their way through. Often they could scarcely find a spot dry enough to halt upon and kindle their camp-fires, to cook their food and sleep by. All day long it was tramp, tramp through the ice-cold water splashing around them; but they pushed on for nearly one hundred miles above the Ohio, and at last reached the fork at White River.

This was about fifteen or twenty miles, as I have told you, south of Vincennes; and they soon hoped, now, to reach the fort. But suddenly they found that the prospect before them was worse than ever. At this point the "drowned lands" were more forbidding than before. The whole country between the forks was flooded to the depth of many feet, and there were only a few spots of dry land here and there, some of them five miles apart. It seemed almost impossible to plunge on through such an expanse of freezing water, but Clarke determined to try. There was no "give up" either in him or his men, and at the word they marched into the water and struggled on.

As they proceeded, the water grew deeper and deeper. At first it only came up to their knees, then it reached to their waists, and at last the waves washed backward and forward just under their armpits. The water was freezing, and enough to benumb their limbs. But the work was so hard that it probably kept them warm; and they struggled along, holding their guns and powder above their heads to keep them from becoming wet, until they reached dry land again, and stopped for a short rest.

I have often shut my eyes and thought of this strange march. It would make a very fine picture. You would see in the picture—if it was like the real scene—the long line of hunters, up to their shoulders nearly in the cold water, toiling along, and stumbling perhaps now and then, but recovering their foothold again, and at the head of them the tall form of brave Colonel Clarke moving, like a good soldier, in front of all.

IV.

On the evening of the 18th of February they had passed through the worst of these "drowned lands" of the Wabash, and were near Vincennes—so near that they heard the boom of the "evening gun," which was a cannon fired off at the fort to tell people that it was time to come in for the night.

Clarke knew by this that he had not much farther to march, and ordered his men to lie down and sleep, which they did. But at the first streak of dawn they were up, and their leader issued his orders. These orders were that they were to blacken their faces with gunpowder, to frighten their enemies, and advance upon the fort. Clarke then found a large boat, into which the men crowded. They crossed the river, and pushed on through water again, and at last landed near Vincennes.

The time for fighting had now come, and Colonel Clarke wrote a letter to Colonel Hamilton, in the fort, demanding his surrender. This he sent by a countryman living near, and it was delivered by him to the commandant. No man could have been more perfectly astounded than Colonel Hamilton. If Clarke and his men had dropped down suddenly from the sky, his surprise could not have been greater. He knew all about the "drowned lands," and thought that no soldiers on earth would dare to march through them in the depth of winter, and he could scarcely believe that his enemies were really near him. But there they were, and there was Clarke's letter demanding that he should surrender. The families at the place were in favor of this, but Colonel Hamilton would not hear of it. He was a brave soldier, and the governor of all Canada, and he did not mean to give up his fort without fighting.

Hamilton accordingly sent back word that he would not surrender, and Clarke at once attacked the fort. His cannon, which had been dragged on in the boats, were brought up, and a furious fire was opened on Fort Vincennes. Colonel Hamilton replied to this by a shower of balls and grape-shot from his cannon in the fort, and for fourteen hours the guns went on thundering through the chill winter fields and woods. This was kept up long after night had come; and it must have been a grand sight to see the red glare of Clarke's cannon, and the flashes coming back from the walls of the fort, lighting up all around. At last both sides stopped, and Clarke's men lay down to get some sleep, intending to begin the fight again at daylight.

But the matter was decided. Colonel Hamilton came to the conclusion that he could not resist the Kentuckians; and when, next morning, Clarke once more demanded a surrender, the English commander gave up, and the Kentuckians marched into the fort, shouting and waving their hats. We are not told how Colonel Clarke and Colonel Hamilton met each other; they probably bowed and shook hands, as soldiers do after fighting with each other; and then the Red Cross flag of St. George, which was the flag of England, was pulled down from the staff, and the American Stars and Stripes were run up in its place, amidst the shouts and cheers of the Kentuckians.

Colonel Hamilton and some of his officers were then sent to Williamsburg, Virginia, with the captured papers; and as these papers showed that they had excited the Indians to attack the Americans, they were all "put in irons," that is, fettered, for their conduct. But these fetters were soon removed, and they were allowed to go to their homes. And that was the end of Governor Hamilton and his doings.

I have told you all about this march through the wilderness and the Wabash low grounds, to show you what a brave race of men the Americans of that time were. I hope it has interested you, for it was an adventurous and romantic exploit. But it was far more than that in its consequences, that is, in what followed it. A few words will explain this, and let you know just what I mean.

Some years afterward the Revolutionary War ended, and peace was made; and then the question was, What land was to belong to England and what to the United States? England still owned Canada, and there was no dispute about that; but there was the great country around Vincennes south of the Great Lakes—who was to be the owner of *that?* This was a hard matter to decide, and there was a great deal of talk about it. But at last it was agreed that a rule called the *Uti possidetis* should govern in the matter. These are Latin words, and

I will tell you what they meant. They meant that each side was to keep what they *had possession of* at the end of the war; and now you will see how this rule worked as to the great north-western country.

By capturing the small fort of Vincennes, Clarke had driven the English out of the country, and taken possession of it in the name of America. They never could drive him away afterward, and so it remained ours; and when the treaty of peace was made, England gave up all claim to it. Thus the march of about two weeks through the "drowned lands" of the Wabash, and the one day's fighting at Fort Vincennes, won for us the great States of Ohio, Michigan, Indiana, Illinois, and Kentucky, to say nothing of all the other States springing up every day in the great West.

General George Rogers Clarke passed through many other remarkable scenes, but of these I cannot tell you at present. You must take the capture of Vincennes as a specimen. I thought I would tell you about that, as he was a Virginian, and the land he fought upon was then a part of his State. Rich and prosperous commonwealths, full of happy families, now cover this fine region, which was given up by Virginia to her sisters of the Union. If she had not done so, the people would still be called Virginians; and in this little book I am trying to show you why they ought not to be ashamed of the name.

JOHN MARSHALL, THE CHIEF-JUSTICE.

I.

As in my three last stories I have endeavored to give you some idea of life in the western woods, I will now return to Eastern Virginia, and tell you about some famous personages there, after which I will finish with some scenes of the Revolution.

Do you remember the Culpeper "Minute-men," with

JOHN MARSHALL.

their rattlesnake flag and its motto, "Don't tread on me?" These brave men took part in the battle of Great Bridge against Lord Dunmore; and I will now tell you about a young lieutenant of these "Minute-men," who pursued the British after the fall of Fordyce.

His name was John Marshall, and he was, afterward, the Chief-justice of the United States. This ought to make you desire to hear all about him; but besides this, he was so great and good a man that he deserves a place in any book relating to the distinguished men of Virginia.

He was the son of Colonel Thomas Marshall, of Fauquier — a brave soldier who had fifteen children. His property was small, and his means very moderate; his wife and daughters, it is even said, had to use thorns instead of pins to pin their dresses. This they did not mind, however; and the small farm was managed so well that Colonel Marshall gave his children a good education, besides teaching them always to be true and honest. They lived near Manassas Gap, in the Blue Ridge Mountains, and here young John passed his boyhood till the Revolution, when he was elected lieutenant of the "Minute-men," and marched down to Norfolk. He fought bravely there, and everybody was fond of him. He was not a very handsome person. He was tall and thin, but his face beamed with good-humor, and his black eyes seemed to smile at everybody; so he was very much liked. He also read poetry in a very sweet voice; and when the "Minutemen" marched to Yorktown after the fighting, young John Marshall used to go to General Nelson's house and read poems to the young ladies, and it is said they thought his reading the sweetest in the world.

I tell you this, which may seem very trifling, because almost anything about so great a man ought to interest us. And, for that matter, in my little story I mean to tell you scarcely anything but anecdotes; and I am glad to do so, and leave out the rest, for, after all, these little details about distinguished people often give you a better idea of them than the *facts* in regard to their public lives.

John Marshall continued in the army during the whole

war, and those who fought with him said that he was not only brave, but that nothing could put him in low spirits. When Washington spent the dreary winter with his little army at Valley Forge, near Philadelphia, the times were so dark, and the sufferings of the soldiers so great, that they nearly gave way to despair. But John Marshall never did. Like the rest, he had to tramp through the deep snow to gather a little wood to keep from freezing; but in the midst of all, his friends said afterward, he was still bright and hopeful. Seated by the camp-fire, he would tell stories, and laugh, and cheer up his comrades, and thus keep them in good spirits when they were downhearted.

He was an excellent soldier, you see, and bore all the hardships of that hard time without a murmur. He had scarcely clothes to wear, and no money to buy them; and it is related that, when he visited home once, he was obliged to return to the army on foot, and was so shabbily dressed that a tavern-keeper in Philadelphia would not let him come into his house. But for this he did not care. He knew that he was doing his duty, and he went on cheerfully performing it without a murmur to the last.

When the Revolution ended, John Marshall came back to Virginia—a poor young fellow, with scarcely a penny in the world. But he was not disheartened. He resolved to go to work, and as he had managed to learn a little law, he began the practice, and soon got married. His wife was one of the young ladies whom he had read poetry to at Yorktown in 1775, after the battle at Great Bridge, and her name was Mary Willis Ambler. She had never forgotten the bright black eyes and sweet smile and voice of the tall young soldier, and now gave him her hand. He was so poor at the time that he gave the parson who married them the last golden guinea he had in the world.

But, poor as he was, he was happy with his young wife, and he loved her so much that he seemed to think of no one else in comparison with her. When they were old, and she was sick, he would walk about the house and yard with his shoes off, and hardly speak above his breath; and any one could see that she was dearer to him than when she was a rosy-cheeked young girl. After her death he wrote these words: "On the 3d of January, 1783, I was united by the holiest bonds to the woman I adored. From the moment of our union to that of our separation, I never ceased to thank Heaven for this, its best gift. Not a moment passed in which I did not consider her a blessing, from which the chief happiness of my life was derived. Hers was the religion taught by the Saviour of man. I have lost her, and with her have lost the solace of my life."

II.

Some of these days you will read all about the great Chief-justice Marshall, and find what people thought of him. He began, you know, only as a poor young lawyer, but everybody soon saw that he was a man of wonderful genius. There was scarcely any office which he would accept that the people did not offer him. He served in the Legislature; then in the Convention to ratify the Constitution; then was sent as envoy to France; then was made Secretary of State; and then Chief-justice of the United States, where the greatest judges, even the great Judge Story, my father told me, looked up to him, and listened to what he said, as if that decided everything. When he died, at the age of eighty nearly, he was one of the greatest and most famous men in America.

Now for a few anecdotes about him, for I wish you to know *the man* John Marshall. My father knew him very well, and loved him, and told me many things about him. He was very tall and thin, and dressed very plainly. He wore a suit of plain black cloth, and common yarn stockings, which fitted tightly to his legs, and showed how thin they were. He was a very great walker, and would often walk out to his farm, which was several miles from Richmond, where he lived, and back, without thinking of ordering his carriage. But sometimes he went on horseback; and old Bishop Meade said he met him one day riding out to his farm with a bag of clover-seed on the saddle before him.

His manners were simple and friendly, and he liked to talk about every-day matters with plain country people, and laugh and jest with them. As to this poorly dressed man being the great Chief-justice Marshall, it was hard to make a stranger believe such a thing. He never seemed to remember that he was a great man at all, and played games of "quoits" with his coat off at Buchanan's Spring, near Richmond, as full of fun as a boy, and ready to laugh with everybody. In a word, he was so great a man that he was plain and simple, and I will wind up my little talk about him with an anecdote or so which will show you this.

At that time it was the fashion among the gentlemen of Richmond to walk to market early in the morning, and buy fresh meats and vegetables for their family dinners. This was a good old fashion; and some famous old gentlemen—among them the distinguished Benjamin Watkins Leigh, whom I knew and loved—used to do so to the end of their lives. It was the habit of Judge Marshall, and very often he took no servant with him. He would buy what he wanted, and return home with his "marketing;" and on one of these occasions the little incident I will speak of took place.

Judge Marshall had gone to market and made his purchases, when, just as he was going home, he heard somebody swearing angrily not far from him. He turned round and saw what the hubbub was about. A finely dressed young man, who seemed to be a stranger, had come to market and bought a turkey. He then looked round for some one to take it home; but as no one could be found, he grew angry, and began to curse and swear. Judge Marshall listened, and stepping up to him asked, politely, "Where do you live, sir?"

The young man looked at the plainly dressed old countryman, as he supposed, and told him where he lived.

"That is my way," said Judge Marshall, with a smile, "and I will take it for you."

The young man handed him the turkey and left the market, followed by Judge Marshall, and they soon reached the house where the former lived. Marshall then politely handed him the turkey, and turned to go.

"What shall I pay you?" said the young man.

"Oh, nothing," replied Marshall; "you are welcome. It was on my way, and no trouble." With which he bowed and walked on, while the young man looked after him with a puzzled expression. He had, no doubt, begun to think that he had made some mistake; and, as a citizen was passing, he said, pointing after Marshall,

"Who is that polite old gentleman who brought home my turkey for me?"

"That is John Marshall, Chief-justice of the United States," replied the citizen.

The young man was perfectly astounded, and exclaimed, "But why did he bring home my turkey?"

"To give you a reprimand, and learn you to attend to your own business!" replied the citizen, walking off.

This little anecdote will show you the character of John

Marshall; but I do not believe that he brought home the young man's turkey to "give him a reprimand." Another person might have done so, but John Marshall never seemed to have any desire to reprimand people. He was too sweet-tempered and kindly to take pleasure in doing so, and I have no doubt he carried the turkey from a pure wish to be obliging.

III.

I might tell you more stories—how, among other things, he once met an old army comrade, who said he would be ruined unless he could get three thousand dollars, when Marshall privately left a check for the amount to be handed to him, and then rode away to escape his thanks. These anecdotes you will read some day, but those I have related will give you a true idea of this great man, and show how simple and unpretending he was, as all really great men are.

He did nothing "for effect," as the phrase is, and never seemed to feel that he was greater than the very humblest countryman of his acquaintance; and this was all the stranger, if you remember what I said about the public opinion of him. The greatest judges of the United States at Washington looked up to him as their superior; and whenever he passed, men took off their hats, to show their respect for him. But this did not have any effect upon him. He was the same simple old gentleman, with his friendly smile, ready to chat with anybody or do them a kindness, and just as devoted a Christian too, which was more than all, and as humble before God as the humblest.

I said that I had no time to relate other anecdotes of John Marshall, but I cannot pass over one referring to his faith in Christianity.

One day an old gentleman was seen to drive up to a tavern in the Valley of Virginia, in a shabby one-horse gig, the shafts of which were broken, and tied together with hickory bark. He was a plain-looking old man, and wore common yarn stockings, and when he went in and sat down, nobody took any notice of him. In the tavern were some young lawyers, and as night came on they got into an argument about the truth of Christianity, one of them sneering at it, and another speaking in favor of it. All this time the old man in the yarn stockings had been sit-

OLD TAVERN.

ting in a corner, smiling and listening, until at last they were tired out. They laughed, and gave up the argument; but one of them turned round and said,

"Well, old gentleman, what think you of these things?"

They all turned round and looked at him, expecting, probably, that he would have nothing to say. Never were any persons more mistaken. The old gentleman began quietly, and went on for nearly an hour without stopping. What he said was all in favor of the truth of the Christian religion, and his arguments were so powerful that the young lawyers listened in perfect amazement. If a streak of lightning had flashed before them, one of them afterward said, they could not have been more startled than by hearing such grand reasoning from such a plain-looking old countryman. They were all keen lawyers, but they felt that this old stranger was their master. And another of them said that to try to describe his language would be like attempting to paint the beams of the sun. At last he finished, and, with a smile on his lips, retired; and then everybody was anxious to find who this wonderful old countryman, with the shabby coat and yarn stockings, could be. This they soon discovered. He was John Marshall, the Chief-justice of the United States.

I have told you this anecdote because I wish you to see that the greatest intellects are the first to bow their heads before the majesty of Christianity. It is well to remember this, when we find so many people of weak minds sneering at holy things. John Marshall's mind was one of the greatest and strongest that man ever had, and he was an humble believer, if the young lawyers were not. He was such to the day of his death, and never went to bed at night without kneeling down and saying the Lord's Prayer, and the old verse which his mother had taught him:

"Now I lay me down to sleep,
I pray the Lord my soul to keep:
If I should die before I wake,
I pray the Lord my soul to take—
And this I ask for Jesus' sake."

This is all I have to tell you about the great John Marshall. It is not very much, and I might say a great deal more, but you must have a good idea of him, and see what sort of person he was. There never was a finer example of our good old Virginia country stock of people, which gave so many great men to the land we live in. He was honest, brave, simple-minded, and had a vast intellect. You may not have an intellect like his—few human beings ever had—but you can imitate his sweet temper and good heart. He lived before my time, but I know a great deal about him, and I can tell you that he valued goodness far above any mere strength of mind.

JOHN RANDOLPH OF ROANOKE.

I.

ONE morning, many years since, I visited an old house called "Matoax," on the north bank of the Appomattox

JOHN RANDOLPH.

River, near Petersburg, and spent some time thinking, beside a time-worn slab of marble, under a clump of trees not far from the river. It was a beautiful spot, and the tall trees waved in the wind above the marble tombstone, which was nearly sunk in the grass; and, looking at the stone, I thought of the time when the great orator, John Randolph of Roanoke, came there one day and cried beside it, for it was the grave of his mother.

As I have said in the case of John Marshall, it is hard to leave out of my stories any celebrated Virginians who were connected in any manner with the days of the Revolution. John Randolph was one of the most famous men who ever lived in the old Commonwealth, and knew Jefferson well, and made his first public speech in reply to Patrick Henry's last; and so I will now tell you a few incidents of his life, which was remarkable, and even splendid, although not happy.

Many of the celebrated men we have talked of were of plain origin, and began life poor; but John Randolph was rich, and belonged to an old and influential family. He was therefore never called upon to struggle with poverty, like Patrick Henry and others, and raise himself from a low station by the strength of his talents. He was born to a good estate, and bore a distinguished name; but, as you will see, neither of these two things can make a man happy.

I have spoken of the visit I paid to the old house, "Matoax," which was one of the names of Pocahontas, from whom John Randolph was descended. This was his father's house, but he was born at "Cawsons," the residence of his mother's father, Mr. Bland, in the year 1773, just after the marriage of Thomas Jefferson, who was his cousin. Cawsons stood near the mouth of the Appomattox River, below Petersburg, and here he passed many hours of his childhood with his beautiful dark-eyed mother, Frances Bland Randolph. She became a widow before he could remember his father, and this pious Virginia mother instilled into her child all the best and purest principles and feelings of his after-life. Up to the age of fifteen nothing of interest occurred to young John Randolph, except a visit to the beautiful Bermuda Islands, in the midst of the Atlantic Ocean, where he read Shakspeare's "Tempest," and no doubt thought of the little winged spirit of the air, *Ariel*, who is one of the characters in that drama. But he soon came home, and was sent to school, from which he suddenly came back on hearing of his mother's death.

The death of his mother was a dreadful blow to poor young John Randolph. He loved her with the deepest tenderness; and now, at the early age of fifteen, he came back to his old home, to find that he would never again see the face which was dearer to him than everything in the world besides. There was no pretence at all in this fond love, or any wish to make it out greater than it was, in order to have himself looked upon as a tender-hearted person. John Randolph was not at all tender-hearted toward the world in general, and never tried to gain people's good opinion by pretending to anything; he was far too proud, and indifferent to what was thought of him, for that. When he spoke to his few warm friends of his love for his mother, he was in earnest, and he never forgot her to the last day of his life.

When he was an old gray-headed man, lonely, sick, and nearly out of his mind, he crossed James River one day in a boat, with the spray dashing over him, to Cawsons, and stood for a long time in silence, looking at the old spot where he had played with his brothers when he was a little child. There was the same old house where he once ran, laughing, to tell his mother some childish trifle—that he had found a bird's-nest, perhaps, or that the buttercups were in bloom—and where he had knelt with his head on her knees, with her arms around him and her head bending fondly over him, to repeat "the Lord's Prayer and the Ten Commandments," which he said she taught him. There was every familiar scene in which he had passed his happy childhood; but his mother was long dead, and he was only a poor, old, unhappy, famous man!

You see I am trying to tell you about the *feelings* of John Randolph, and show you what his real character was, as I have tried to do when speaking of other celebrated people. Many persons who hated him because he was so bitter against them, and made people laugh at them by his terrible tongue, said that he had no *feeling* at all, and never *had* had any. But that was a very great injustice. Like many other poor human beings, he was made gloomy and bitter by disease and trouble; but no man that loves his mother faithfully, and thinks of her with deep tenderness to the last hour of his life, can be truly said to be without feeling, or really bad.

After his mother's death, John Randolph was never like the same person, and other troubles soon came. These were not money troubles, for he was quite rich, as I have said; they arose from disappointment in connection with a young lady. This lady was a beauty, and had something about her which attracted everybody. John Randolph met her when they were both children and the British invaded Virginia, under Lord Cornwallis, of which I will soon tell you. As Cornwallis was marching toward Petersburg, and "Matoax" was very near it, the family hastened away, and stopped for the night at the house of a friend of theirs. He was the father of the young lady I have mentioned, and here the children became acquainted; and when John Randolph grew to be a young man, he became deeply attached to her and wished to marry her. The marriage never took place for some reason, and the disappointment was a terrible one to the youth. He never got over it, and never married any one, and this made him more and more unhappy. You may think it was unreasonable in him to let it trouble him so much, and perhaps it was. But he said himself that he was always "thin-skinned," and small matters troubled him; and so poor young John Randolph moped and brooded, scarcely knowing what he would do.

At last he determined to try whether he could not serve his country in Congress. He was a large landholder, and at that time it was considered that men of this sort were better for public place, as there was no reason why they should use their offices to make money. So young John Randolph "ran for Congress," as the phrase is, in Charlotte and other counties about the time when he was twenty-five years old.

II.

I must say a few words about the occasion of his first speech, as it was quite a remarkable one. It was in the year 1799, the last year of the century, and Patrick Henry made his last speech on the same day that John Randolph made his first. They were not opposed to each other to win the same office, for Patrick Henry was "running" for the Virginia Legislature, where Washington wished him to go and speak against some famous laws, called the "Resolutions of '98," while John Randolph was a candidate for Congress.

It was Charlotte County court day, and a great crowd had assembled. Everybody came to hear Patrick Henry, who was now old and celebrated, and he mounted the platform and made them a great speech. He was not the same Patrick Henry who had made the fiery speeches at Williamsburg and Richmond before the Revolution. He was nearly seventy, and his form was bowed with age;

but he soon began to kindle, and spoke with as splendid an eloquence as ever. The crowd shouted and hurrahed, and when he finished seemed ready to carry him on their shoulders, as they had done in Hanover after his speech against the parsons. One of them exclaimed, "The sun has set in all its glory!"—meaning the fame of Patrick Henry; and when, a few moments afterward, a boyish-looking young fellow mounted the same platform to speak, they were ready to hiss him, and turn their backs at his presumption in daring to address them after Patrick Henry.

The youth was John Randolph. He was a mere stripling, with a smooth rosy face, smiling lips, and "remarkable for his beauty," it is said, by those who saw him. He began in a thin, shrill voice, which made everybody laugh; but he did not mind that, and went on speaking in the same voice. What made matters worse was that he was denying the truth of every argument of Patrick Henry's, and this excited strong indignation in those who listened. But he did not seem to care. The shrill voice did not falter; it seemed to pierce every ear to the farthest skirts of the crowd, and they were forced to listen to him, whether they would or not. At last he stopped and came down from the platform, and there in the crowd was Patrick Henry. The old man came up to young Randolph and put his hands upon his head.

"Keep faith and honor, my son!" said Patrick Henry, as if he foresaw how famous the youth would become; and thus ended what has always seemed to me a very striking incident. It was the old world and the new standing face to face—the gray-haired "man of the people" about to die, and the beardless young "aristocrat" just beginning life. As the old man's sun was setting, the young man's was just rising; and the words of Patrick Henry were worthy of his noble character.

They were both elected, but Patrick Henry's sun had set. He never took his seat, and soon afterward died—the greatest orator the Western world has produced.

III.

I cannot tell you all about John Randolph's long and remarkable life. He ran a famous and splendid career, and attracted the attention of the whole country by his wonderful oratory, which was so sharp and bitter that men hated him, and spoke ill of him very often when he did not deserve it. But all this would lead us far into this century, and you know I am only telling you stories of "old times," and the great men of the far past. I will, therefore, only say that John Randolph became famous, and was minister to Russia, and remained in public life for thirty years or more, and from first to last loved Virginia, and defended her against every one.

Instead of speaking of all this, which you will read about for yourselves some of these days, I will pass over the whole of it, and tell you how John Randolph appeared and acted as an old man.

This I can do easily from what I have read of him, and also from what my father told me about him. There was a great convention in Virginia, of which both were members; and as he and my father differed in opinion about many things, they often spoke against each other, and knew each other well. So, although I never saw him, I can describe his appearance and character, which were very different from what they were when he was *young* John Randolph.

I have told you that when he was youthful he was remarkable for his beauty, and his portrait, which was taken by a famous painter of that time, shows that he certainly was. The cheeks in the picture are rosy, and the eyes bright and happy. His hair is parted in the middle, and very soft and silky. He looks, indeed, like a sweet-tempered, happy young fellow, ready to love everybody and to make himself beloved by them; and it is hard indeed to believe that the portrait was ever like him, as it really was.

The "Virginia Convention" I have mentioned took place in the year 1829, and it is said to have had more famous men in it than any other body which ever sat in the United States. I need only tell you that its object was to make a new Constitution for Virginia; and the eastern part of the State and that beyond the Blue Ridge Mountains were opposed to each other. The Valley and Western Virginia came to ask for more votes in the government, and John Randolph said he came to the Convention to say "No" to everything.

He was a remarkable sight as he sat in the Capitol—very different, as you will see, from the *young* John Randolph of the portrait. He was now an old, stooping man, with thin gray hair, and a sallow face, worn by pain and suffering. His health was very bad, and his mind diseased, some people said; but his sharp black eyes, which were deeply sunken in his head, did not seem to show that he had lost any of his power of mind; and when he rose to speak, people could see that he was as brilliant as ever. He did not speak much. He generally sat quiet, holding a large walking-stick in his hand, and passing his hands up and down it, looking keenly all the time at anybody who was speaking. But at last one day the people of Richmond were seen running through the streets toward the Capitol. They hastened on as if they were going to a fire; and when a stranger asked what the matter was, one of them exclaimed,

"John Randolph is speaking!"

There he was on his feet, indeed, with every one listening in silence, and the crowd at the doors and in the galleries growing every moment larger. He was the queerest-looking figure you can possibly imagine. He wore an old cloak, and his cap, with a straight brim, was on the desk by him. His slender legs were clad in silk stockings, and his long, sharp forefinger was stretched straight out, pointing before him, as he went on, in his high, shrill voice, to address the Convention. Nobody ever before heard such a voice. It was more like a woman's than a man's, but was clear and sweet, in spite of its shrillness. Every word was distinct and deliberate, and heard by all; and the long forefinger seemed to point every sentence which he uttered.

You know how he looked now in that famous old Convention, where he had come to say "No" to everything. He did not wish the old Constitution to be changed; and, in fact, he never wished *anything* concerning *old* Virginia to be altered. All his life he had loved Virginia with his whole heart and soul—her old times, old habits, old manners, and old glory. He could not bear to think that these would ever be changed in the least; and in his feelings he might be compared to the famous Mary Queen of Scots. She came from France, you know, and said one day that if people opened her heart when she died they would find "France" written on it. Well, I think if people had opened the heart of John Randolph they would have found "Virginia" written on his.

IV.

I must end my story, which is carrying us too far. I thought you would be interested in this strange man. He was not a happy man. His distress at his mother's death, and then his disappointment with the young lady whom he wished to marry, made him gloomy. His temper became irritable under all these trials, and his tongue was fearfully sharp against people whom he did not like. It seemed to cut like a knife, and everybody became afraid of him. They wondered at his brilliant eloquence, but hated him for his ill-nature; and this will show you how ill-advised it is to indulge such feelings. No one likes a person who is always saying unkind things, and few people had any personal regard for John Randolph besides his intimate friends. These knew that he had very warm feelings, and they loved him deeply, and he loved them; but all the rest of the world feared him, or looked upon him with astonishment.

At last his mind gave way—I do not mean that he lost it, but the bright sun was overclouded, and he was like a great ship beating on the breakers. But to the last he was a very great man in the eyes of the Virginia people. He was looked upon as a mighty ruin, which might not be what it once was, but still was grand and majestic, even in its decay. At length he passed away, and was buried on his farm, called "Roanoke," in Virginia, under two great trees, and there the ashes of this remarkable man now rest.

As I have said more than once, the main object of my stories is to set before you high examples. This great man is not one of them. He allowed bitter feelings to carry him away, and was much more ready to frown than to smile on his fellow-men. He ought to have remembered that it is a far more beautiful thing to love than to hate, and that kindness and charity are better than the most splendid genius if it is only used to wound the feelings of others.

Still, John Randolph had noble traits. He loved his native State and his friends dearly, and was open-handed and generous. His black slaves were tenderly attached to him and he to them, and by his will he gave them their freedom, and means to live. We must not do as *he* often did—that is, look on the dark side—but remember that he had much to try him and make him irritable and bitter. I have heard his old friends speak of him, and read many of his letters which have never been published, and visited the spots where he had his troubles, and I cannot feel other than kindly toward this great unhappy man. The old house is still standing where he visited the young lady who refused to marry him, and I have often seen her name, cut with a diamond ring on a window-pane there. In the room are two pictures of her, one when she was a little girl, with her hair on her shoulders, and the other when she was a middle-aged lady, with a veil over her forehead. It was curious to think that the young people met here so long ago, and how unhappy young John Randolph must have looked as he went away down the old steps to where his horse was tied and rode away.

I have mentioned my visit to "Matoax," near Petersburg, where his father and mother were buried. He used to go there when he was an old man, and lean his face down in the grass and cry. It was pitiful to imagine that scene as I stood by the grave under the old trees; and I think everybody who supposes that John Randolph was only bitter and hateful, ought to do as I did, that is, go to the spot where he thus shed tears over the grave of his mother.

ROSEWELL, AND SELIM THE ALGERINE.

I.

As we go on with our stories we often meet, you know, with persons who have already been mentioned in former talks, and find them playing their parts in other incidents.

One of the persons thus spoken of was a young Mr. John Page, you remember, perhaps, to whom Thomas Jefferson wrote the letters from Williamsburg about "Belinda," and dancing with her in the "Apollo," when they were all young people. As time wore on, they all became staid men and women; and this John Page was first a delegate to the General Congress, then Governor of Virginia, and throughout his life an excellent, pious man, whom every one loved and respected. He lived at a house called "Rosewell," on York River, not far from the spot where Pocahontas rescued Captain Smith, and this house, which is still standing, was a very large and fine one.

It was built on a hill not far from the river, and, people say, was the largest in all Virginia at that time. The rooms had lofty ceilings, and the mantel-pieces were of fine marble. The staircases and pillars were carved into leaves and bunches of grapes, and on top of the house there was a flat space, covered with lead, from which you could look up and down the broad York River for miles and miles. On this high platform it is said that Governor Page and Thomas Jefferson used to sit in the evening and talk about religious matters while looking out upon the river, where white-sailed ships were passing, either up the broad current or down toward the sea.

It is an interesting old place, and was built a long time ago. How it came by its name is not exactly known, but two explanations are given of it. Down the hill, not far from the house, there was a fountain which bubbled up in a marble basin, and the path to this led through a double row of fine cedar-trees, while a shady path ran beyond, called "The Lovers' Walk." All around were multitudes of flowers, especially roses, and the place, it is said, was called Rose Well, or fountain, for that reason. Others say that the name was given to it because a little girl called Rose Page, a daughter of the owner, loved the well or fountain, so the house was called Rose Well after *her*. But, whether or no, that was the name of it; and here John Page, Jefferson's old friend, lived with his wife and children at the time of the Revolution, greatly respected by everybody, and entertaining a great deal of company, who loved to come to the hospitable old place.

These guests were always met in the kindest manner; but what surprised them was to see a very singular-looking person who came in and out, as if he was entirely at home. He was a strange sort of old man, with bright, piercing eyes, and long scattered locks of hair floating down over his forehead from beneath a straw hat, which was tied on with a check handkerchief. Around his shoulders he wore a bright-colored blanket, and on his legs and feet were leggings and moccasins like those worn by the Indians, made of deer-skin. He wandered around in a curious manner, as if he was looking for something; and whenever he met any one, he would wave his hand and exclaim, "God save ye!" Altogether he was a singular sight, and persons who saw him supposed he was a common lunatic, without sense or education. In this they were mistaken. He was a little out of his mind, it is true; but he could read Greek, and Hebrew also, it seems, and had more learning than many who pitied him. His name was Selim, and I will now tell you his story.

II.

Selim was first seen in Virginia about the time of General Braddock's march to Fort Duquesne, and he made his appearance under very unusual circumstances.

There was a worthy old hunter who lived in Augusta County, west of the Blue Ridge, and one day he went out hunting deer to supply his family with fresh venison. It is the habit with deer to bound off as soon as they hear any one approaching, but sometimes they stand still and watch the persons who are hunting them, out of their soft bright eyes, as if curious to know what they have come for. On this occasion the old hunter tramped on through the mountains for some time without discovering any game, but at last he thought he had certainly come on a fine deer. Right in front of him was a fallen tree, which had probably been uprooted by some storm, for the top was still bushy, with green leaves growing closely together. In this bushy top the hunter now saw two eyes gleaming. He had no doubt that they belonged to a deer which was hidden and looking at him; so he raised his rifle, took dead aim at the eyes behind the leaves, and was about to fire.

All at once, however, the eyes disappeared from view, and the next moment there came out from the fallen tree one of the strangest-looking creatures ever seen. It was hard to say at first whether he was a man or a wild animal. He was entirely naked, and covered all over with blood. His body was hairy, and his head was a mass of elf-locks tossing about his face. He came toward the old hunter, who probably kept a keen eye on him, thinking he might be some strange wild animal; but the poor thing made signs, and muttered something in a strange language; so the hunter knew that it was a man. He soon saw that there was no danger, as the wild man had a very pitiful and humble expression of countenance. It was plain that he was nearly starved, from his hollow cheeks and meagre limbs; so the hunter went up to him, and at last took him home to his house.

The poor wild man could not speak English, people soon found, and could give no account of himself: besides, he was evidently suffering for want of food and clothing, and the first thing to do was to dress him and give him something to eat. This was done by the kind hunter, and the poor creature remained with him. But pitiful as he seemed, it was very soon plain that he did not want sense. He began to read all the books he could find, and learn English. In this he made very rapid progress, and it was not long before he could speak the language and tell who he was.

His story was strange indeed. His name was Selim, he said, and he was born in Algiers, a country in the north of Africa, on the banks of the Mediterranean Sea. His parents were wealthy people, and Mohammedans, like the rest of the Algerines, and when he was a youth he was sent to the city of Constantinople to be educated. Here he remained some time studying languages, ancient and modern, until at last his education was nearly finished, and he set sail to return to his family in Algiers. He was not destined to see them again, however, for many a long year. Spain was then at war with Turkey or Algiers, and on the way they met a Spanish ship, which attacked them, and captured them. The Spanish ship then sailed on, but met with a French vessel outward bound. On this vessel Selim was placed with others, and the ship crossed the ocean, and reached New Orleans, in America.

Selim's fate was now melancholy, and hard to bear with

patience. He had been brought up in a wealthy home, surrounded by every comfort and luxury; but he now found himself a slave, set to work on a Louisiana plantation. He had been sold to the planter who owned the property, and he soon found that he was a cruel and brutal man. He was not only made to work like a slave, but one day his master grew angry with him, and struck him so heavy a blow on the head that it affected his mind, and he never afterward recovered from it.

Good-fortune seemed at length to come to his relief. He was sent up the Mississippi River, probably to some other plantation, and this removed him from his cruel master. But new troubles were coming. He was captured by the Indians, and taken as their prisoner to the Shawnee towns, as they were called, on the Ohio, where he found he was a greater slave than ever. The Indians loaded him with heavy burdens, and kicked and cuffed him, and nearly starved him; so he determined, if he could, to escape from them. This seemed almost impossible, as he was closely watched; and even if he succeeded in getting away, he was so ignorant of the country that the chance was that he would starve in the woods before he reached the abodes of white people.

But at last he determined to try. There was a white woman with the Indians, who was a prisoner like himself, and she pitied the poor Algerine, and advised him what to do. She told him that the Virginia settlements were toward the rising sun, and he had only to travel straight in that direction and he would reach them. He resolved to escape and try the long and toilsome journey; so he managed to get away without being seen by the Indians, and was soon in the Great Woods, going toward the rising sun.

All day long he tramped on, keeping his eyes upon the direction which he supposed to be the east, and after sleeping in the woods, again started on the next morning toward the sunrise. Very soon he began to suffer from hunger, and knew not what to do. His moccasins were worn out, and his clothes torn to shreds by the thorns and briers through which he was obliged to force his way. He, however, struggled on, barefooted and in rags, eating berries and such roots as he could dig, until his rags were entirely torn from him, and he was almost starved. He bound the last of his rags around his feet to protect them from the rocks, and still tottered along, nearly dead with hunger, until at last he had sunk to the ground in the top of a fallen tree, and prepared to die. But Providence was watching over him. His friend, the old hunter, had come; he was saved at last. And that was the poor fellow's whole story.

III.

Selim was treated most kindly by every one, and soon made a number of friends by his kindliness and inoffensive temper. People saw that his mind was affected, but he was far better educated than most of those around him, and this gave them a certain respect for him. As he was a heathen in his religious belief—for, as you know, his parents were followers of Mohammed—there was a great desire to convert him to Christianity; and this conversion now occurred in a somewhat singular manner.

Selim had a horse given him, and one day he rode with his friend to Staunton, where court was sitting. As soon as he reached the place, he was seen to stop suddenly and look at a person in the crowd with great intentness. This person was the Rev. Mr. Craig, a Presbyterian minister; and Selim went and spoke to him, and said he wished to go home with him. Of course this very much surprised Mr. Craig, but he at once replied that he would be very glad to see him. So they rode to the house, which was near Staunton, and Mr. Craig then asked Selim why he had come up and spoken to him in the crowd, as he was an entire stranger.

Selim replied that he had done so on account of a very remarkable dream he had had. This dream he now related. In his sleep he thought he was back in his native country of Algiers, and on a vast plain he saw the greatest multitude of men his eyes had ever looked upon. They were all in uniform of some sort, and drawn up in a line, like soldiers about to begin a battle. The plain stretched away in front of them, and was a dead level, without any object upon it; but far off in the distance he saw a dim, mysterious figure, resembling a man, and all that he could discover in regard to this figure was that he was some great Personage, to whom the multitude were looking for something.

From time to time some one of the multitude drawn up on the plain left the ranks and tried to reach this Personage; but in this they did not succeed. As soon as they had gotten about half-way across the plain they would drop into a great pit in the ground, and disappear from sight. At last he saw an old man standing at some distance from the crowd, and some of the multitude applied to him for advice and directions how to reach the great Personage. He gave them the directions they wished, and they followed them, and safely crossed the vast plain without falling into the pit. This was his dream, Selim said, and, what was strangest of all, was that Mr. Craig exactly resembled this old man who had given the directions. As soon as he saw him he knew him, and that was the explanation of his accosting him, and his desiring to go and live with him.

This was certainly a very remarkable dream, and it is a difficult matter to account for it. Selim was "half out of his head," you know, and we may understand some portion of the dream. The men drawn up on the plain were no doubt Mohammedans, that is, believers in the false religion of Mohammed, who was the great impostor of the East, and the uniforms worn by them were those worn by the Algerine or Turkish soldiers. The great Personage in the distance was also, no doubt, our Saviour, and the deep pit between was Selim's idea of the difficulty of coming to Jesus Christ through the dangers of this world. It was also very natural that he should have fancied that there was some good man present who directed those who tried to cross the plain and enabled them to pass it safely. But why did he suppose that Mr. Craig was this person? If the minister had belonged to the Episcopal Church, in which clergymen wear black gowns in the pulpit, he might have thought he was the same, as the figure he remembered might have worn a similar robe. But Mr. Craig was a Presbyterian, and wore no gown in preaching; so the whole matter was as mysterious and unaccountable as ever.

It was plain, however, that Selim wished to be a Christian, and Mr. Craig began to explain the true doctrine to him. But Selim studied it himself. He found a New Testament in the original Greek in which it was written, and hugged it to his breast, and began to read it quickly, for he knew Greek far better than he knew English. In two weeks he had studied the whole question of the truth of Christianity, and said he was convinced that there was no other true religion. He was therefore baptized, and said that now he meant to go back to Algiers and convert his family from their belief in the false doctrine of Mohammed.

His friends gladly aided him. He was supplied with money, and set sail for Africa by way of England, and then for some years nothing was heard of him. At last he came back to Virginia suddenly, and his friends saw that his mind was more diseased than ever. He had evidently passed through great sufferings, and of these he gave an account. He had returned to his home in Algiers, he said, and attempted to convert his family to Christianity; but they would listen to nothing he had to say. They plainly looked upon him as a lunatic, and turned him off upon the world again, to go where he chose and take care of himself as he could, as he refused to give up his religion and become a Mohammedan again. He could not do this, and left them, to go and live in England among Christians. But he found no friends there, and came back to Virginia now, where he passed nearly all the rest of his life.

This is a singular story, but it is entirely true. Selim was very well known to many of the most respectable families of Virginia, who vouched for the truth of what I have told you. He was a wild, erratic being, and wandered from place to place, waving his hand when he met any one, and exclaiming, "God save ye!" At other times he would pass his hand constantly up and down over his face, exclaiming, "It is the blow—that disgrace to a gentleman — given me by that Louisiana planter. But, thank God! thank God! but for the Saviour I could not bear it!"

He seldom slept in a house, his favorite place being an old windmill near Yorktown, where he would lie down at night, wrapped in his blanket. . Sometimes he would go to Williamsburg and read Greek with an old professor at William and Mary College. Now and then, too, he would wander into Yorktown; and one day he was persuaded to take a seat in Lady Nelson's sedan-chair, which was a sort of small vehicle with shafts at each end, which servants lifted and carried along, with a lady or gentleman inside. Selim took his seat in the sedan-chair, and he was carried into Governor Nelson's house. As they set down the chair he rose up and began to sing, in a sweet voice, the hymn for children,

"How glorious is our heavenly King!"

His latter days were spent in thus wandering about Lower Virginia, and he and Mr. Page, of Rosewell, were very great friends. They read Greek together, and Selim became fond of the whole Rosewell family. When Mr. Page went to Philadelphia to attend the meeting of Congress, Selim followed him on foot, and his portrait was painted for Mr. Page by the distinguished artist Peale. This was sent home in a box to Rosewell, and the family and servants thought the box contained a portrait of Mr. Page. When it was opened, however, the servants exclaimed, "God save ye!" as Selim always did. The likeness was so perfect that they recognized him at once. This portrait is still in Williamsburg, where any one may see it. From Philadelphia he wandered off to South Carolina, and after that nothing more was ever heard of him.

I have thus told you of this singular person, and his life spent at Rosewell and in the vicinity, with his kind friends the Pages and others. I think his story is an interesting one; and in spite of his being a poor wanderer, without house or home, he is worthy of our respect. If he had consented to give up his belief in Christianity he might have been a rich man, and lived in luxury in Algiers, for his family were wealthy, and he was their heir. But this he refused to do. He clung to his religion like a good Christian; and you may see that he understood what Christianity meant by his forgiving his enemies. The Louisiana planter had beaten him so cruelly that it destroyed his reason, but he struggled to forgive him. His blood boiled when he remembered the blow the planter had struck him on the head, but he exclaimed, you remember, "Thank God! thank God! *but for the Saviour* I could not bear it!"

This meant that *he* could bear blows and insult as our Saviour had borne them; and to feel thus and forgive injuries is to be a true Christian.

MORGAN, THE "THUNDER-BOLT OF THE REVOLUTION."

I.

I HAVE often visited an old stone house which stands on a grassy hill not far from the little village of Millwood, beyond the Blue Ridge, in the Valley of Virginia. As it

DANIEL MORGAN.

may be called a historic spot, it is very interesting. At the foot of the hill there is a very fine spring, which bubbles up beneath some weeping-willows, and on all sides are green fields and woods and blue mountains. The house is old and large. To the right of the front door is a long apartment with tall windows, and a fireplace so large that it holds quite a load of wood; and in this apartment I have often mused about former days, and thought of the old soldiers gathered there once, talking about the days of the great Revolution.

This was the place of residence of Daniel Morgan, the brave soldier who really won the battle of Saratoga, though another person got the credit of it, and defeated Tarleton badly at the Cowpens. He was supposed to be a native of New Jersey, but he came to Virginia when he was young, and worked as a farm-laborer, for he was poor, and plain in his origin, it is said. But you will see that he was a braver and truer man than many who had greater advantages in beginning life. A story is told of his having been a wagon-driver in Braddock's expedition, and of his receiving a terrible lashing by order of an English officer, whom he had beaten with his wagon-whip for insulting him. He was sentenced to receive five hundred lashes, it is said, but they stopped at four hundred and ninety-nine; and Morgan always said, with a laugh, afterward, that he owed them one lash yet. If this whipping made him an enemy of the English they had better have let him alone, for he made them pay for it in blood on many occasions.

Morgan's early manhood was not very quiet or respectable. He was a rough young fellow, and so much given to fist fighting that the village of Berryville, near which he then lived, took the name of *Battletown*. He lived at a place called "Soldier's Rest," near by, and this old house still stands, and is interesting; for young George Washington used to sleep in it when he was a boy-surveyor here, which I have told you about.

But Morgan was too brave a man to spend his time in these idle brawls. He was probably led into them, and was sorry for them afterward; and his want of education ought to be some excuse for such things. He soon showed that he was fit for better things. No sooner did the Revolution begin than he raised a company of riflemen, and set out for Boston, where Washington then was. They were all hardy young fellows in linen hunting-shirts, with "Liberty or Death" on the breasts of their shirts, and they marched six hundred miles, and at last were near Boston. It was in the evening, and Washington, who was riding out, saw them and stopped. Morgan stepped in front, and, saluting, said,

FLAG OF MORGAN'S RIFLE CORPS.

"General, from the right bank of the Potomac!"

At this Washington displayed great emotion. He dismounted from his horse, walked along the line of riflemen, shaking hands with every man, while the tears rolled down his cheeks, and then mounted his horse again, and, touching his hat, rode away without a word.

He believed that Morgan and his men were the real stuff for soldiers, and in this he was not mistaken. The Americans determined to attack Quebec, in Canada, which the English held, and Morgan was sent to help in this undertaking. The march, which took place in winter, was a fearful one, for a great wilderness had to be traversed, and the sufferings of the men were terrible; but at last they reached Quebec, and attacked it. This attack was at night, from the "Plains of Abraham," as they are called, west of the old city, and was a desperate and bloody affair. General Montgomery, who led the assault, was killed, and Morgan was taken prisoner; and I have told you about this assault to inform you of Morgan's brave speech on the occasion.

He had led the attack on what was called the St. Roche bastion, and had fought so desperately that the English were filled with admiration for him. He was their prisoner now, and the British general sent for him. He told him how much he thought of him, and said that if he would join them he should have the commission of colonel in the English army. This was a splendid offer to so poor and humble a man, but Morgan only frowned and grew angry.

MONTGOMERY'S MONUMENT.

"I hope," he said, looking sternly at the English general, "that you will never again insult me, in my distressed and unfortunate situation, by making me offers which plainly imply that you think me a rascal!"

That was a brave reply, and shows the stuff Morgan was made of. He did not mean to sell himself for rank or pay. And on another occasion, some years afterward, he made another speech of very much the same sort. He had gone on fighting bravely after getting away, as he soon did, from the British, and at the battle of Saratoga was a general and a rising man. General Gates, who commanded the Americans in this battle, had been an Englishman, and as the English army had surrendered to him, he thought he was a greater man than Washington. He therefore set a scheme on foot to have Washington removed, and himself appointed commander-in-chief; and the American officers were sounded, as it is called, to find if they would support Gates. At last they came to Morgan, but he stopped them very quickly.

"I have one favor to ask of you," he said, in the same stern tone he had used at Quebec, "which is never to mention *that detestable subject* to me again; for under no other man than Washington, as commander-in-chief, will I ever serve!"

You may see at a glance that men of this sort may be counted on; and old Daniel Morgan, as he always called himself, soon showed everybody that he was true as steel. No man was ever braver, and whenever he fought, as he did all through the war, from north to south, he showed that nothing could daunt him. This same battle of Saratoga was one instance, and his daring attack there was the cause of the British defeat.

His most important victory was the battle of the Cowpens, in the Carolinas. The Americans had been defeated everywhere, and were retreating before the English, and on their heels rushed Colonel Tarleton, who commanded the British cavalry, certain that he was about to destroy them. I will tell you more at another time of this famous Colonel Tarleton. He was a very brave soldier, but as cruel and boastful as he was courageous. He now hastened after Morgan, who was in command of the Americans; and wherever he stopped, as he often did to plunder houses, he boasted that he would soon overtake Morgan and cut him to pieces.

It seemed that he would be able to do this, as he had in addition to his cavalry a considerable force of infantry and plenty of cannon. He supposed that Morgan would not dare to stop and fight him; but in this he was much mistaken. Suddenly he came on the Americans drawn up in line of battle, and instead of flying Morgan awaited his attack. The English fought hard, but they had found a tough obstacle in "Old Morgan." He would not yield, and the end of it was that, before night, Colonel Tarleton was himself flying, with all his men and cannon, with Morgan following close on his heels.

II.

I should like to tell you more about the hard fighting of brave old Daniel Morgan, but this you may read of in larger books: I shall now only give you some idea of him as he was in private, after the war.

The old house which I have spoken of near Millwood was built by him, and there are some stories told in the neighborhood as to how this was done. At Winchester, which is only a few miles distant, a number of English prisoners were kept at that time under guard. They were Hessians, who came to fight us, to win pay only, and were much despised; so Morgan determined that he would make them work. He therefore ordered them to quarry large stones for him on the Opequon, which is a stream near by; and these stones, which were for his house, he compelled them to carry for miles on their shoulders. It was hard work, and they often growled and grumbled, but Morgan did not mind that. He told them that, as they were eating bread and meat which belonged to the Americans, he would make them work, and if they *did not work they should not eat.* So they were compelled to obey his orders, and certainly deserved no better treatment. They were not Englishmen, and had come to kill the Americans for money; and Morgan was right in looking on them as little better than beasts of burden, unworthy of much respect.

The house was built at last, and he called it "Saratoga,"

after the battle which he had really won. It was an excellent piece of stone-work, and here Morgan lived in his old days. He had come back to the same neighborhood in which he used to have his quarrels and fist fights; and, judging from a speech which he made one day, he often thought of those times, and remembered what a gay, careless, young fellow he had been.

"To be young once more," he said, "I would be willing to be stripped naked and hunted through the Blue Ridge with wild dogs."

But he soon gave up all this idle feeling and

GATES'S HEAD-QUARTERS AT SARATOGA.

talk, and became a very different man. Instead of looking back and longing for the scenes of his youth, which were not much to his credit, he looked forward to the future in another world, and got ready for his long journey. He became a good Christian, and joined the Presbyterian Church in Winchester; and in his last days at "Saratoga," or in Winchester, he often talked with his friends about the battles in which he had fought.

"People think old Morgan never was afraid," he said, "and never prayed, but people did not know."

He then went on and described the assault on Quebec. It was at night, he said, and he had drawn up his men, waiting for the order to advance. It was a fearful moment. It seemed almost hopeless to make such an attack on so strong a place, so well defended, and his heart sunk within him. A miracle was all that could save them, and he determined to ask the help of God. He therefore stepped aside and knelt down by one of the cannon, and prayed to God to protect him. He was still on his knees when the word was passed along the line to advance on the enemy, and his protection from death on that terrible night he said was due, he fully believed, to this prayer.

At the battle of the Cowpens he had felt afraid in the same way, he said. The British were coming on in a long glittering line to attack him, and, as he looked at his own poor little army, he felt that God only could enable him to conquer. He therefore rode into the woods, and dismounting from his horse, knelt down in the top of a fallen tree and prayed long and earnestly. When he had finished his prayer he felt far more cheerful, and returning to his men, made them a speech which they answered with cheers. The bloody battle followed, and Tarleton was defeated, and this, too, he attributed to his prayers.

While talking about these old times Morgan would shake his head, and say that people might speak of him as the "thunder-bolt of war, who never knew fear," but they were greatly mistaken.

"Old Morgan," he said, "was often miserably afraid."

And now I have told you these incidents of Daniel Morgan to show you what true courage is. It is not mere foolhardiness and thoughtlessness. Many persons have that sort of courage, but it is not the best sort, and does not make the hardest fighters. The truest courage, and the sort which is most dangerous to an enemy, is that of the man who, though he may feel afraid of death, still resolves to trust in God, and do his duty without flinching. It is hard to overcome such people, because they see the worst from the beginning, and are never cast down by anything which takes place. They mean to meet death if necessary, doing their duty and looking to God, and the result generally is that no enemy can stand before them.

Morgan died in Winchester, a celebrated old man, with his gold medal from Congress, and enjoying the respect and regard of Washington. But the old house which I have described—I mean "Saratoga"—is more closely connected with his last days than any other spot. It is interesting to visit it, and think of the tall soldier who once walked about the grounds and down to the old spring. Such spots make us remember the old days of the Revolution, and the brave men who won American liberty.

CORNWALLIS, AND THE BOY LAFAYETTE.

I.

We have come at last to the final scenes of the Revolution, which ended on the soil of Virginia. These were the termination of a long and remarkable drama, and I shall tell you a few of them, and first of Lafayette and Cornwallis. You will see from this story that the British general looked on the young Frenchman as "a boy," and I will then proceed to tell you how the boy proved himself a better soldier than the general.

It was the opening of the year 1781. The long Revolutionary War was very nearly over, and it was going to end in a manner which very few persons expected. It began, you know, in the north, near the city of Boston, where most of the English troops were, and then drifted down to New York, and afterward to New Jersey and Pennsylvania. Year after year the two armies went on fighting, one sometimes getting the best of it, and then the other; but at length things began to look very dark for the Americans, and the English felt sure that they were going to conquer. Washington's army was very small, and had scarcely any clothes to wear or anything to eat. Often the soldiers had no shoes, and one winter day when an officer came to visit General Washington, he told him that he had followed the track of his army by the marks of blood left on the snow by the naked and bleeding feet of his men.

At last the whole North seemed to be conquered, or

very nearly, and the British commander-in-chief, whose name was Sir Henry Clinton, sent one of his generals, named Lord Cornwallis, to conquer the States of Georgia and North and South Carolina. Sir Henry also determined to get possession of Virginia, and accordingly sent a fleet of ships to Chesapeake Bay to sail up James River and capture Richmond, to which the capital had been removed from Williamsburg.

This fleet of ships, with the soldiers in them, was placed under command of General Benedict Arnold. You must have heard the name of this infamous person. He was an American by birth, and had fought bravely for the Americans; but he turned against them at last, and attempted to commit a great crime; and as the story is interesting, I will stop and tell you about it in as few words possible:

BENEDICT ARNOLD.

In the summer of 1780 Sir Henry Clinton, the British commander, had possession of the city of New York with his army, and General Washington, with the American troops, was along the Hudson River above, around the strong fortress of West Point. The officer commanding at West Point was named Benedict Arnold, and the Americans thought that they could not intrust this important fort to a better man. Arnold was a general in the American army, and had showed, in more battles than one, that he was as brave as steel. But he was a cunning and treacherous man, and thought he had been treated badly by Congress. He was also very much in debt, owing to his extravagance in living; so, in consequence of his hatred and his money troubles, he determined to turn traitor, and give up the great fortress of West Point for a large sum of money and a post of rank in the British army.

Arnold had no sooner made this resolution than he attempted to carry it out; and you will see that when a man determines to be a rascal, he begins to act in the most secret and underhand manner. He sent word secretly to the British general in New York that he was ready to sell West Point, and his offer was at once accepted. You may feel surprised at this, as Sir Henry Clinton was a highly honorable soldier and gentleman, but it is one of the bad rules of war to get the better of your enemy in almost any possible manner; so Sir Henry sent back word, in the same secret way, that Arnold should be paid, and determined to send one of his officers to finish the bargain.

The officer chosen was named John André. He was quite a young man, and so handsome and friendly in his manners that everybody loved him. If he had not often shown how brave he was—and you will soon see there was no doubt about that—people might have supposed that he was too soft and easy in disposition to be a good soldier. He was very fond of ladies' society, and one of his greatest pleasures was to laugh and talk with them. He also wrote poetry, and played on musical instruments, and drew well, and was very accomplished in every way. So it was hard to believe that he was so fearless as he really was, and was now about to show.

Young André, who was a major and adjutant-general on Clinton's staff, went up the Hudson River in a British ship to meet Arnold. It was at night, and the two men met in a thicket in the dark, on the west shore of the river. For many hours they went on talking about the surrender of West Point, and had not finished the business when daylight came. At this Arnold grew uneasy. He told André that they must go to a house near by, where they could talk over everything, and when the next night

JOHN ANDRÉ.

came, André could return to his ship. To this the young soldier consented, and went with Arnold, but was startled at suddenly hearing an American sentinel cry out, "Who goes there?" This showed him that they were going to pass the lines of the American army, and André told Arnold that he had never intended to do anything of that sort, as he might be taken for a spy, which was considered infamous, and tried and shot for it. Arnold, however, told him there would be no trouble, and André went on. Arnold gave the watchword to the sentinel, as he knew what it was, and so they got to the house and finished the whole bargain.

The great point with André was now to get back to New York; but his ship had sailed away. An American fort on the other side of the river had seen the ship, and fired at her with cannon. So the *Vulture*, as her name was, dropped down the river, and André was there in Washington's lines, in danger of being caught and shot.

Arnold now acted as all men do when they know they are traitors—he looked out for himself. He told André that when night came he could get back to the *Vulture;* but in case he could not, he could cross the river, and return to New York by land. To this poor André had to agree; and soon afterward Arnold left him, first giving him some papers containing a full description of West Point, and the number of soldiers there, for Sir Henry Clinton. He also gave André a pass, which he signed himself, but, of course, did not write, "Pass *Major André*." What he wrote was, "Pass *Mr. John Anderson* through the lines," and André was to tell any one who stopped him that he was an American on "secret service," as it is called, for the Americans.

With this he had to be satisfied. Arnold rode off for fear of being discovered; and as soon as night came André asked the man to whom the house belonged to row him down to the *Vulture*. But the man refused. It would be dangerous to try that, he said, and the best thing to do was to cross the Hudson River and go by land; and he promised to show the way. To this André had to agree, and he then proceeded to take off his uniform and put on plain clothes. He knew how dangerous this was, for, unimportant as it seemed, it made everything very different. As long as a soldier goes into an enemy's lines dressed in his uniform, he is looked upon as a soldier, doing a soldier's duty; but if he dresses in plain clothes, so that no one can know who he is, he is looked upon as a spy, and shot or hung if he is caught. André knew this very well, and did not wish to take off his British uniform; but this he was obliged to do to get back to his friends; so he put on the plain suit of clothes, and, after hiding the papers about West Point, given him by Arnold, in his boot, mounted a horse, and crossed the river on his way to New York.

He was soon stopped by the American sentinels, but he showed General Arnold's pass, in which he was called "Mr. John Anderson," you know, and they handed it back, telling him it was all right. He then rode on down the river in the direction of New York, and had nearly reached the city, when his journey came to a sudden end. Some young men belonging to the American side saw him passing, and ran and stopped him. From something that they said he took them for friends of the English, and said he was a British officer, and they must stand aside, as he was on important business. At this they told him who they really were, and searched him to find what was in his pockets. Nothing was found but his purse and his watch; but they made him take off his boots, and there between his foot and the sole of his stocking were the papers given him by Arnold.

All was now over for poor André, and he was conducted back at once, under guard, to the American army. Word was sent to General Arnold, who was in command of the troops in the vicinity, that Major André, of the British army, had just been captured, and had a pass from him, General Arnold, under the name of "John Anderson." At this Arnold saw that all was discovered, and he knew that his only hope was to make his escape to the British. The news reached him just at the moment when General Washington was coming to his house, opposite West Point, to breakfast with him. But he did not mean to eat breakfast with Washington on that morning if he could help it. He kissed his wife and baby, and told the former in a few words how matters were: the poor lady shrieked aloud, and fell fainting on the floor; and then Arnold

CAPTURE OF ANDRE.

sprung on a horse and galloped at full speed down the bank to his barge, or large boat, and the men in it were ordered to row rapidly down the river. They obeyed, and Arnold stood at the prow, looking out for the *Vulture*. At last it came in sight, and he waved a white handkerchief. The boat darted on, and soon reached the ship, which Arnold went on board of, and was safe.

I have scarcely the heart to tell you the fate of young André. He wrote to General Washington, giving him a true account of everything; but he had come on a terrible errand, which might have ruined the Americans if it had succeeded; and a court-martial was assembled to try him. From first to last André never showed the least sign of fear. He said that he never had the least intention of becoming a spy; that he wore his uniform; that General Arnold had betrayed him into entering the American lines; and if he died, he would die like a soldier and a gentleman, feeling that he had done no more than an honorable soldier's duty. But all was of no avail. The court decided that as he had entered the lines by night, without a flag, he "ought to be considered as a spy;" and they would not even consent that he should be shot like a soldier—he was to be hung like a criminal. This was done, and poor André was marched out and hung: he remained brave and cool to the very last, and those who saw him could not help loving and admiring him, and shedding tears at his fate.

Perhaps you will ask me if this was right. That is a hard question to answer. According to army law it was not right, for André was in reality no spy. But the times were terrible, and it was necessary to make a terrible example. This no doubt led the court-martial to condemn him to death, and even to refuse to let him be shot. They condemned him to be hung, in order to warn British officers not to venture on any such thing in future, and Washington approved the sentence. They were brave and honorable men, and admired André as much as other people did; but they did what they thought was their duty under all the circumstances, and were ready to bear the blame, if there was any attached to their action.

This is the story of brave young André and the traitor who betrayed him. Arnold reached New York safely, and Sir Henry Clinton paid him his money, and made him

ANDRÉ'S MONUMENT.

a British general. But every officer in their army despised him as a traitor, and refused to associate with him, except when they were obliged to do so.

Now you know all about the man who was sent with the ships and soldiers to make war on the people of Virginia.

II.

Benedict Arnold did not do much in Virginia, after all, but I thought I would take this occasion to tell you, in a few words, one of the most sorrowful stories in American history.

Although the English despised him, they knew he was a brave and determined soldier, as he certainly was; and as a man often hates old friends, when he turns against them, worse than he hates other people, the English probably thought Arnold would do everything in his power to injure the Americans; and he soon showed that they were right in supposing so. He sailed up James River to Richmond, which was now the Virginia capital, and plundered and burned and laid waste wherever he went. Thomas Jefferson, who was governor at the time, had to mount his horse and gallop away, and then Arnold and his soldiers committed all the depredations they could; after which they went back to their ships in the river, and sailed down to Portsmouth again.

Soon afterward General Phillips was sent to take the place of Arnold, and sailed up James River, landing here and there, and destroying everything he thought would be of any use to the American army. He then landed with three thousand five hundred men at City Point, and marched up the Appomattox to Petersburg. Here he intended to wait until he was joined by Cornwallis, who had been fighting the Americans in the Carolinas. Cornwallis had been successful, and had taken the whole country, together with the chief city, Charleston. He was therefore ready to march northward to Virginia, where Sir Henry Clinton had determined to bring the war to an end.

General Phillips, who was very proud and high-tempered, but very brave and honorable too, marched into Petersburg, and captured the place without any trouble. But

LAFAYETTE.

suddenly he received intelligence that Washington had sent troops from the North to attack him, and that these troops were coming toward Richmond from the direction of the Rappahannock River. He therefore determined to go and meet them, and was soon at Manchester, opposite Richmond. But here he was stopped. On the hills across the river were long lines of Americans, waiting with their cannon to receive his attack.

The Americans were commanded by the brave young French marquis, Lafayette. At this time he was only twenty-three years of age, but he was already considered one of the best soldiers in the army, and everybody had the highest respect for him. At home, in France, he had been very rich, and ranked high among the nobility. He was also married to a beautiful young wife; but in spite of his wealth and high rank and his pretty young wife, he determined to cross the ocean and fight for the Americans. He did so, and told them that he was ready to go into the ranks as a private soldier, and would not take any pay; but they saw what a good officer he would make, and would not allow that. He was made major-general, in spite of his being a boy almost, and soon showed people that he had as much sense and courage as the oldest generals. Washington had a high opinion of him, and this you will easily see, as Lafayette was now sent to take command of an army of four thousand men, and meet the old British generals in Virginia.

He soon let people see that, if he was a mere boy, he knew his business, and was the man for the place. He got to Richmond before General Phillips, and drove him

BOLLINGBROOK.

back to Petersburg, to which place he followed him, and attacked the British.

Poor Phillips was now taken very ill. He had caught a fever, and it grew worse and worse. His head-quarters were at "Bollingbrook," a house in the town belonging to a Mrs. Bolling; and as Bollingbrook was on a hill, it was exposed to the fire of the American cannon. The balls crashed through the house, for Lafayette did not know that the British general was lying ill there, and poor Phillips was heard to groan out from his bed,

"Can't they let me die in peace!"

None of the balls injured him, however; his fever ended his life. He soon afterward died, and his men buried him in the graveyard around "Old Blandford" church, which is still standing in ruins, covered with green ivy. They fired a salute over the grave of their general; and that was the last of "the proudest man of the proudest nation on earth," as he was called by Thomas Jefferson.

III.

It was now the month of May, 1781. Lord Cornwallis had arrived with his army from the South, and Lafayette was obliged to retreat from Petersburg up James River again, toward Richmond. Here he stopped not far from "Wilton," an old house some miles below the city, and began to watch his enemy.

If you will now think for a moment how matters stood, you will see that the contest between the two generals was very unequal. Lord Cornwallis was an experienced soldier of forty two or three years of age, and had a well-disciplined army of regular soldiers; while Lafayette had far fewer men, and nearly three-fourths of them were untrained militia. Another thing which seemed to be against the Americans was Lafayette's age. It seemed unreasonable to suppose that a youth of twenty-three could fight successfully against a man of forty-three, who was acknowledged to be a good soldier, and had a victorious army at his orders; and Lord Cornwallis took this view of the subject. When he heard that the Americans were only commanded by Lafayette, he laughed at the intelligence, and said,

"*The boy* cannot escape me!"

But *the boy*, as he was called, had a better head than Lord Cornwallis thought he had. No doubt the English general supposed that Lafayette was brave and reckless, as many young men are, and would be ready at any time

CORNWALLIS.

to fight, which was just what he wished. He knew that Lafayette's men were not disciplined soldiers, only untrained country people; and as the English cavalry rode strong horses and were hard fighters, he expected to ride over the American militia, and soon make an end of them. The boy Lafayette, however, had not the least idea of standing still and waiting to fight Cornwallis. He was brave enough, and nothing would have pleased him better than a good bloody battle, in which he might win distinction; but he knew that he ought not to think of such a thing. Washington had sent him to take charge of things in Virginia, and if he fought the English and was defeated, it would be a terrible blow to the American cause. So Lafayette kept his eyes on every movement of the British; and when they came up the river, as they soon did, to attack him, he retreated slowly before them toward the Rappahannock.

For this time, at least, you see, the boy had escaped Lord Cornwallis. This probably mortified the English general, and he saw that his youthful adversary was a better and cooler soldier than he supposed. He resolved, however, to lay waste Virginia, and capture, if he could, the members of the Legislature, then in session at Charlottesville; so he marched up the country for that purpose.

In front of him went Colonel Tarleton, the young cavalry general who had laid waste the Carolinas with fire and sword. Tarleton was as brave as possible, but cruel, boastful, and quick-tempered. He pretended to have a great contempt for the Americans, and told an American lady once that Colonel William Washington was an "illiterate fellow, hardly able to write his name." Now Colonel Washington had just defeated Tarleton in a cavalry fight, and the lady replied,

"You ought to know better, for you bear on your person proof that he knows very well how to *make his mark!*"
—by which she meant to allude to the way uneducated people have of making a cross-mark when they cannot write.

At this Tarleton grew angry, and exclaimed, with a sneer,

"I would be happy to see Colonel Washington!"

"If you had *looked behind you* at the Cowpens, you

would have enjoyed that pleasure!" replied the lady, referring to the battle in which Tarleton had been defeated.

This made him furious, and, without thinking, probably, he laid his hand on his sword, when General Leslie, of the English army, who was present, and very angry at his doing so, exclaimed, addressing the lady,

"Say what you please, Mrs. Ashe. Colonel Tarleton knows better than to insult a lady in *my* presence!"

Tarleton now marched with his troopers, in front of Lord Cornwallis, toward the mountains, committing all sorts of depredations wherever he went. He plundered many of the houses, carried off all the horses which were fit to ride, and when they were too young he ordered their throats to be cut, in order to prevent the Americans from riding them. Some fine colts, which he found at a place called Elk Hill, belonging to Thomas Jefferson, were treated in this manner, as the British had a particular spite against him for doing so much to bring on the Revolution; and other acts were committed by Colonel Tarleton which were very cruel. He burned all the mills for grinding flour or meal, and destroyed the barns containing the grain to make bread. This, he pretended, was only to prevent the bread from being sent to the American soldiers; but it was very convenient to make that excuse. The effect of it was to nearly starve the women and children, who did no fighting; and no side ever really prospers or comes to good in the end when the "cry of the widow and the fatherless," as the Bible says, goes up to Heaven against them.

Cornwallis did not succeed in catching the "legislators" at Charlottesville. A man on horseback galloped in and told them the British were coming; so they hurried away, and made their escape. Some cavalrymen were then sent to capture Thomas Jefferson at "Monticello," where he and his young wife, you remember, had laughed and sung in the little pavilion on that snowy night nearly ten years before. But they were warned in time. Jefferson sent off his family to "Blenheim," where they had stopped that day, and, mounting his horse, rode into the mountains. The British cavalry thus failed to take him prisoner. They drank his fine wine, but did no other mis-

GENERAL ANTHONY WAYNE.

chief. They then returned to Cornwallis, and the whole army soon afterward retreated down the country.

Lafayette followed them at once, for all this time he had been watching them. He had now been joined by more troops, which were sent to him by Washington, and these were commanded by "Mad Anthony" Wayne, as he was called, for his love of fun and his dashing courage. "Mad Anthony" was a Pennsylvanian, and one of the very bravest soldiers in the army. He was always in high spirits, and ready to do anything that Washington told him; and there never was any "give up" in him when he once began to fight. He showed this at a place called Stony Point, on the Hudson River, a year or two before this time. The British held the fort, and "Mad Anthony" attacked it, and succeeded in capturing it. During the attack he was shot down, and fell on his knees. But he sprung to his feet, exclaiming to his men,

"March on, and take me into the fort, for I will die at the head of my column!"

These were the words of a brave soldier, and ought to have been cut on his tombstone. They will show you that the Pennsylvanian was the man for the times; and Lafayette, who knew him well, and admired him as much as other people did, must have been rejoiced to see his bold laughing face in Virginia.

IV.

"The boy" Lafayette now acted like an experienced soldier. He knew that it would be dangerous to fight a regular battle with Cornwallis, one army against the other; but he meant to watch for an opportunity, and see if he could not take his enemy unawares.

He therefore followed the British closely as they retreated down James River, and near Williamsburg he had a hot skirmish with them, in which neither side had much to boast of. After the skirmish the British continued to retreat, and at last Lord Cornwallis reached Jamestown, where he intended to cross James River.

But first he made up his mind to draw "the boy" Lafayette into a trap, and this he proceeded to set for him. Jamestown, where Smith and the first settlers had landed, you know, was a sort of island, separated from the main-land by a marsh and a small stream. All around were thick woods, and these enabled Cornwallis to lay his trap. He hid his soldiers in the woods along the marsh on the land side, and then did everything to make Lafayette believe that his main army had crossed to the island. Into this well-laid trap Lafayette now fell. He thought nothing but the rear-guard of the British army was before him, and at once resolved to attack it.

"Mad Anthony" was selected to head the attack, and got his men ready. It was a summer day (July 6th, 1781), and the woods and swamps were covered with fog. This made it all the easier to get up to the enemy without being seen, and about three o'clock in the afternoon Wayne advanced to attack them. In front marched some riflemen to look for the English, then came some cavalry, and behind came the foot-soldiers—about eight hundred men.

Cornwallis was waiting for him, with nearly his whole army hidden in the woods, while the Americans thought they were only going to attack his small rear-guard. The battle soon began. Wayne's riflemen, who went in front, saw redcoats in the woods, and opened a hot fire on them. At this the American cavalry charged at a gallop, and the infantry behind them rushed on, firing and cheering. But suddenly the woods swarmed with the redcoats on every side. The Americans found themselves attacked by an army instead of a small force, as they expected; and Wayne, who was just as cool and prudent as he was brave, saw that they had fallen into a trap. Lafayette sent word to him to retreat at once; and he fell back, fighting at every step, and at last made a stand, where he hoped he would be able to hold his ground.

This he soon found was impossible. Suddenly heavy lines of the English, to the number of two thousand men, burst out of the woods on his right and left, as well as in front. It seemed just as impossible for the Americans to retreat as to stand their ground. Wayne saw that his situation was desperate almost, and that his only hope was to get back to Lafayette. But how could he do so? The enemy were upon him, and if he tried to fall back, they would rush upon his flying men and destroy them.

Wayne saw all this at a single glance, and determined what he would do. Instead of flying, he drew up his men in close line of battle, and charged the enemy, ordering his cannon to open a hot fire upon them as he did so. The charge was made, and it was so impetuous that it drove the British back. They did not know what to make of it, as they thought the Americans were defeated, and now supposed that Lafayette's whole army was ready to surround them. They therefore halted, and this was just what Wayne wanted. Lafayette, he knew, was far in his rear, and could not help him: the only thing to do was to get out of the trap; and taking advantage of the enemy's surprise at his bold attack, he ordered his men to retreat, and they got safely out of the woods back to their friends again.

This was a brave and skilful act in Wayne. He deserved all the credit of it, and the Pennsylvania soldiers, who did most of the fighting, were entitled to their full share of the honor. It was a Pennsylvania fight, you see, as both general and soldiers came from that State, and I have no doubt the Virginians cheered their friends as they came back.

After this there was no more fighting. Night was coming on, and Lord Cornwallis was perplexed in his mind. As he did not know what force Lafayette had, he was afraid to attack him; so he retired to Jamestown Island, and three days afterward crossed James River and marched toward Norfolk.

I thought you would like to hear this story of the brave "boy" Lafayette and "Mad Anthony" Wayne, and how they got the better at last of old Lord Cornwallis. There is a saying that "he laughs best who laughs last"—that is, who succeeds in the end in what he undertakes; and Lafayette could now indulge in a good laugh at his enemy. Cornwallis had called him *a boy*, and said he could not escape from him; but, instead of being a thoughtless youth, Lafayette proved himself a good general, and it now looked very much as if Lord Cornwallis was himself retreating to escape from this very same "boy."

All this happened, as I have told you, in the month of July, 1781; and in October of the same year the great war was to come to an end. How this took place I will tell you in my last story.

THE SURRENDER AT YORKTOWN.

I.

This is the last of my stories of Virginia history, and in it I will tell you how the Revolution ended at Yorktown, not far from Williamsburg, where, in 1765, Patrick Henry sounded the first note of resistance to England.

After the battle at Jamestown with Lafayette, Lord Cornwallis crossed James River, and finally retired with his army to Yorktown. Here he began to throw up earthworks to protect himself from the Americans; and this will show you what a change had suddenly taken place in everything. In fact, General Washington was every day expected. He had left his camp near New York with very great secrecy, and was marching southward to attack the British in Virginia. The news went before him, and Lord Cornwallis no doubt heard it, and it could not have put him in very good spirits. The Americans were closing in on him from every side; and, what made matters worse, a French fleet under Comte de Grasse, which had come over to help Washington, was lying in Chesapeake Bay, ready to cut him off if he tried to escape by water. If he was attacked at Yorktown by the

LE COMTE DE GRASSE.

American army and the French ships, there seemed small probability that he would be able to make much resistance; and Sir Henry Clinton, who was at New York, understood this perfectly well. He saw that there was no time to lose, if he intended to help Cornwallis; so he sent a fleet of English ships, under an officer named Admiral Graves, to sail into Chesapeake Bay, and carry more soldiers to Yorktown. With these he hoped that Cornwallis would be able to hold his ground against the Americans, or if he could not, there would be the ships to safely carry away him and his men.

Admiral Graves accordingly sailed down and soon reached the shores of Virginia. But Comte de Grasse, with his French ships, was on the lookout, and meant to fight him; so as soon as they heard that the English ships were near, the Frenchmen sailed out to attack them.

The Americans saw the French ships sail away to attack the English, and soon lost sight of them in the direction of the ocean. But before long they heard, borne on the ocean wind, the distant roar of cannon, from which they knew that the two fleets were fighting. Hour after hour the dull, far-off muttering of the cannon went on, and then at length there was silence. The Americans hoped that this meant that the English fleet was driven back; and so it indeed proved. The French and English ships had attacked each other and fought until night. The English vessels were not destroyed; but as Admiral Graves did not renew the attack on the next day, or try to get to Yorktown, Comte de Grasse was satisfied, and waited for what was to come next. For five days the two fleets sailed about in sight of each other without any more fighting; and at last the French ships returned to Chesapeake Bay, and the English did not follow them.

Lord Cornwallis must have listened to that faint roar

WASHINGTON AS COMMANDER-IN-CHIEF.

of cannon from the ocean with very great anxiety. He knew just what his situation was, and that his only hope of safety was the defeat of Comte de Grasse by Admiral Graves. If the English ships were driven off, he saw that he would be caught like a rat in a trap; so he probably stood on his earthworks at Yorktown, listening anxiously to the sound of the guns, and trying to form an opinion how the fight would end. This, you know, he could do in some measure by the sound. If it grew louder and nearer, it would mean that De Grasse was coming back toward the bay; while if it grew fainter, it would signify that Admiral Graves was sailing away toward the ocean. But the sound did neither. It went on steadily until it stopped; and Lord Cornwallis was obliged to wait until news was brought to him of the result of the fighting.

It was bad enough news, you see, and he must have felt that the end of the struggle was now near. The sea-fight took place in the first week of September, and on the fourteenth of the same month General Washington reached Williamsburg, which is not far from Yorktown. As he rode along the lines of his war-worn troops the soldiers waved their hats and burst forth into cheers. Every man felt that there would be hot work now when the great commander-in-chief had arrived, and nothing pleased them better than the prospect. They were anxious to beat the British and return home to their families, and the expression on every face seemed to say, "We are ready!"

II.

Washington listened while Lafayette told him all that had happened, and probably praised the young soldier highly for all his movements in the summer campaign.

If Lafayette had not beaten Lord Cornwallis in battle, he had followed and worried him until he had shut himself up in Yorktown; and from this corner there seemed no means of his escaping. With the land forces on one side, and the ships on the other, the English were caught; and Washington set out at once in a small vessel to visit Comte de Grasse.

He found the brave sailor in his ship, named the *Ville de Paris*, in the bay, and was received with a salute of honor. In the midst of the thunder of cannon Washington went on board the ship, and Comte de Grasse came to meet him, making him a low and respectful bow. They then went into the cabin and had a long talk. De Grasse did not wish to stay and take part in the siege of Yorktown. He was burning to follow the English ships and attack them again; but Washington told him that the great thing now was to capture Cornwallis, and at last the bold sailor was convinced that this was best. He promised not to sail away, but remain where he was, and Washington then went back in his small vessel, which was named the *Queen Charlotte*, to Williamsburg.

Everything was now ready for the march upon Yorktown, and the soldiers set out through the beautiful autumn weather (September 28th, 1781) for the place. It was only twelve miles from Williamsburg, and the road led through cultivated fields, and woods of lofty pines, hollies, laurels, and other forest-trees, which cast refreshing shadows on the troops as they marched along. They were all in fine spirits, and the French soldiers who had come from the North with Washington were dressed in bright uniforms. But the Americans, or "Continentals," as they were called at that time, presented a much less imposing appearance. Their clothes were faded and worn, and some of them were almost in rags; for America was poor, and could not give them good uniforms. But they were just as well satisfied and in the highest spirits; and if their clothes were worn and soiled, their muskets were bright.

It was not long before they came in sight of Yorktown. This old village is still standing, and looks pretty much the same as it did at that time. It was built on high ground on the south bank of York River, and had in it only about sixty houses. Just opposite, across the river,

VIEW AT YORKTOWN.

which becomes much narrower at this place, was Gloucester Point, which the British also held. In the direction from which the Americans were coming toward the south and west, they had thrown up a number of redoubts or field-works, as they are called; that is, small banks of earth, behind which were placed cannon. Inside of these were heavier works still; and then, just in the edge of the town, were others, fifteen or twenty feet high, to retreat to, in case they were driven out of those in front of them.

You can now fancy how everything looked as the Americans marched up. The bright autumn sunshine lit up the whole landscape. There on the left was York River, and in front were the houses of the town; and in front of all were the British redoubts, with their cannon waiting.

As Lord Cornwallis expected to have more soldiers sent him by Sir Henry Clinton, he ought to have fought in these redoubts, I think, in order to gain time. But he determined that he would give them up, and retreat to his stronger works behind them. The Americans at once rushed in and took possession of them; and then the next thing to be done was to make what are called parallels. These are trenches and banks of earth thrown up by the army which is attacking earthworks, behind which they fight, as those who are besieged fight behind their own. The parallels were begun, and the men worked at them day and night: at last one of them was finished and mounted with cannon, and the Americans then prepared for the attack. Their army lay around Yorktown in the shape of a new moon; the left, composed of French troops, resting on York River, and the right, of Americans under Lafayette, extending down beyond the town. In this way Yorktown was regularly invested from the land side; the French fleet watched on the water, ready to meet any British ships which attempted to approach; and on the 9th of October General Washington began the attack.

It was begun in the afternoon, and for eight hours the cannon thundered from the opposing works. Darkness soon came, but this did not stop the fire, and the spectacle is said to have been magnificent. The red glare of the artillery lit up the night, and all at once a still more splendid sight was presented, which I will now proceed to describe.

III.

Opposite the left of the American line, in York River, were some English ships, which they determined to make an effort to destroy. One of them was named the *Charon* and the other the *Guadaloupe*, and, as their lights were visible, there was no difficulty in firing at them. This was done with red-hot cannon-balls from the American redoubts toward York River, and both the ships were soon set on fire. One who saw them described it as a wild and beautiful

CORNWALLIS'S CAVE.

spectacle, full of "terrible grandeur" and attraction. The flames speedily caught the sails and rigging of the ships and ran to the summits of the masts, and the shores were lit up by the conflagration. The ships had slipped their cables and attempted to get away, but the red-hot balls caught up with them, and they became the mark of all the batteries as they fled, like mountains of fire, toward the bay. The *Guadaloupe* managed to extinguish the fire on board, and escaped, but the *Charon* was completely destroyed and sunk. Another English ship was also set on fire by shells and destroyed; and the cannonade did not cease until next morning.

Day after day the fighting continued, and the prospect became darker and darker for Lord Cornwallis. There was a cave, it is said, in the river bluff, where he consulted with his officers, but his head-quarters, it seems, were in what was called the "Nelson House," a residence belonging to General Nelson. The Americans fired at it, although they at first did not wish to do so, from reluctance to injure the fine mansion. But of this General Nelson would not hear. When the artillery officers hesitated, he himself aimed the cannon and fired at his own house; and this, if nothing else were known of him, would prove his noble character and self-sacrificing patriotism.

Day after day and night after night the fighting went on, and the situation of Lord Cornwallis grew every hour more critical. A second parallel was constructed by the Americans in front of their right wing, very close to two of the strongest of the English works; and these redoubts Washington now resolved to assault.

NELSON HOUSE.

The attack took place on the evening of the 14th of October. The column on the right consisted of the troops under Lafayette, and was led by Alexander Hamilton, afterward one of the greatest statesmen of America. On the left were the French *chasseurs* and *grenadiers*, as they were called; and when the word was given, the two columns rushed forward toward the British redoubts. They were received with a storm of bullets and cannon-shot, but did not return the fire. The only way to take the works was at the point of the bayonet, and the men rushed on over the felled trees and other obstacles, and mounted the earthworks, where they fought with clubbed muskets hand to hand with the English troops.

The Americans under Hamilton carried everything before them, and were at last in possession of the redoubt. The French were still fighting on the left, and Lafayette sent word to Baron Viomenil, who commanded the French, that "*He* was in *his* redoubt; when would the baron be in *his?*"

"Tell the marquis," replied Viomenil, "that I am not in mine, but I will be in five minutes!"

He was as good as his word. Suddenly cheers were heard all along the front. Both redoubts were captured, and the shouts of the French and Americans rang aloft and mingled together.

Washington was standing on his works in the rear, listening. As he heard this shout he closed his field-glasses, and said to General Knox, who was standing by him,

"The work is done—and well done!"

IV.

Lord Cornwallis was now in a desperate situation. He had lost all hope of having more soldiers sent him by Sir Henry Clinton, and he saw that he could not resist Washington much longer. He made one attempt to attack the French above the town before daylight one morning, but was soon driven back; and then he determined to make an effort to escape.

The manner in which he attempted to do this shows how desperate he had become. You will remember what I told you about Gloucester Point, across the river from Yorktown. The British had some soldiers there, and a party of French were also across the river watching them. Lord Cornwallis's plan was this: As the river was not more than a mile wide at the place, he resolved to leave all his cannon and baggage in Yorktown, and cross his men over in boats by night to the Point. Then he meant to make a sudden attack on the French there and cut them to pieces. Then he and his men could mount the horses of the French legion, gallop off toward the Rappahannock, and, forcing their way through Maryland, Pennsylvania, and New Jersey, arrive safely in the city of New York, where their main army was.

When a man is desperate he is ready to undertake desperate things, and you see this was now the case with Lord Cornwallis. He was like Colonel M'Culloch, who leaped over the precipice at Wheeling. It was his only chance of safety, and he resolved to try it.

The boats were soon ready, and on the night of the 16th of October the British began to cross from Yorktown to Gloucester. It was about ten o'clock at night when the boats pushed from shore, and they moved in such deep silence that no one in the American camps dreamed of their design. The greatest secrecy had been kept about the whole affair, and none of the people in the town knew of it; so the first boat-loads were landed on the Gloucester side, and then the boats set out to return and carry over more. But Providence had determined that Lord Cornwallis should not escape. His plan might have succeeded, as desperate plans sometimes do; but when Heaven has decreed that certain things in this world shall not take place, the power of man is vain, and everything comes to nothing. No sooner had the boats started back toward Yorktown than the sky clouded over, and a violent storm began. The thunder roared, the lightning flashed, and the waves of the broad river dashed the boats up and down, rendering it impossible to carry over the rest of the army. All night the storm went on, and when morning came it was not yet over. Cornwallis saw that there was no hope now, as the Americans would discover his attempt to escape; so he brought back the soldiers who were at

THE SURRENDER AT YORKTOWN. 331

Gloucester Point, and sent word to General Washington that he was ready to surrender.

V.

Such was the end of the famous siege, and the long agony of the Revolution was over. One ceremony only

SURRENDER OF CORNWALLIS AT YORKTOWN.

remained to be observed—to receive the surrender of the British troops; and this was fixed for the 19th of October.

On that day it took place. The terms were as liberal as possible. The men and officers were to retain their baggage and side-arms, and all their personal property. Only one disagreeable condition was exacted by Washington. This was that the English flags should be "cased," as it was called, that is, rolled up, when the troops marched out. This was considered a great disgrace; but Lord Cornwallis had inflicted it upon General Lincoln, of the

MOORE HOUSE.

American army, when he surrendered at Charleston, and now Washington resolved that he should submit to it in his turn.

The surrender took place in a field south of Yorktown, and the scene was long remembered. Through the field a road ran, and on one side of this road the American troops were drawn up. The French were facing them on the other side, and the lines were more than a mile long.

Washington rode a white horse, and took his place at the head of the American line; and General Rochambeau, on a fine bay, was at the head of the French. A great crowd had assembled from all the surrounding country, and at the hour appointed the British troops were seen defiling out of Yorktown. Their colors were cased, in compliance with the terms of surrender, and they came on slowly, with sullen faces, in the midst of a deep silence.

THE SURRENDER AT YORKTOWN. 333

Lord Cornwallis did not make his appearance. He sent word that he was unwell, and General O'Hara, of the British army, took his place. This officer rode up to Washington, made a bow, and presented Lord Cornwallis's sword. Washington bowed in return, but pointed to General Lincoln, to signify that the surrender must be made to him. General O'Hara therefore presented the sword to Lincoln, who received it with a bow, and then returned it, requesting that it should be restored to Lord Cornwallis.

The rest of the ceremony was soon over. The British troops marched between the two lines, and stacked their

MOUNT VERNON.

arms and colors. This seemed to mortify and enrage them in the highest degree. The officers looked furious, and Colonel Abercrombie, of the English Guards, covered his face and bit the hilt of his sword with rage.

The British troops were then marched back to their quarters in Yorktown, and the ceremony of the surrender was over.

From that hour the Revolutionary War was at an end. British troops remained upon American soil, but the fighting was over, and in 1783 a formal treaty of peace was made between England and the United States. As soon as intelligence of this was received the British prepared to leave New York. This ceremony took place in November, 1783; and in December of the same year Washington, who was then in the city of New York, took leave of his old friends and comrades, who had fought under him so long. It was an affecting scene. Washington came into the room where his generals were all assembled, and raising a glass of wine, addressed them in a voice full of the deepest feeling:

"With a heart full of love and gratitude I now take leave of you," he said. "I most devoutly wish that your latter days may be as prosperous and happy as your former ones have been glorious and honorable."

He then drank to their health and happiness, and looked at them with deep emotion. The tears were running down their cheeks, and they seemed unable to utter a word.

Washington then said, "I cannot come to each of you to take my leave, but shall be obliged to you if each will come and take my hand."

General Knox, who was next to him, grasped his hand, and Washington kissed him. He then shook hands with and kissed each of the generals in turn, after which he left the room. Long lines of his old soldiers were drawn up in the street. Between these he walked to a boat on the river; raised his hat in reply to the cheering; the boat was rowed away, and thus ended one of the most affecting scenes of history.

A LAST WORD TO THE BOYS.

I HAVE thus told you a good many stories of Virginia history, and have tried to do so in a manner to interest you. Whether I have succeeded I do not know; but I have done my best, and I hope, at least, that some of them have pleased you.

But pleasing you was not my main object in telling you my stories. It is a great thing to interest young people, and make them acquainted with facts which they ought to know; but what is far more important is to improve their characters, by showing them how great and good men did their duty wherever and whenever they were called upon. If you will go back and remember the stories in our little book, you will see that I have never lost sight of this, or allowed it to pass out of my mind. I first told you about John Smith and his adventurous career—how he began life as a poor boy, but was always so brave and true that every one respected him, and how he came at last to found a great country, and died leaving a famous name. Then you were told of Nathaniel Bacon and his patriotic life; and then all about Washington, and his courage and high character, from the time when he was a boy whom scarcely any one had heard of, to that day in New York when he was looked upon as the greatest man living in the whole world. You heard next about Thomas Jefferson and Patrick Henry, and other patriots; and in my stories of Andrew Lewis, and Elizabeth Zane, and Colonel Rogers, I showed you how brave and true the men and women and very children of the border were, in the dark days when they were called upon to show what was in them. All these and other stories still I have gone on telling you day after day—never tired telling them, if you were willing to listen; and now when I have finished, and am about to bid you good-bye, I think I can say that some, at least, of these true stories will be of profit to you.

You are boys now, but you will soon be men. Then you will have your own way to make in the world. Do you mean to be idle, and fearful, and deceive people, and give them a bad opinion of you? Or do you intend to go to work, and act bravely and nobly, and do your duty, and leave a name behind you when you die which the world will love and respect? Take care—now is the time! Did you ever notice a large tree that grew crooked, and was an ugly eyesore on that account? Perhaps it stood on the lawn, right in front of the porch, and your father would have liked very much to straighten it. It was impossible to do so. A hundred horses could not have dragged it erect. And yet think of the time when that large tree was a small sapling: a child might have straightened it then, and it would have grown properly, and every one would have admired it.

By this I mean that boys ought to *grow straight*, not crooked. You are young now, as the tree was once: begin in time, and you will be as straight as an arrow when you are a man. If you wait, it will be too late. The way to make men erect and noble is to take them, when they are boys, and show them that there is nothing in this world so noble as doing their duty. Once more I say, remember that, though you are boys now, you will be men soon. The old people will die, and you must take their places; and woe to these old people if they set you a bad example! Did you ever hear what a great and good man said one day? He was walking in the snow, and his little son was following him, and stepping in the prints which his father's feet had made in the snow. His father saw this, and shook his head:

"I must mind how I walk," he said to himself; "that fellow is following in my footsteps!"

We old people must mind how we walk, if you young fellows are walking after us, and take care where we go and what we do. You will do good or evil, just as you have been taught. If you are false and worthless, you and everybody else will have a hard time of it. You may be soldiers, judges, statesmen, and presidents. What you say or do may decide the fate of millions of other people. These will look to you; and, more than all, God will watch you, and hold you to a strict account. If you are brave, and true, and unselfish, Heaven will bless you, and every one who knows you will love and respect you. If you are mean and cowardly, and think of nothing but your own pleasure, God and man will hate you. Which will you be?

The greatest of all things is to be pure, and to do your duty. Boys, and grown people too, learn this best by example, I think, and I have tried to show you these examples in American history.

I might have made my book longer, and written it in a different style; but I think I acted wisely in never forgetting that I was writing for boys. If I have interested you, I am more than content. I am sure of one thing—that I would not write what would make you worse, for all the world. I hope my little stories, by showing you great examples, will make you wiser and better.

THE END.

VALUABLE AND INTERESTING WORKS
FOR
PUBLIC AND PRIVATE LIBRARIES
PUBLISHED BY HARPER & BROTHERS, NEW YORK.

☞ *For a full List of Books suitable for Libraries, see* HARPER & BROTHERS' TRADE-LIST *and* CATALOGUE, *which may be had gratuitously on application to the Publishers personally, or by letter enclosing Nine Cents in Postage stamps.*

☞ HARPER & BROTHERS *will send their publications by mail, postage prepaid [excepting certain books excluded from the mail by reason of weight], on receipt of the price.* HARPER & BROTHERS' *School and College Text-Books are marked in this list with an asterisk (*).*

MACAULAY'S HISTORY OF ENGLAND. The History of England from the Accession of James II. By THOMAS BABINGTON MACAULAY. New Edition, from new Electrotype Plates. 8vo, Cloth, Gilt Tops, Five Volumes in a Box, $10 00 per set. Sold only in sets. Cheap Edition, 12mo, Cloth, $4 00.

MACAULAY'S LIFE AND LETTERS. The Life and Letters of Lord Macaulay. By his Nephew, G. OTTO TREVELYAN, M.P. With Portrait on Steel. Complete in 2 vols., 8vo, Cloth, uncut edges and gilt tops, $5 00; Sheep, $6 00; Half Calf, $9 50. Popular Edition, two vols. in one, 12mo, Cloth, $1 75.

HUME'S HISTORY OF ENGLAND. The History of England, from the Invasion of Julius Cæsar to the Abdication of James II., 1688. By DAVID HUME. 6 vols., 12mo, Cloth, $4 80; Sheep, $7 20; Half Calf, $15 30. *New Edition, from new Electrotype Plates, nearly ready.*

GIBBON'S ROME. The History of the Decline and Fall of the Roman Empire. By EDWARD GIBBON. With Notes by Rev. H. H. MILMAN and M. GUIZOT. With Index. 6 vols., 12mo, Cloth, $4 80; Sheep, $7 20; Half Calf, $15 30. *New Edition, from new Electrotype Plates, in Press.*

HILDRETH'S UNITED STATES. History of the United States. FIRST SERIES: From the Discovery of the Continent to the Organization of the Government under the Federal Constitution. SECOND SERIES: From the Adoption of the Federal Constitution to the End of the Sixteenth Congress. By RICHARD HILDRETH. 6 vols., 8vo, Cloth, $18 00; Sheep, $21 00; Half Calf, $31 50.

MOTLEY'S DUTCH REPUBLIC. The Rise of the Dutch Republic. A History. By JOHN LOTHROP MOTLEY, LL.D., D.C.L. With a Portrait of William of Orange. 3 vols., 8vo, Cloth, $10 50; Sheep, $12 00; Half Calf, $17 25.

MOTLEY'S UNITED NETHERLANDS. History of the United Netherlands: from the Death of William the Silent to the Twelve Years' Truce—1609. With a full View of the English-Dutch Struggle against Spain, and of the Origin and Destruction of the Spanish Armada. By JOHN LOTHROP MOTLEY, LL.D., D.C.L. Portraits. 4 vols., 8vo, Cloth, $14 00; Sheep, $16 00; Half Calf, $23 00.

MOTLEY'S LIFE AND DEATH OF JOHN OF BARNEVELD. The Life and Death of John of Barneveld, Advocate of Holland: with a View of the Primary Causes and Movements of "The Thirty-years' War." By JOHN LOTHROP MOTLEY, LL.D., D.C.L. Illustrated. 2 vols., 8vo, Cloth, $7 00; Sheep, $8 00; Half Calf, $11 50.

FIRST CENTURY OF THE REPUBLIC. A Review of American Progress. 8vo, Cloth, $5 00; Sheep, $5 50; Half Morocco, $7 25.

*HAYDN'S DICTIONARY OF DATES, relating to all Ages and Nations. For Universal Reference. Edited by BENJAMIN VINCENT, Assistant Secretary and Keeper of the Library of the Royal Institution of Great Britain, and Revised for the Use of American Readers. 8vo, Cloth, $3 50; Sheep, $3 94.

HUDSON'S HISTORY OF JOURNALISM. Journalism in the United States, from 1690 to 1872. By FREDERIC HUDSON. 8vo, Cloth, $5 00; Half Calf, $7 25.

JEFFERSON'S DOMESTIC LIFE. The Domestic Life of Thomas Jefferson: Compiled from Family Letters and Reminiscences, by his Great-granddaughter, SARAH N. RANDOLPH. Illustrated. Crown 8vo, Cloth, $2 50.

JOHNSON'S COMPLETE WORKS. The Works of Samuel Johnson, LL.D. With an Essay on his Life and Genius, by ARTHUR MURPHY, Esq. 2 vols., 8vo, Cloth, $4 00; Sheep, $5 00; Half Calf, $8 50.

KINGLAKE'S CRIMEAN WAR. The Invasion of the Crimea: its Origin, and an Account of its Progress down to the Death of Lord Raglan. By ALEXANDER WILLIAM KINGLAKE. With Maps and Plans. Three Volumes now ready. 12mo, Cloth, $2 00 per vol.; Half Calf, $3 75 per vol.

LAMB'S COMPLETE WORKS. The Works of Charles Lamb. Comprising his Letters, Poems, Essays of Elia, Essays upon Shakspeare, Hogarth, &c., and a Sketch of his Life, with the Final Memorials, by T. NOON TALFOURD. With Portrait. 2 vols., 12mo, Cloth, $3 00; Half Calf, $6 50.

LAWRENCE'S HISTORICAL STUDIES. Historical Studies. By EUGENE LAWRENCE. Containing the following Essays: The Bishops of Rome.—Leo and Luther.—Loyola and the Jesuits.—Ecumenical Councils.—The Vaudois.—The Huguenots.—The Church of Jerusalem.—Dominic and the Inquisition.—The Conquest of Ireland.—The Greek Church. 8vo, Cloth, Uncut Edges and Gilt Tops, $3 00.

MYERS'S REMAINS OF LOST EMPIRES. Remains of Lost Empires: Sketches of the Ruins of Palmyra, Nineveh, Babylon, and Persepolis, with some Notes on India and the Cashmerian Himalayas. By P. V. N. MYERS. Illustrated. 8vo, Cloth, $3 50.

LOSSING'S FIELD-BOOK OF THE REVOLUTION. Pictorial Field-Book of the Revolution: or, Illustrations by Pen and Pencil of the History, Biography, Scenery, Relics, and Traditions of the War for Independence. By BENSON J. LOSSING. 2 vols., 8vo, Cloth, $14 00; Sheep or Roan, $15 00; Half Calf, $18 00.

LOSSING'S FIELD-BOOK OF THE WAR OF 1812. Pictorial Field-Book of the War of 1812: or, Illustrations by Pen and Pencil of the History, Biography, Scenery, Relics, and Traditions of the last War for American Independence. By BENSON J. LOSSING. With several hundred Engravings on Wood by Lossing and Barritt, chiefly from Original Sketches by the Author. 1088 pages, 8vo, Cloth, $7 00; Sheep or Roan, $8 50; Half Calf, $10 00.

FORSTER'S LIFE OF DEAN SWIFT. The Early Life of Jonathan Swift (1667-1711). By JOHN FORSTER. With Portrait. 8vo, Cloth, $2 50.

GREEN'S ENGLISH PEOPLE. History of the English People. By JOHN RICHARD GREEN, M.A. In 4 vols. Vols. I. and II. ready. 8vo, Cloth, $2 50 per volume.

HALLAM'S MIDDLE AGES. View of the State of Europe during the Middle Ages. By HENRY HALLAM. 8vo, Cloth, $2 00; Sheep, $2 50; Half Calf, $4 25.

HALLAM'S CONSTITUTIONAL HISTORY OF ENGLAND. The Constitutional History of England, from the Accession of Henry VII. to the Death of George II. By HENRY HALLAM. 8vo, Cloth, $2 00; Sheep, $2 50; Half Calf, $4 25.

HALLAM'S LITERATURE. Introduction to the Literature of Europe during the Fifteenth, Sixteenth, and Seventeenth Centuries. By HENRY HALLAM. 2 vols., 8vo, Cloth, $4 00; Sheep, $5 00; Half Calf, $8 50.

SCHWEINFURTH'S HEART OF AFRICA. The Heart of Africa. Three Years' Travels and Adventures in the Unexplored Regions of the Centre of Africa—from 1868 to 1871. By Dr. GEORG SCHWEINFURTH. Translated by ELLEN E. FREWER. With an Introduction by WINWOOD READE. Illustrated by about 130 Wood-cuts from Drawings made by the Author, and with two Maps. 2 vols., 8vo, Cloth, $8 00.

M'CLINTOCK & STRONG'S CYCLOPÆDIA. Cyclopædia of Biblical, Theological, and Ecclesiastical Literature. Prepared by the Rev. JOHN M'CLINTOCK, D.D., and JAMES STRONG, S.T.D. 7 vols. *now ready.* Royal 8vo. Price per vol., Cloth, $5 00; Sheep, $6 00; Half Morocco, $8 00.

MOHAMMED AND MOHAMMEDANISM: Lectures Delivered at the Royal Institution of Great Britain in February and March, 1874. By R. BOSWORTH SMITH, M.A., Assistant Master in Harrow School; late Fellow of Trinity College, Oxford. With an Appendix containing Emanuel Deutsch's Article on "Islam." 12mo, Cloth, $1 50.

MOSHEIM'S ECCLESIASTICAL HISTORY, Ancient and Modern; in which the Rise, Progress, and Variation of Church Power are considered in their Connection with the State of Learning and Philosophy, and the Political History of Europe during that Period. Translated, with Notes, &c., by A. MACLAINE, D.D. Continued to 1826, by C. COOTE, LL.D. 2 vols., 8vo, Cloth, $4 00; Sheep, $5 00; Half Calf, $8 50.

HARPER'S NEW CLASSICAL LIBRARY. Literal Translations. The following Volumes are now ready. 12mo, Cloth, $1 50 each.

    CÆSAR. — VIRGIL. — SALLUST. — HORACE. — CICERO'S ORATIONS.— CICERO'S OFFICES, &c.—CICERO ON ORATORY AND ORATORS.—TACITUS (2 vols.).— TERENCE.— SOPHOCLES.— JUVENAL.— XENOPHON.—HOMER'S ILIAD.—HOMER'S ODYSSEY.—HERODOTUS.—DEMOSTHENES (2 vols.).—THUCYDIDES.—ÆSCHYLUS.—EURIPIDES (2 vols.).—LIVY (2 vols.).—PLATO [Select Dialogues].

LIVINGSTONE'S SOUTH AFRICA. Missionary Travels and Researches in South Africa: including a Sketch of Sixteen Years' Residence in the Interior of Africa, and a Journey from the Cape of Good Hope to Loanda on the West Coast; thence across the Continent, down the River Zambesi, to the Eastern Ocean. By DAVID LIVINGSTONE, LL.D., D.C.L. With Portrait, Maps, and Illustrations. 8vo, Cloth. $4 50; Sheep, $5 00; Half Calf, $6 75.

LIVINGSTONE'S ZAMBESI. Narrative of an Expedition to the Zambesi and its Tributaries, and of the Discovery of the Lakes Shirwa and Nyassa, 1858–1864. By DAVID and CHARLES LIVINGSTONE. With Map and Illustrations. 8vo, Cloth, $5 00; Sheep, $5 50; Half Calf, $7 25.

LIVINGSTONE'S LAST JOURNALS. The Last Journals of David Livingstone, in Central Africa, from 1865 to his Death. Continued by a Narrative of his Last Moments and Sufferings, obtained from his Faithful Servants Chuma and Susi. By HORACE WALLER, F.R.G.S., Rector of Twywell, Northampton. With Portrait, Maps, and Illustrations. 8vo, Cloth, $5 00; Sheep, $5 50; Half Calf, $7 25. Cheap Popular Edition, 8vo, Cloth, with Map and Illustrations, $2 50.

GROTE'S HISTORY OF GREECE. 12 vols., 12mo, Cloth, $18 00; Sheep, $22 80; Half Calf, $39 00.

RECLUS'S EARTH. The Earth: a Descriptive History of the Phenomena of the Life of the Globe. By ÉLISÉE RECLUS. With 234 Maps and Illustrations, and 23 Page Maps printed in Colors. 8vo, Cloth, $5 00; Half Calf, $7 25.

RECLUS'S OCEAN. The Ocean, Atmosphere, and Life. Being the Second Series of a Descriptive History of the Life of the Globe. By ÉLISÉE RECLUS. Profusely Illustrated with 250 Maps or Figures, and 27 Maps printed in Colors. 8vo, Cloth, $6 00; Half Calf, $8 25.

NORDHOFF'S COMMUNISTIC SOCIETIES OF THE UNITED STATES. The Communistic Societies of the United States, from Personal Visit and Observation; including Detailed Accounts of the Economists, Zoarites, Shakers, the Amana, Oneida, Bethel, Aurora, Icarian, and other existing Societies. With Particulars of their Religious Creeds and Practices, their Social Theories and Life, Numbers, Industries, and Present Condition. By CHARLES NORDHOFF. Illustrations. 8vo, Cloth, $4 00.

NORDHOFF'S CALIFORNIA. California: for Health, Pleasure, and Residence. A Book for Travellers and Settlers. Illustrated. 8vo, Cloth, $2 50.

NORDHOFF'S NORTHERN CALIFORNIA, OREGON, AND THE SANDWICH ISLANDS. Northern California, Oregon, and the Sandwich Islands. By CHARLES NORDHOFF. Illustrated. 8vo, Cloth, $2 50.

PARTON'S CARICATURE. Caricature and Other Comic Art, in All Times and Many Lands. By JAMES PARTON. With 203 Illustrations. 8vo, Cloth, Gilt Tops and uncut edges, $5 00.

*RAWLINSON'S MANUAL OF ANCIENT HISTORY. A Manual of Ancient History, from the Earliest Times to the Fall of the Western Empire. Comprising the History of Chaldæa, Assyria, Media, Babylonia, Lydia, Phœnicia, Syria, Judæa, Egypt, Carthage, Persia, Greece, Macedonia, Parthia, and Rome. By GEORGE RAWLINSON, M.A., Camden Professor of Ancient History in the University of Oxford. 12mo, Cloth, $1 46.

NICHOLS'S ART EDUCATION. Art Education applied to Industry. By GEORGE WARD NICHOLS, Author of "The Story of the Great March." Illustrated. 8vo, Cloth, $4 00.

BAKER'S ISMAILÏA. Ismailïa: a Narrative of the Expedition to Central Africa for the Suppression of the Slave-trade, organized by Ismail, Khedive of Egypt. By Sir SAMUEL WHITE BAKER, PASHA, F.R.S., F.R.G.S. With Maps, Portraits, and Illustrations. 8vo, Cloth, $5 00; Half Calf, $7 25.

BOSWELL'S JOHNSON. The Life of Samuel Johnson, LL.D., including a Journal of a Tour to the Hebrides. By JAMES BOSWELL, Esq. Edited by JOHN WILSON CROKER, LL.D., F.R.S. With a Portrait of Boswell. 2 vols., 8vo, Cloth, $4 00; Sheep, $5 00; Half Calf, $8 50.

6 Valuable and Interesting Works for Public and Private Libraries.

VAN-LENNEP'S BIBLE LANDS. Bible Lands: their Modern Customs and Manners Illustrative of Scripture. By the Rev. HENRY J. VAN-LENNEP, D.D. Illustrated with upward of 350 Wood Engravings and two Colored Maps. 838 pp., 8vo, Cloth, $5 00; Sheep, $6 00; Half Morocco, $8 00.

VINCENT'S LAND OF THE WHITE ELEPHANT. The Land of the White Elephant: Sights and Scenes in Southeastern Asia. A Personal Narrative of Travel and Adventure in Farther India, embracing the Countries of Burma, Siam, Cambodia, and Cochin-China (1871-2). By FRANK VINCENT, Jr. Illustrated with Maps, Plans, and Woodcuts. Crown 8vo, Cloth, $3 50.

SHAKSPEARE. The Dramatic Works of William Shakspeare. With Corrections and Notes. Engravings. 6 vols., 12mo, Cloth, $9 00. 2 vols., 8vo, Cloth, $4 00; Sheep, $5 00. In one vol., 8vo, Sheep, $4 00.

SMILES'S HISTORY OF THE HUGUENOTS. The Huguenots: their Settlements, Churches, and Industries in England and Ireland. By SAMUEL SMILES. With an Appendix relating to the Huguenots in America. Crown 8vo, Cloth, $2 00.

SMILES'S HUGUENOTS AFTER THE REVOCATION. The Huguenots in France after the Revocation of the Edict of Nantes; with a Visit to the Country of the Vaudois. By SAMUEL SMILES. Crown 8vo, Cloth, $2 00.

SMILES'S LIFE OF THE STEPHENSONS. The Life of George Stephenson, and of his Son, Robert Stephenson; comprising, also, a History of the Invention and Introduction of the Railway Locomotive. By SAMUEL SMILES. With Steel Portraits and numerous Illustrations. 8vo, Cloth, $3 00.

SQUIER'S PERU. Peru: Incidents of Travel and Exploration in the Land of the Incas. By E. GEORGE SQUIER, M.A., F.S.A., late U.S. Commissioner to Peru, Author of "Nicaragua," "Ancient Monuments of Mississippi Valley," &c., &c. With Illustrations. 8vo, Cloth, $5 00.

STRICKLAND'S (Miss) QUEENS OF SCOTLAND. Lives of the Queens of Scotland and English Princesses connected with the Regal Succession of Great Britain. By AGNES STRICKLAND. 8 vols., 12mo, Cloth, $12 00; Half Calf, $26 00.

THE "CHALLENGER" EXPEDITION. The Atlantic: an Account of the General Results of the Exploring Expedition of H.M.S. "Challenger." By Sir WYVILLE THOMSON, K.C.B., F.R.S. With numerous Illustrations, Colored Maps, and Charts, from Drawings by J. J. Wyld, engraved by J. D. Cooper, and Portrait of the Author, engraved by C. H. Jeens. 2 vols., 8vo, Cloth, $12 00.

BOURNE'S LIFE OF JOHN LOCKE. The Life of John Locke. By H. R. FOX BOURNE. 2 vols., 8vo, Cloth, uncut edges and gilt tops, $5 00.

ALISON'S HISTORY OF EUROPE. First Series: From the Commencement of the French Revolution, in 1789, to the Restoration of the Bourbons in 1815. [In addition to the Notes on Chapter LXXVI., which correct the errors of the original work concerning the United States, a copious Analytical Index has been appended to this American Edition.] Second Series: From the Fall of Napoleon, in 1815, to the Accession of Louis Napoleon, in 1852. 8 vols., 8vo, Cloth, $16 00; Sheep, $20 00; Half Calf, $34 00.

WALLACE'S GEOGRAPHICAL DISTRIBUTION OF ANIMALS. The Geographical Distribution of Animals. With a Study of the Relations of Living and Extinct Faunas, as Elucidating the Past Changes of the Earth's Surface. By Alfred Russel Wallace. With Maps and Illustrations. In 2 vols., 8vo, Cloth, $10 00.

WALLACE'S MALAY ARCHIPELAGO. The Malay Archipelago: The Land of the Orang-Utan and the Bird of Paradise. A Narrative of Travel, 1854–1862. With Studies of Man and Nature. By Alfred Russel Wallace. With Ten Maps and Fifty-one Elegant Illustrations. Crown 8vo, Cloth, $2 50.

BLUNT'S BEDOUIN TRIBES OF THE EUPHRATES. Bedouin Tribes of the Euphrates. By Lady Anne Blunt. Edited, with a Preface and some Account of the Arabs and their Horses, by W. S. B. Map and Sketches by the Author. 8vo, Cloth, $2 50.

GRIFFIS'S JAPAN. The Mikado's Empire: Book I. History of Japan, from 660 B.C. to 1872 A.D. Book II. Personal Experiences, Observations, and Studies in Japan, 1870–1874. By William Elliot Griffis, A.M., late of the Imperial University of Tōkiō, Japan. Copiously Illustrated. 8vo, Cloth, $4 00; Half Calf, $6 25.

THOMPSON'S PAPACY AND THE CIVIL POWER. The Papacy and the Civil Power. By the Hon. R. W. Thompson, Secretary of the U. S. Navy. Crown 8vo, Cloth, $3 00.

THE POETS AND POETRY OF SCOTLAND: From the Earliest to the Present Time. Comprising Characteristic Selections from the Works of the more Noteworthy Scottish Poets, with Biographical and Critical Notices. By James Grant Wilson. With Portraits on Steel. 2 vols., 8vo, Cloth, $10 00; Half Calf, $14 50; Full Morocco, $18 00.

*THE STUDENT'S SERIES. With Maps and Illustrations. 12mo, Cloth.

France.—Gibbon.—Greece.—Hume.—Rome (by Liddell).—Old Testament History.—New Testament History.—Strickland's Queens of England (Abridged). — Ancient History of the East. — Hallam's Middle Ages. — Hallam's Constitutional History of England.—Lyell's Elements of Geology.—Merivale's General History of Rome. — Cox's General History of Greece.—Classical Dictionary. Price $1 46 per volume.

Lewis's History of Germany. — Ecclesiastical History. Price $1 75 per volume.

CARLYLE'S FREDERICK THE GREAT. History of Friedrich II., called Frederick the Great. By THOMAS CARLYLE. Portraits, Maps, Plans, &c. 6 vols., 12mo, Cloth, $12 00; Sheep, $14 40; Half Calf, $22 50.

THE REVISION OF THE ENGLISH VERSION OF THE NEW TESTAMENT. With an Introduction by the Rev. P. SCHAFF, D.D. 618 pp., Crown 8vo, Cloth, $3 00.

This work embraces in one volume:

I. ON A FRESH REVISION OF THE ENGLISH NEW TESTAMENT. By J. B. LIGHTFOOT, D.D., Canon of St. Paul's, and Hulsean Professor of Divinity, Cambridge. Second Edition, Revised. 196 pp.

II. ON THE AUTHORIZED VERSION OF THE NEW TESTAMENT in Connection with some Recent Proposals for its Revision. By RICHARD CHENEVIX TRENCH, D.D., Archbishop of Dublin. 194 pp.

III. CONSIDERATIONS ON THE REVISION OF THE ENGLISH VERSION OF THE NEW TESTAMENT. By C. J. ELLICOTT, D.D., Bishop of Gloucester and Bristol. 178 pp.

ADDISON'S COMPLETE WORKS. The Works of Joseph Addison, embracing the whole of the *Spectator*. 3 vols., 8vo, Cloth, $6 00; Sheep, $7 50; Half Calf, $12 75.

ANNUAL RECORD OF SCIENCE AND INDUSTRY. The Annual Record of Science and Industry. Edited by Professor SPENCER F. BAIRD, of the Smithsonian Institution, with the Assistance of Eminent Men of Science. The Yearly Volumes for 1871, 1872, 1873, 1874, 1875, 1876, 1877, 1878 are ready. 12mo, Cloth, $2 00 per vol.

BROUGHAM'S AUTOBIOGRAPHY. Life and Times of Henry, Lord Brougham. Written by Himself. 3 vols., 12mo, Cloth, $6 00.

BULWER'S HORACE. The Odes and Epodes of Horace. A Metrical Translation into English. With Introduction and Commentaries. By LORD LYTTON. With Latin Text from the Editions of Orelli, Macleane, and Yonge. 12mo, Cloth, $1 75.

BULWER'S KING ARTHUR. King Arthur. A Poem. By LORD LYTTON. 12mo, Cloth, $1 75.

BULWER'S PROSE WORKS. The Miscellaneous Prose Works of Edward Bulwer, Lord Lytton. 2 vols., 12mo, Cloth, $3 50. Also, in uniform style, *Caxtoniana*. 12mo, Cloth, $1 75.

DAVIS'S CARTHAGE. Carthage and her Remains. being an Account of the Excavations and Researches on the Site of the Phœnician Metropolis in Africa and other Adjacent Places. Conducted under the Auspices of Her Majesty's Government. By Dr. N. DAVIS, F.R.G.S. Profusely Illustrated with Maps, Woodcuts, Chromo-Lithographs, &c. 8vo, Cloth, $4 00; Half Calf, $6 25.

Valuable and Interesting Works for Public and Private Libraries. 9

CAMERON'S ACROSS AFRICA. Across Africa. By VERNEY LOVETT CAMERON, C.B., D.C.L., Commander Royal Navy, Gold Medalist Royal Geographical Society, &c. With a Map and Numerous Illustrations. 8vo, Cloth, $5 00.

CARLYLE'S FRENCH REVOLUTION. The French Revolution: a History. By THOMAS CARLYLE. 2 vols., 12mo, Cloth, $3 50; Sheep, $4 30; Half Calf, $7 00.

CARLYLE'S OLIVER CROMWELL. Oliver Cromwell's Letters and Speeches, including the Supplement to the First Edition. With Elucidations. By THOMAS CARLYLE. 2 vols., 12mo, Cloth, $3 50; Sheep, $4 30; Half Calf, $7 00.

BARTH'S NORTH AND CENTRAL AFRICA. Travels and Discoveries in North and Central Africa: being a Journal of an Expedition undertaken under the Auspices of H.B.M.'s Government, in the Years 1849-1855. By HENRY BARTH, Ph.D., D.C.L. Illustrated. 3 vols., 8vo, Cloth, $12 00; Sheep, $13 50; Half Calf, $18 75.

THOMSON'S LAND AND BOOK. The Land and the Book; or, Biblical Illustrations drawn from the Manners and Customs, the Scenes and the Scenery, of the Holy Land. By W. M. THOMSON, D.D., Twenty-five Years a Missionary of the A.B.C.F.M. in Syria and Palestine. With two elaborate Maps of Palestine, an accurate Plan of Jerusalem, and several hundred Engravings, representing the Scenery, Topography, and Productions of the Holy Land, and the Costumes, Manners, and Habits of the People. 2 vols., 12mo, Cloth, $5 00; Sheep, $6 00; Half Calf, $8 50.

TENNYSON'S COMPLETE POEMS. The Poetical Works of Alfred Tennyson, Poet Laureate. With numerous Illustrations by Eminent Artists, and Three Characteristic Portraits. 8vo, Paper, $1 00; Cloth, $1 50.

CRUISE OF THE "CHALLENGER." Voyages over many Seas, Scenes in many Lands. By W. J. J. SPRY, R.N. With Map and Illustrations. Crown 8vo, Cloth, $2 00.

DU CHAILLU'S AFRICA. Explorations and Adventures in Equatorial Africa: with Accounts of the Manners and Customs of the People, and of the Chase of the Gorilla, the Crocodile, Leopard, Elephant, Hippopotamus, and other Animals. By PAUL B. DU CHAILLU. Illustrated. 8vo, Cloth, $5 00; Sheep, $5 50; Half Calf, $7 25.

DU-CHAILLU'S ASHANGO LAND. A Journey to Ashango Land, and Further Penetration into Equatorial Africa. By PAUL B. DU CHAILLU. Illustrated. 8vo, Cloth, $5 00; Sheep, $5 50; Half Calf, $7 25.

WHITE'S MASSACRE OF ST. BARTHOLOMEW. The Massacre of St. Bartholomew: Preceded by a History of the Religious Wars in the Reign of Charles IX. By HENRY WHITE, M.A. With Illustrations. Crown 8vo, Cloth, $1 75.

DRAPER'S CIVIL WAR. History of the American Civil War. By JOHN W. DRAPER, M.D., LL.D. 3 vols., 8vo, Cloth, Beveled Edges, $10 50; Sheep, $12 00; Half Calf, $17 25.

DRAPER'S INTELLECTUAL DEVELOPMENT OF EUROPE. A History of the Intellectual Development of Europe. By JOHN W. DRAPER, M.D., LL.D. New Edition, Revised. 2 vols., 12mo, Cloth, $3 00; Half Calf, $6 50.

DRAPER'S AMERICAN CIVIL POLICY. Thoughts on the Future Civil Policy of America. By JOHN W. DRAPER, M.D., LL.D., Professor of Chemistry and Physiology in the University of New York. Crown 8vo, Cloth, $2 00; Half Morocco, $3 75.

WOOD'S HOMES WITHOUT HANDS. Homes Without Hands: being a Description of the Habitations of Animals, classed according to their Principle of Construction. By J. G. WOOD, M.A., F.L.S. Illustrated. 8vo, Cloth, $4 50; Sheep or Roan, $5 00; Half Calf, $6 75.

FLAMMARION'S ATMOSPHERE. The Atmosphere. Translated from the French of CAMILLE FLAMMARION. Edited by JAMES GLAISHER, F.R.S., Superintendent of the Magnetical and Meteorological Department of the Royal Observatory at Greenwich. With 10 Chromo-Lithographs and 86 Woodcuts. 8vo, Cloth, $6 00; Half Calf, $8 25.

ABBOTT'S DICTIONARY OF RELIGIOUS KNOWLEDGE. A Dictionary of Religious Knowledge, for Popular and Professional Use; comprising full Information on Biblical, Theological, and Ecclesiastical Subjects. With nearly One Thousand Maps and Illustrations. Edited by the Rev. LYMAN ABBOTT, with the Co-operation of the Rev. T. C. CONANT, D.D. Royal 8vo, containing over 1000 pages, Cloth, $6 00; Sheep, $7 00; Half Morocco, $8 50.

ABBOTT'S FREDERICK THE GREAT. The History of Frederick the Second, called Frederick the Great. By JOHN S. C. ABBOTT. Illustrated. 8vo, Cloth, $5 00; Half Calf, $7 25.

ABBOTT'S HISTORY OF THE FRENCH REVOLUTION. The French Revolution of 1789, as viewed in the Light of Republican Institutions. By JOHN S. C. ABBOTT. Illustrated. 8vo, Cloth, $5 00; Sheep, $5 50; Half Calf, $7 25.

ABBOTT'S NAPOLEON BONAPARTE. The History of Napoleon Bonaparte. By JOHN S. C. ABBOTT. With Maps, Illustrations, and Portraits on Steel. 2 vols., 8vo, Cloth, $10 00; Sheep, $11 00; Half Calf, $14 50.

ABBOTT'S NAPOLEON AT ST. HELENA. Napoleon at St. Helena: or, Interesting Anecdotes and Remarkable Conversations of the Emperor during the Five and a Half Years of his Captivity. Collected from the Memorials of Las Casas, O'Meara, Montholon, Antommarchi, and others. By JOHN S. C. ABBOTT. Illustrated. 8vo, Cloth, $5 00; Sheep, $5 50; Half Calf, $7 25.

www.ingramcontent.com/pod-product-compliance
Lightning Source LLC
Chambersburg PA
CBHW031850220426
43663CB00006B/561